Black Missionary in an Age of Enslavement

The Life and Times of George Liele

Noel Leo Erskine
Emory University

ROWMAN & LITTLEFIELD
Lanham • Boulder • New York • London

Acquisitions Editor: Richard Brown
Acquisitions Assistant: Victoria Shi
Sales and Marketing Inquiries: textbooks@rowman.com
Credits and acknowledgments for material borrowed from other sources, and reproduced with permission, appear on the appropriate pages within the text.

Published by Rowman & Littlefield
An imprint of The Rowman & Littlefield Publishing Group, Inc.
4501 Forbes Boulevard, Suite 200, Lanham, Maryland 20706
www.rowman.com

86-90 Paul Street, London EC2A 4NE

Copyright © 2024 by The Rowman & Littlefield Publishing Group, Inc.

All rights reserved. No part of this book may be reproduced in any form or by any electronic or mechanical means, including information storage and retrieval systems, without written permission from the publisher, except by a reviewer who may quote passages in a review.

British Library Cataloguing in Publication Information available

Library of Congress Cataloging-in-Publication Data
Names: Erskine, Noel Leo, author.
Title: Black missionary in an age of enslavement : the life and times of George Liele / Noel Leo Erskine, Emory University.
Description: Lanham : Rowman & Littlefield, [2024] | Includes bibliographical references. | Summary: "This book reframes conventional understanding of mission studies and outreach by exploring the legacy and life of the enslaved American Baptist George Liele (1750-1825)-the first African American ordained to the Christian ministry"-- Provided by publisher.
Identifiers: LCCN 2024006713 | ISBN 9781538180051 (cloth) | ISBN 9781538180068 (paperback) | ISBN 9781538180075 (epub)
Subjects: LCSH: Liele, George, approximately 1750-approximately 1825. | African American clergy--Biography. | African American missionaries--Biography. | African American Baptists--Biography.
Classification: LCC BX6455.L54 E77 2024 | DDC 266.0092 [B]--dc23/eng/20240513

LC record available at https://lccn.loc.gov/2024006713

Contents

Preface v

Chapter 1: Liberation 1

Chapter 2: Theologian of Hope 39

Chapter 3: Patriarch of the Native Baptist Movement. 65

Chapter 4: The Coming of Missionaries 103

Chapter 5: The Man and His Legacy 145

Bibliography 187

Index 191

About the Author 209

Preface

Growing up on the beautiful island of Jamaica, I was told by the elders in the community that an African American, George Liele, was instrumental in opening doors that were closed to Afro-Jamaicans caught in the terrible scourge of New World slavery. The elders pointed out that slavery in Jamaica and many of the Caribbean islands was inhuman and cruel and that children and women were often flogged and had to work on plantations from sunrise until sunset.

What really got my attention was that doors—school doors, church doors, and social doors—were closed to enslaved persons and that an African American, George Liele, a liberated slave from the American colonies of Virginia and Georgia, the first Black missionary to Jamaica, had opened school doors and church doors to enslaved Jamaicans. Liele was the first person to place the Bible in the hands of enslaved Jamaicans, and he started schools wherever he began a mission to introduce Afro-Jamaicans to "the Lord and master" who was above all masters. This was Liele's way of communicating that the plantocracy did not have the last word in relation to the lives of enslaved persons.

There are several persons who have served as inspiration for this project. A special recognition to theologian David Shannon, who gathered several scholars and church leaders in the Atlanta area to put together a text honoring Liele's life and ministry. There were about twelve of us women and men who engaged this project, which was published as *George Liele's Life and Legacy: An Unsung Hero*, by Mercer University Press, in 2012, edited by David Shannon, Julia Frazier, and Deborah Bingham Van Broekhoven. *Black Missionary in an Age of Enslavement: The*

Life and Times of George Liele joins in conversation with this important contribution.

Primary sources for Liele's work are found in letters Liele wrote to John Rippon, published in *The Baptist Annual Register for 1790, 1791, 1792, and part of 1793* (n.p. [London]), 332–44, 540–43. Rippon edited Liele's letters with quotation marks that indicated words Liele wrote.

Special thanks are accorded the librarians at the Angus Library, Regents Park College, at Oxford University, for their diligent search for evidence of Liele's visit to the Baptist Missionary Society of London during his trip to London in 1822. Expressions of thanks are also offered to the staff and librarians at the American Baptist Historical Society for their care in sourcing Liele's mission and ministry as a Black missionary both in Georgia and Jamaica.

I am grateful to the Society for the Study of Black Religion, which made space for Peter Paris and me to lecture on David George and George Liele at its annual meetings; to the American Missiological Society for their invitation to lead a discussion on George Liele as the first missionary from the United States; and to the Baptist World Alliance for the opportunity to present at its annual meeting in Jamaica, on "George Liele, Liberated Slave and Missionary to Jamaica."

It is with much gratitude that I thank my editor, Richard Brown, for his patience and guidance during the writing of this project. And to my father, Leo Erskine, who planted seeds for research on the life and times of George Liele.

Chapter 1

Liberation

IN THE FIELD OF CHRISTIAN MISSIONS, THE WORK OF ENGLISH missionary William Carey and American missionaries Adoniram and Ann Judson are well known. William Carey traveled to India in 1793 and Adoniram and Ann Judson to Burma in 1813. What is not equally well known is that an African American, George Liele, had begun Christian missions in Jamaica eleven years earlier. Liele's work reached beyond a nation-state framework and included regions of Nova Scotia, Canada, and Freetown, Sierra Leone, Africa, through his protégé David George. Writing from Jamaica, Liele stated:

> The last accounts I had from Savannah were, that the Gospel had taken very great effect both there and in South Carolina. Brother Andrew Bryan, a black minister at Savannah, has TWO HUNDRED MEMBERS, in full fellowship, and had certificates from their owners of ONE HUNDRED MORE, who had given in their experiences and were ready to be baptized. Also I received account from Nova Scotia of a black Baptist preacher, Brother David George, who was a member of the church at Savannah; he had the permission of the governor, to preach in three provinces; his members in full communion were then SIXTY, white and black, the Gospel spreading. Brother Amos is at Providence (Bahama Island), he writes that the Gospel has taken good effect, and is spreading greatly; he has about THREE HUNDRED MEMBERS.[1]

Chapter 1

Liele maintained an active correspondence with John Rippon of the British Baptist Community, which he visited in 1822, and mentees in the Bahama Islands; Sierra Leone, Africa; Nova Scotia, Canada; Savannah, Georgia; and Silver Bluff, South Carolina. This manuscript seeks to look at Christianity and indigenous expressions of religion in Africa and the African diaspora in which Liele and his mentees participated. The lens employed will be the life and times of George Liele, with the hope that a better understanding of the Black Atlantic world will emerge.

In a letter to Rippon, Liele wrote "The Covenant of the Anabaptist Church, begun in America, December 1777 and in Jamaica, December 1783." In a discussion of Liele's covenant, Robert G. Gardner contends that "Liele expressly fixed December 1777 as the constituting date for his Savannah Church. Of course, this does not preclude earlier black Baptist in preaching in and near Savannah."[2] There were twenty-one articles included in this covenant. Through this covenant Liele established himself as a thought leader and theologian in his own right.

The Early Years

Liele was only fourteen years old when he arrived in New Georgia as an enslaved youth of Henry Sharp. Liele wrote to John Rippon, secretary of the British Baptist Missionary Society, with important biographical information:

> I was born in Virginia, my father's name was Liele, and my mother's name was Nancy. I cannot ascertain much of them, as I went to several parts of America when young, and at length resided in New Georgia; but was informed by both white and black people, that my father was the only black person who knew the Lord in a spiritual way in that county. I always had a natural fear of God from my youth, and was often checked in conscience with thoughts of death, which barred me from many sins and bad company. I knew no other way at that time to hope for salvation but only in performance of my good works. About two years before the war, The Rev. Matthew Moore, one sabbath afternoon, as I stood with curiosity to hear him, he unfolded all my dark views, opened my best behavior and good works to me, which I thought I was saved by, and I was convinced that I was not in the way to heaven,

but in the way to hell. . . . I saw my condemnation in my own heart, and I found no way wherein I could escape the damnation of hell, only through the merits of my dying Lord and savior Jesus Christ; which cause[d] me to make intercession with Christ, for the salvation of my poor immortal soul; and I full well recollect, I requested of my Lord and Master to give me a work, I did not care how mean it was, only to see how good I could do it.[3]

Liele seems to call attention to a master who transcended his earthly master in his claim, "I requested of my Lord and Master to give me a work, I did not care how mean it was, only to see how good I could do it." It was clear that the one called "Lord and Master" was above all earthly masters, and it was his work that was of first importance.

Liele was enslaved by Henry Sharp, who was a deacon in the Baptist church in which Liele was converted to Christianity. Licensed to preach in the congregation to which he was converted and baptized by Rev. Matthew Moore, Liele was set aside to read verses of hymns and texts from the Bible to enslaved persons on plantations in the vicinity of Savannah. The Bible and the hymnal were important resources for Liele in his reaching out to fellow enslaved persons. Impressed with his gifts of communication to fellow enslaved persons and his fidelity to the church in which he was converted and baptized, Liele was invited to preach at one of their church meetings and set aside to minister to the enslaved community.

> I felt such love and joy as my tongue could not express. After this I declared before the congregation of believers the work which God had done for my soul, and the same minister, the Rev. Matthew Moore, baptized me, and I continued in this church for about four years till the "vacuation" of Savannah by the British. . . . Desiring to prove the sense I had of my obligations to God, I endeavored to instruct the people of my own color in the word of God. The white brethren seeing my endeavors, and that the word of God seemed to be blessed, gave me a call at a quarterly meeting to preach before the congregation.[4]

Chapter 1

Liele saw the world, his world, in terms of black and white. His turn to God in conversion and baptism and his being set aside for ministry to fellow enslaved persons awakened in him a profound obligation to serve fellow enslaved persons by reading texts from the Bible and verses from the church hymnal. It was this commitment in ministry to people of his own color that led the white congregation to set him aside and apart for ministry on plantations in the vicinity.

Liele was offered the license to preach as a probationer in 1773 and ordained to the Christian ministry May 20, 1775.[5] The freedom to boat along the Savannah River and explain verses of hymns to fellow enslaved persons took Liele to Silver Bluff, South Carolina, where he became reacquainted with David George. David George became converted through Liele's preaching, was baptized by Elder Palmer, and was set aside as an elder of the Silver Bluff Church.

In conversation with John Rippon and Samuel Pearce in his visit to London, David George, who had settled in Freetown, Sierra Leone, shares stories of his life under slavery and his success in running away from masters in Virginia to Silver Bluff, South Carolina, where he became reunited with George Liele. David George comments on his reacquaintance with Liele:

> I used to say the Lord's prayer, that it might make me better, but I feared that I grew worse; and I continued worse and worse, as long as I thought I would do something to make me better; . . . Soon after I saw that I could not be saved by any of my own doings, but that it must be by God's mercy—that my sins had crucified Christ; and now the Lord took away my distress. I was sure that the Lord took it away, because I had such pleasure and joy in my soul, that no man could give me. Soon after I heard brother George Liele preach, who, as you both know is at Kingston in Jamaica. I knew him ever since he was a boy. I am older than he; I am about fifty. His sermon was suitable, on *Come unto me all ye that labor, and are heavy laden, and I will give you rest*. When it was ended, I went to him and told him I was so; That I was weary and heavy laden, and that the grace of God had given me rest. Indeed his whole discourse seemed for me. . . . Brother Palmer appointed a Saturday evening to hear what the Lord had done for us, and the next day he

baptized us in the Mill-stream. . . . Brother Palmer formed us into a church, and gave us the Lord's supper at Silver Bluff. . . . Afterwards the church advised with Brother Palmer about my speaking to them and keeping them together. . . . So I was appointed to the office of an Elder and received instruction from Brother Palmer how to conduct myself.[6]

According to David George, Liele would come frequently to visit and preach at Silver Bluff. On one occasion, shortly after he was baptized, he confided to Liele that he was ashamed to pray and witness to friends.

Sometime afterwards, when Brother George Liele came again, and preached in a corn field, I had a great desire to pray with the people myself, but I was ashamed, and went to a swamp and poured out my heart before the Lord. I then came back to Brother George Liele, and told him my case. He said, "In the intervals of service you should engage with service with the friends." At another time, when he was preaching, I felt the same desire, and after he had done, I began in prayer—it gave me great relief, and I went home with a desire for nothing else but to talk to the brothers and sisters about the Lord.[7]

Liele's witness to David George and others in the congregation at Silver Bluff sets Liele apart as the first Black preacher at Silver Bluff and one who was instrumental in the founding of that community.

The Silver Bluff Church was formed on the plantation of George Galphin in Aiken County, South Carolina. David George and George Liele, friends of their childhood in Virginia, renewed their friendship at this plantation church and provided important leadership for the congregation at Galphin Mill.

Milledge Galphin Murray, the great-grandson of George Galphin, frames the priority and centrality of Baptist witness at Silver Bluff.

[David] George, who became the first black minister in South Carolina, was an escapee slave from Virginia taken in by one of Galphin's Indian traders. Galphin purchased David George, who became Galphin's personal servant. Throughout his service at Silver Bluff, George described Galphin as kind. David George wrote that in 1770 a black

5

evangelist named George Liele visited Silver Bluff and preached a sermon to some and he learned about repentance from a sinful life, forgiveness of sins through Jesus Christ's sacrifice on the cross, and a new relationship in Jesus Christ as personal savior.[8]

We can see the emergence of Liele as a contextual preacher and theologian. With a sense of the situation of David George and his need for spiritual and existential liberation, Liele shared with him the comforting words of Jesus, in John's gospel, "Come unto me all ye who labor and are heavy laden." David George informs us that Liele's sermon spoke to his spiritual and physical situation. This sermon moved David to confess that he was heavy laden and open to the gift of divine grace. On another occasion David was moved to prayer with Liele preaching in the cornfield as he embraced the power of prayer. Galphin calls attention to the centrality of the sermon in Liele's ministry as themes of repentance, forgiveness through Christ's death on the cross, and a new relationship with Jesus as savior is forged. The suffering of Jesus on the cross found resonance among enslaved persons to whom Liele preached and begins to explain why David George confessed that he was heavy laden and in need of a savior.

Walter H. Brooks calls attention to the priority of the Silver Bluff Church as the first independent Black church in either the North or South of the American colonies, in which David George and George Liele had significant leadership roles. According to Brooks, Baptist polity that emphasized the autonomy of the local church and a democratic style of church government was appealing to enslaved persons as they were able to constitute their own congregations and choose their own preachers.

> In speaking of the beginning of Negro churches in the United States, those of the Baptist faith must not be forgotten. Nor must we err in thinking that the first churches of this faith were planted in the North. It is true that there were Negro Baptists in Providence, Rhode Island, as early as 1774, and doubtless much earlier, but they had no church of their own. . . . Negro Baptist churches, unlike other Negro churches, had their beginning in the South, and at a somewhat earlier date. The

first church of Negro Baptists, so far as authentic and trustworthy writings of the eighteenth century established, was constituted at Silver Bluff, on Mr. Galphin's estate. A year or two before the Revolutionary War.[9]

Albert Raboteau supports the claim of Silver Bluff community having the distinction of being the first separate Black church whether in the North or in the South of the United States. "This church owed its beginning to the preaching of a white Baptist minister named [Wait] Palmer who preached to the slaves of one George Galphin at Silver Bluff," Raboteau wrote. "David George, George's wife, Jesse Galphin (or Jesse Peter), and five other slaves were converted and baptized by Palmer at Galphin's Mill. These eight formed the nucleus of the Silver Bluff Church. David George had a talent for exhorting and was appointed to the office of elder on the recommendation of Palmer."[10]

As signs of the Revolutionary War became obvious at the Galphin Mill, the membership of the church was informed that Palmer and Liele would not be allowed to visit Silver Bluff, perchance they should share with the enslaved population possibilities of their freedom. "This undoubtedly was not later than November, 1775," wrote church historian Walter H. Brooks, "when the Earl of Dunmore issued on American soil a proclamation of emancipation, in which the Black slaves and the white indentured bondmen were alike promised freedom, provided they espoused the cause of England, in its struggle with the colonists.... The Negroes along the Savannah River were abandoning their masters, and now going to the British in scores and hundreds, to the detriment of their owners, and the menace of the cause of American Independence."[11]

Galphin, a Patriot, in attempts to escape from the British, abandoned his slaves and fled for safety. David George, Jesse Galphin, and about fifty of the enslaved members of the community fled to Savannah, where they were emancipated by the British. Carter G. Woodson suggests that although David George and Jesse Galphin were in fact pastors of this community from Silver Bluff, now in exile, they may not have had the influence to secure the permit to preach in Savannah. It was George Liele who had the influence among the British as a friend of Col. Moses

CHAPTER 1

Kirkland, who in fact served as pastor of this congregation in exile. It was from this relationship with a congregation in exile that Liele formed "the first Negro Baptist Church in the city of Savannah, which flourished during the British occupancy from 1779 to 1782. The oldest Negro Baptist church in this country, however, was that of the Silver Bluff church which, in another meeting place and under a new name, became established at Augusta, having existed from the year 1773 to 1793 before the time of Andrew Bryan's organizing efforts in Savannah."[12]

During the British occupation of Savannah, 1779 to 1782, there was much upheaval among the membership of the Silver Bluff community as they sought community in the Savannah area under the patronage of the British. Walter H. Brooks makes it clear that because of Liele's close relationship with Col. Moses Kirkland, who was in charge of the British military, Liele was able to provide worship experience for the little flock from Silver Bluff that was now in the Savannah area. Brooks cites much of the disposition of the colonists toward African Americans who by the thousands had taken sides with the British in the promise that they would receive their freedom. "How well these slaves understood and appreciated the preferred boon may be inferred from a letter which was written by Stephen Bull to Col. Henry Laurens, President of the Council of Safety, Charleston, South Carolina, March 14, 1776. In that letter he says: 'It is better for the public, and the owners, if the deserted Negroes who are on the Tybee Island be shot, if they cannot be taken.'"[13]

According to Stephen Bull, many enslaved persons were abandoning their masters and siding with the British cause. Liele, although not a runaway slave, spent much time at Tybee Island when he could no longer visit Silver Bluff. It is important to note that at this time Liele's master, Henry Sharp, took up arms against the Americans and had given Liele his freedom with the understanding that he would remain with the Sharp family until his master's death. Liele's freedom came early as Sharp was soon killed in action. Although his freedom was challenged after his master's death by members of Sharp's family, Liele was able to produce his manumission papers. Liele spent much time preaching to the refugees at Tybee Island.

As cited earlier, when Liele was set apart to minister to enslaved persons by reading verses of hymns and texts from the Bible to fellow enslaved persons in neighboring estates, he mentioned the unspeakable joy he had in sharing the gospel of Christ with fellow enslaved persons. Liele's passion to be with fellow enslaved persons in the area of Tybee Island begins to highlight his passion of being in solidarity with the "least of God's children" (Matthew 25:45 RSV).

A TIME OF TRANSITION

The British occupation of Savannah introduced a time of transition for Liele. The Americans took back Savannah from the British in 1782, and this triggered an exodus of the British and their sympathizers from the Savannah area to several Caribbean islands and Canada. David George left the group for Charleston, South Carolina, and then went with the British to Nova Scotia, where he preached to members of his own race for about ten years prior to his journey along with hundreds of fellow people of African descent to Sierra Leone, in British Central Africa, where he established the first Baptist church in Africa. John Davis sums up the scattering of the leadership of Liele's church at the end of the British occupation of Savannah in 1782. Liele and several of the leadership of the first African Baptist Church in Savannah prepared to leave for Nova Scotia, Canada; New Providence, The Bahama Islands; or Jamaica. It is interesting that Rev. Jesse Gaulsing and a more recent convert, Andrew Bryan, chose to remain in slavery with the Americans.

According to John W. Davis, "Among these early members of the Yamacraw church were Reverend David George, who later labored, with permission from the Governor, in the ministry of Nova Scotia, with sixty communicants, white and black; Reverend Amos, who preached with good results at New Providence, one of the Bahama Islands, to about three hundred members; and Reverend Jesse Gaulsing, who preached near Augusta, in South Carolina, to sixty members. Preaching from Chapter iii Saint John, and the clause of verse 7, 'Ye must be born again,' George Liele moved to repentance a more useful man, Andrew Bryan, and a noted woman named Hagar."[14]

CHAPTER 1

It was Andrew Bryan who carried on Liele's work in the church in Savannah when Liele left for Jamaica with the British in 1782.

> Probably because of the antagonism engendered by the exodus of slaves with the British, the work of Bryan was frequently interrupted by the whites. More than once he was personally molested and put in jail . . . opposition grew so strong that Bryan and fifty of his followers were once severely whipped. A certain eyewitness on this occasion reports that while Bryan was under their lashes, "he held up his hand, and told his persecutors that he rejoiced not only to be whipped, but would freely suffer death for the cause of Jesus Christ."[15]

Andrew began to preach in Savannah about nine months after Liele left for Jamaica. As with Liele, his parents were slaves. Andrew's brother Sampson would preach for him in his absence, and when he saw fit to divide the congregation it was named Second African Baptist Church. Andrew's church was First African Baptist Church of Savannah. The pastor of Second African Baptist Church was a fellow enslaved person, Henry Francis. Indeed, Liele's labors through his mentee Andrew Bryan bore much fruit.

Historian Walter H. Brooks reminds us that Jesse Peter, sometimes referred to as Jesse Galphin, returned to Silver Bluff and through his instrumentality revived the work that formerly had David George, Jesse Peter, and George Liele as founding pastors.

"The man who was instrumental in resuscitating the work at Silver Bluff was Jesse Peter, who, according to an old custom of applying to the slave the surname of the master, was better known as Jesse Galphin, or Gaulfin," Brooks wrote. "Having been connected with the Silver Bluff Church from the very first, and only separated from it during the Revolutionary War and the period of readjustment immediately thereafter, Jesse Peter was eminently fitted . . . to take up the work at Silver Bluff. Silver Bluff was his home and there he was held in high esteem."[16]

Brooks raises an important question: why would Jesse Peter, who had obtained freedom because of his identification with the British, turn his back on freedom and elect to remain in slavery?[17] Brooks suggests that unlike George Liele, Jesse Peter did not have a pioneering spirit. Further, Brooks wagers that it could be the case that Jesse Peter stayed in his former condition of bondage and returned to Silver Bluff in order to preach where he, along with George Liele and David George, labored. In any case, it is clear that George Liele, writing from Jamaica, kept abreast of the preaching and ecclesial activities of Jesse Peter. As John Rippon wrote, "George Liele, writing from the West Indies, in 1791, had said to Joseph Cook, of South Carolina, 'Brother Jesse Galphin, another black minister, preaches near Augusta, in South Carolina, where I use[d] to preach.'"[18]

THE EMERGENCE OF MOREHOUSE COLLEGE

Jesse Peter, the sole pastor of the Silver Bluff Church, was not satisfied with the location of the Silver Bluff Church in South Carolina. He relocated the church to Augusta, Georgia, and renamed it First African Baptist Church of Augusta, Georgia. The history of Silver Bluff Church was linked with Elder Palmer, David George, George Liele, and Jesse Peter. This distinguished array of pastors somehow pointed to a new future and was filled with new possibilities with the power of a new name. In a profound sense, the "curtain falls" on the Silver Bluff Church. "Here we lose sight of the Silver Bluff Church," writes Walter H. Brooks, "just as the First African Baptist Church, of Augusta, Georgia, better known as the Springfield Baptist Church, comes into being. Jesse Peter had secured standing and recognition for the first African Church in Savannah, Georgia."[19]

It is fitting that a church that has its roots in the ministry of George Liele would combine education and the Christian faith. It was the Springfield Baptist Church that gave birth to Morehouse College in 1867. Also, this historic church gave birth to the now disbanded Georgia Education Association, which fought hostile opposition in order to build public schools for Black children during the era of Jim Crow.[20] It should be kept in mind that Jesse Peter brought along a group of members from Silver Bluff who formed First African Baptist Church in 1791. The church was later renamed Springfield Baptist Church. In the evolution of the church, as it expressed its mission in keeping with traditions initiated by George Liele and David George in their respective ministries, education had a pivotal role in the framing of its mission and understanding of community. According to Alfred Pugh, in 1867, the Augusta Institute, "a school for the primary purpose of preparing Black men for ministry and teaching, was founded by a Baptist minister and cabinet maker, The Reverend William J. White. It was located, in the basement of the Springfield Baptist Church. Augusta Institute, later renamed Morehouse College, is presently located in Atlanta, Georgia, its student body composed of mostly black males." And of course, Pugh adds, the Rev. Dr. Martin Luther King Jr. "was one of its most renowned graduates."[21]

Alfred Pugh quite rightly attributes the impact of Liele's ministry on the life of his protégés David George, Jesse Peter (Galphin), Andrew Bryan, and Brother Amos (Williams). According to Pugh, Liele's impact was not only realized in areas of church growth in terms of membership rolls and baptism but also in building schools and making literacy an important index of salvation. Of first importance for Liele, and his mentees, was both preachers and members of the congregation being able to read the Bible. Liele, who was often imprisoned for his convictions, was a pioneer in the area of education who insisted that wherever he built a church it was also of first importance to plant a school. Sometimes the school preceded the church. In the tradition of Augusta Institute, which had its basis in the mission and ministry of Jesse Peter, the Baptists in Jamaica, drawing on the legacy of George Liele, founded Calabar College in 1843, the first theological college for the training of native ministry. Calabar College has a basis in Liele's work, as Liele was the first person in Jamaica to found a school and offer education to enslaved persons. Liele's legacy in Calabar College preceded the Augusta Institute by twenty-four years. A personal aside: I had the privilege as a son of Jamaica to attend this college, as did my father, Leo Erskine.

Brother Amos and the Bahamas

The last of Liele's protégés from the American context, whose impact on the social and religious areas of ministry we will examine, is Amos Williams, often referred to by George Liele as Brother Amos. "Amos Williams, also known as Brother Amos," Alfred Pugh writes, "frequently heard George Liele preach at the Dead River Church on the Galphin plantation. It is also probable that, following the outbreak of the Revolutionary War, he was also a member of a church Liele organized near Savannah.... Walter Brooks, one of the early writers about the history of the black church, referred to a letter written by George Liele to John Rippon, the editor of *The Baptist Register*, in which he mentions correspondence received from friends in Savannah with news that 'Brother Amos' had organized a Baptist Church building for worship services."[22]

Historian Antonina Canzoneri writes that Amos Williams received a Redd Pass, indicating that he had received his freedom from the British. Also, his wife, Judy, and children are free. His children are Lisey, Caesar, Prince, Elsey, and Rachall. He designates himself as a carpenter on land deeds. This may be the Amos who started Baptist work in the Bahamas, at Nassau, since he is the only person with Amos as a first name in the index of Bahamas Records up to 1815. On May 3, 1789, Amos Williams married Selina Bedon; apparently Judy had died. He died in 1799, and Prince Williams was the executor of his estate.[23] Several Caribbean scholars point out that Brother Amos was the first Baptist preacher to take the Afro-Baptist faith to the Bahamas. In the tradition of Liele, he was confident in sharing a Bible-based faith informed by an ability to read and interpret the Bible.

Jim Lawlor puts this in perspective for us:

> The first Baptist preacher, Brother Amos, was another educated free black man, who came to the Bahamas in 1783 and preached the Afro-Baptist faith under a large spreading tree in the eastern district of Nassau. His followers quickly grew from forty to sixty in 1788. In 1791 he wrote to George Liele in Jamaica to the effect that he had 300 members and by 1812 it was reported that the church in New Providence had 850 members.[24]

The passion to grow churches not only as spaces where the gospel of Christ was proclaimed from an Afrocentric frame of reference but also as centers of literacy for both freed and enslaved children of Africa was embraced by Liele and his mentees. Through Liele's influence,

CHAPTER 1

the ministry he ascribed to in Savannah, Georgia, Silver Bluff, South Carolina, and Jamaica, West Indies, was practiced by mentees Andrew Bryan, Jesse Peter, David George, and Amos Williams, in Georgia and South Carolina; in Canada and Freetown, Sierra Leone, Africa; and in New Providence, Nassau, West Indies. In similar fashion as David George ministered in Nova Scotia and Freetown, and Amos Williams in New Providence, Liele began his ministry in Jamaica, West Indies, in 1783. He was the first person of the Christian faith to take the gospel of Christ combined with a ministry in literacy to both freed and enslaved Africans outside of the United States. Liele also has the distinction of participating in the organization of the first church aimed at ministry to African Americans, in Silver Bluff, South Carolina. We noted earlier that when Brother Amos (Amos Williams) arrived in New Providence, Nassau, in 1783, he began his ministry in that country by preaching to enslaved persons under a large tree in the open air. Liele began in similar fashion, preaching in the open air at a park in Kingston, Jamaica, known as the Race Course. Like Jesus their teacher and savior, they taught and preached the gospel in spaces that included trees and running water, especially for baptism, in the midst of the created world.

LIELE IN JAMAICA

In her carefully argued book *Liberty's Exiles: American Loyalists in the Revolutionary World*, Maya Jasanoff gives a flavor of the Jamaica in which George Liele and his family arrived in January 1783. In describing contrasts with Savannah, Georgia, which Liele and his family had left, and their new home in Kingston, Jamaica, Jasanoff points out that although Jamaica represented a fresh start for Liele and family, they had to adjust to an enslaved population that greatly outnumbered the white minority. They had to view the world from a different vantage point—they were now a part of a black majority. However, a consequence of this new reality was that the master class who belonged to a numerical minority would use extraordinary violence to keep enslaved persons subservient and valorize slave culture.

"A dispassionate record of Jamaica's every day sadism survives in the diaries of plantation overseer Thomas Thistlewood, whose thirty-seven-year-long career on the island ended with his death in 1786," she writes. "By then, Thistlewood had scored tens of thousands of lashes across slaves' bare skin, practically flaying some of his victims alive."[25] According to Jasanoff, the realization of a new order in which oppressed Black people would be in the majority while at the same time becoming keenly aware of their lack of power to improve their lives and move from the status of slaves as they affirm their humanity would be signaled to Liele and his family on their voyage to freedom and a fresh start in Jamaica—the ships that took them across the Atlantic also took three thousand white refugees with about eight thousand enslaved persons.

Liele and his family represented a small minority of free Blacks. Liele's freedom would be compromised as he would be indentured to Moses Kirkland, who loaned him funds, which in part made it possible for himself and his family to travel to Jamaica. George Liele and his family "joined about ten thousand mixed-race 'free people of color' and free blacks living in Jamaica. As Liele made his way through Kingston's streets, mud-clogged by the summer rains, he must have marveled to find himself for the first time in his life, in a city where black faces outnumbered white. He was now in a society where he counted in the racial majority . . . yet where that majority was brutally subordinated by laws and violence. Liele knew from his time in a Georgia jail, that being a free black in America was hard enough."[26]

The Rev. John Clark, a missionary from England who served as a Baptist pastor, knew very well and informs us that Liele was very moved with the wretched state of enslaved people in Jamaica. According to Clark, enslaved communities that Liele met in Jamaica "were treated as beasts of burden, bought, sold, branded, driven by the whip, and compelled to labor to the utmost extent of endurance; debarred from self-improvement."[27] Liele, who was not formally commissioned by any organization or church agency to do the work of a Christian missionary to Jamaica, would have to proceed with caution in his attempt to take the church—his version of the Christian gospel—to the enslaved community. He would have learned at Silver Bluff and in the formation of his nascent church in Savannah during the American Revolution that taking the gospel of Christ to the enslaved community could be dangerous; the master class needed assurances that their religion was being offered in a non-threatening way. It was not enough to encourage enslaved persons to attend church when church was not in easy reach and slaves had experiences of feeling unwelcome at church.

In South Carolina, Liele preached to David George and others in a cornfield; now in Jamaica, he begins his ministry at the Race Course, or park. John Clark, a close observer of Liele, mentions that he was moved by the sense of hopelessness that was the lot of the enslaved community he encountered and engaged in Jamaica: "When he [Liele] arrived in Kingston, and saw the wretched state of enslaved brethren living in ignorance and vice, without God, and without hope in the world, his heart was filled with compassion for their souls. He took his stand on the Race Course, and boldly proclaimed the truth as it is in Jesus."[28]

It is appropriate to ask at the beginning of Liele's ministry in Jamaica if there are any clues as to the content of his preaching. Is there any way to begin to frame the scope and content of Liele's proclamation in his early years in Jamaica? In his important essay, "Georgia's Religion in the Colonial Era, 1733–1790," Charles Walker points out that Big Buckhead Creek Baptist Church, where Liele was baptized, licensed to preach, and then ordained to the Christian ministry, was shaped by Matthew Moore, who was in the tradition of the Separatist Baptists. Walker explains: "So many of Whitfield's converts became Baptists that he is reported to have remarked, 'my chickens have turned to ducks.' These converts were soon called 'New Lights' and when they withdrew from the old established churches became known as 'Separate Baptists.'"[29] Over against the Separatists are Regular, or Particular Baptists, who tended more towards a Calvinistic viewpoint and were very conservative in worship, evangelism, and doctrine. Separate Baptists were zealous in making confession of sin and believed in the guidance of the Holy Spirit and the authority of the Bible. "They insisted on an 'Experience of Grace,'" Walker writes, "which was to be publicly confessed before a person was received into the church and baptized. They were much freer in accepting a man's profession of a call to preach than were the Regular Baptists. Yet, they examined him closely and were careful to have a presbytery of ministers for his ordination."[30] This sets the context for beginning to understand the passion and appeal to a theology of grace that Liele exuded as he began a ministry in Jamaica primarily among an enslaved community.

The worldviews that African American preachers confronted in the Caribbean at the turn of the eighteenth and early decades of the nineteenth centuries reflect communities in which the memory of Africa was very strong and Africa served as a controlling metaphor. Ernest Payne, culling from letters that George Liele wrote to John Rippon of the British Baptist Churches from 1791 to 1793, describes the life that confronted Liele and his family in Kingston: "The godlessness of the place filled him [Liele] with concern, and he began boldly preaching at the Kingston, Race Course, forming with a handful of other American refugees, a little Baptist Church. . . . There was much opposition to be met. The life of Kingston was in general wild and dissolute."[31] What Payne, the British theologian, refers to as life in Jamaica that was "wild and dissolute" was the presence and practices of what Du Bois refers to as the African Church. "It was not at first by any means a Christian Church, but a mere adaptation of those heathen rites which we roughly designate as Obe Worship, or 'Voodooism.'"[32] According to Du Bois, African ways of thinking, coupled with faith leaders who interpreted the Christian faith from an African frame of reference, made it extremely difficult if not impossible for the Black church or faith leaders not to meld their Christian faith with African ways of thinking. There was a blending and melding of African and Christian beliefs. Du Bois wagers that there was a bias in churches that were administered by persons of African descent toward a reliance on the centrality of the spirit. Jesus was often understood as one spirit among other spirits. In the naming of his church in Savannah as the First African Baptist Church and the church in Jamaica as the Ethiopian Baptist Church, it is clear an African identity informed Liele's ecclesiology.

I would like to suggest that Liele operated with two views of the church. On the one hand, he sought to articulate an ecclesiology that ameliorated the fears of the planter class and provided confidence that his version of Christianity would not cause the enslaved class to rebel or become agitated against the master class and, on the other hand employed strategies such as hiring a teacher of literacy for both freed and enslaved Jamaicans. Literacy was an important interpretive key in winning the confidence of the enslaved class. When Liele erected the Ethiopian Baptist Church, he secured a bell from the British Baptist Missionary Society with the primary purpose to alert and inform masters of times when church worship would commence and end. Liele played to two audiences, master and slave, and sought church practice and doctrine that would accommodate both. Liele presented the church covenant of the Ethiopian Baptist Church to the master class, who had thrown him in prison on charges of preaching an incendiary sermon intended to make enslaved people dissatisfied with their condition. The covenant was intended to placate the ruling class and to assure the members of his church that they were God's children with rights and privileges.[33]

Liele had a letter of introduction from Col. Moses Kirkland to the governor of Jamaica, Archibald Campbell, who provided him with a job for two years that allowed him to repay his debt to Kirkland. Liele was able to secure for himself and his family a certificate of freedom "from the Vestry and Governor" according to the laws of the country and formally began his ministry in Jamaica in 1784.

Liele seems to distinguish between his preaching at the Race Course, or park, in Kingston and his preaching in a rented room for church services. Preaching at the Race Course was outdoors to large numbers of enslaved persons who gathered in part because of the novelty of seeing a Black man preaching. Liele was perhaps the first person to work among the enslaved in Jamaica, and certainly the first person of color who engaged them with his gospel of freedom. Commenting on the founding of the Ethiopian Baptist Church, Liele stated:

> I began, about September 1784, to preach in Kingston, in a small private house, to a good smart congregation, and I formed the church with four brethren from America besides myself, and the preaching took effect with the poorer sort, especially the slaves. The people, being poor people, at first persecuted us both at meetings, and baptisms, but God be praised, they seldom interrupt us now. We have applied to the Honorable House of Assembly, with a petition to our distress, being

poor people, desiring to worship Almighty God according to the tenets of the Bible, and they have granted us liberty to worship him as we please in Kingston.[34]

Liele's introduction to colonial Jamaica would help him recall what it meant in Savannah, Georgia, to be a Christian slave. Perhaps he did learn from his pastor Matthew Moore, a Separate Baptist who was greatly influenced by George Whitfield, that enslaved persons were also the children of God, and they should have the gospel of Christ proclaimed to them and encouraged to become Christians. But this did not mean challenging and changing the structures of slavery. A Christian slave, they believed, would be obedient, dutiful, and diligent and would serve the master as he or she served Christ. Worship was in the service of keeping things the way they were and not aimed at transformation. Faith and practice were never conjoined with any sense of raising questions about race and enslaved persons being made in the image of God.

In the Jamaican context in which Liele was trying to find his way as preacher, there was a profound disconnect between the practice of the church in matters of social justice and the plight of the oppressed, which enslaved persons concluded, "Master, left him god in England." There was a vast distance in social intercourse between Black and white persons in Savannah and in Jamaica. In Savannah, George Liele attended and became a member of a white congregation from which he received license to preach and his ordination. A contemporary of Liele, a Baptist pastor, points out the situation of oppressed Jamaicans whether in church or in the wider society.

> Not only were they oppressed and bowed down by the operation of unjust and cruel laws, but there was yet another circumstance connected with the condition of the colored and black population, in some respects still more painful. The most inveterate prejudice existed against them on account of their color. Hence they were universally prohibited all intercourse of equality with whites, and if of such an opprobrious distinction they ventured to complain, they were often insultingly told that they were "the descendants of the ourang-outang," that their mothers hunted the tigers in the wilds of Africa; and but for the

generosity of their sires, in place of possessing freedom and property, their lot would have been to dig cane holes beneath the discipline of the driver's whip. At church, if a man of color, however respectable in circumstance or character, entered the pew of the lowest white man, he was instantly ordered out.... With people of color, indeed the whites, like the Egyptians in reference to the Israelites, held it an abomination to eat bread.[35]

According to Missionary Phillippo, "race" was an overarching rubric that governed the relationship of white people to "Colored" and Black people in Liele's Jamaica. It made no difference whether enslaved persons were in the fields offering their bodies to make a profit for the enslaver or at church seeking to worship. In either context, the master-servant, superior-subordinate dynamic held sway. Understandably, enslaved persons in Jamaica preferred to worship among themselves and often resented having to worship with whites, because of the ways Christianity was used to reinforce subordination and subjugation among people of color and the enslaved class. Large numbers of poor people attended Liele's ministry, especially when he preached at the Race Course in Kingston.

In 1791 Liele writes to Dr. Rippon stating that he had purchased three acres of land and had begun to build a meeting place. The congregation was comprised primarily of enslaved persons. Liele suggests that enslaved persons attend worship with permission from their owners. There were also a number of freed persons who attended his church.

"George Liele was probably the first person to do religious work in Jamaica," writes John Parmer Gates. "Up to this time there was not very much effort expended in preaching the Gospel even to the whites. Some early pioneer work was done by three Moravian missionaries in 1754. ... Most of the slaves in Jamaica had probably never heard of the Gospel until the Methodists, and the Baptists under Liele, came at the end of the eighteenth century. Some of the Negroes were undoubtedly not far removed from their primitive state, for slave trade with Africa was still in progress.... Belief in witchcraft, the use of charms and other superstitions were common among them. Is it any wonder that Liele attracted attention when, for the first time, he appeared on the Kingston racetrack preaching the love of God that was in Christ Jesus."[36]

Phillip Curtin suggests that one way in which Liele bridges the gap between his approach to Christianity and that of the enslaved community in Jamaica was to allow a number of African Americans who migrated to Jamaica with him to merge their Baptist faith with the Jamaican Myal religion and create the Native Baptist Church. The loose structure of the Baptist Church allowed them to include African traditional practices such as drumming, dancing, and spirit seizure—in short, practices of Myal. One of the key leaders of the Native Baptist Church who migrated from the United States with George Leile was George Lewis, who rejected the missionary version of Christianity in favor of his more African style. "Lewis had been born in Africa and taken to Virginia as a slave," writes Curtin. "After the American Revolution he was brought to Kingston, where his mistress let him work as a peddler in return for a monthly fee. He mixed peddling with preaching along his route in the parishes of Manchester and St. Elizabeth."[37] Certainly Liele was in the tradition of Lewis in combining his approach to Baptist teaching and polity with African religious practices. Other African American leaders in the tradition of Lewis and Liele were George Gibb and Moses Baker. According to church historian W. J. Gardner, for four years (1783–1787) Baker "lived in utter disregard of religion."[38] It is clear that by "religion," Gardner meant *Christian* religion.

Philip Curtin explained the organizational structure of Native Baptist churches that made it most appealing to many Afro-Jamaicans:

> The organizational basis . . . was the "leader system," and adaptation of the English Wesleyan practice of dividing the church members into classes for teaching. Possibly, the native Baptists picked it up from White missionaries who were already at work in Jamaica, but more likely it was their American training. In any case the leader system underwent some strange transformations. The class-leaders became something more than just a teacher of new converts. They were real spiritual guides, taking a position equivalent to leadership of a Myal cult group, and their power over the classes was authoritarian to the point of tyranny.[39]

Native Baptists adopted a doctrinal position that elevated "the spirit" and neglected the written word. "The followers of Baker and Gibb were required to be possessed by 'the spirit' before baptism was administered," Curtin explains. "This meant the spirit had to descend on the applicant in a dream, which was then described to the leader.... There evolved a regular technique and ceremonial for bringing on spirit-possession, which included a fast according to a set canon followed by a trip into the bush alone at night to wait for the spirit to descend."[40] A theology of spirit provided an openness for Native Baptists to make the theological connection they saw necessary. In this church, John the Baptist had the priority over Jesus Christ, since he baptized and accepted Jesus into his church, so to speak. Jesus was one of the prophets and was not equal with God.

Liele, as one of the first Black persons to introduce Christianity to enslaved persons in the United States, and in Jamaica, was committed to the survival of his people and his family. He believed that Christianity offered the best path to freedom, even if spiritual freedom was seen as a necessary step toward physical freedom. The truth was that often masters and missionaries alike were disappointed with the result of enslaved persons, who would often combine Christian and African practices. In many instances enslaved persons were not willing to abandon Africa nor were they willing to ignore Europe.

In colonial Jamaica, Africa and Europe competed for the souls of Black people. When the lives of enslaved persons were understood from the perspective of missionary teaching, Jesus often meant conformity, obedience to the master class, and even subordination and subservience. One answer to the question, "Where do I stand in relation to Jesus?" was survival within the context of slavery. Liele was a slave in the United States, and yet in Jamaica he owned slaves. He believed that Jesus softened the harshness and terror of slavery because a kinder, gentler slave produced a master who was less inclined to brutalize the enslaved person. For Liele, Jesus did not yet mean fighting for emancipation or breaking the chains of slavery. Liele would test the water to see how the master class would react, and at the first sign of a harsh response, he would recant and fall in line. The truth for Liele is that he would often be satisfied with spiritual freedom for the enslaved persons he served and be content to coexist with their physical chains. What was ultimately at stake was the survival of the church.

One lesson Liele teaches us is that the answer to the Jesus-Africa question, namely, "Where do I stand in relation to Jesus?" or "Where do I stand in relation to Africa?" was *contextual* for him. For the most part Afro-Jamaicans were committed to a hermeneutic of freedom, and survival with dignity was understood as an aspect of that freedom.

It was noted above that Liele and his congregation were focused on the procurement of a place of worship in Kingston, and about three acres of land were purchased on the Windward Road. The noted Baptist historian Horace Russell gives a description of the location of this first dissenting chapel built by George Liele in Jamaica:

> There stands at the corner of Elletson Road and Windward Road in Kingston, Jamaica, a factory which produces foam rubber mattresses and other household furnishings. Next to it is a little chapel which divides the warehouse from the factory itself. On the site where the factory now stands was once located the cemetery, which at one time, was attached to the church. The little wooden church now belongs to the Church of Christ, but it is almost certain that it was on this site that the first Baptist Church in Jamaica stood.[41]

Among Baptists of Jamaica who join the search for the first Baptist church erected by George Liele, this location is often pointed to as the most likely place where Liele erected his church and was buried. In any case, soon after the Ethiopian Baptist Church was completed, Liele preached a sermon from Romans 10:1: "Brethren, my heart's desire and prayer to God for them is that they may be saved." It is reported that in this sermon Liele expressed a strong hope for the salvation and liberation of the enslaved community. "He was charged with preaching sedition and forthwith thrown into prison, where he was treated with the greatest severity," writes F. A. Cox. "He was loaded with irons, his feet made fast in the stocks, and no one was allowed to see him, not even his wife or children. At length he was tried for his life, and some of the leading men in Kingston swore against him, alleging that he sought to stir up the slaves to insurrection."[42]

The tide seemed to turn against Liele and his approach to Christianity and its efficacy as a medium of survival and liberation for the oppressed. Christopher Brent Ballew cites three important sources that claim "another preacher was tried with Liele and hanged."[43] John Parmer Gates reminds us of the history of cruelty and exploitation in Jamaica prior to Liele's presence as a member of the community. In 1509 under Spanish occupation of the island, the Native Indians were hanged "by thirteens" in honor of the thirteen apostles. Further, when the British seized Jamaica from the Spanish in 1655, "Cromwell is supposed to have advised the enslavement of the Negroes 'for their spiritual advantage'" writes Gates. "Rather than be re-enslaved, however, the Negroes who were slaves of the Spanish fled to the mountains. There they became the nucleus of the famous 'Maroon' population, whose number steadily increased through the years by the addition of runaway slaves. These Negroes continued to harass the country until the last Maroon War in 1795."[44] According to Gates, Liele found the enslaved population in worse plight than he was accustomed to in Georgia and South Carolina, where he engaged in ministry prior to his voyage to Jamaica. Liele has been silent concerning the notion that another preacher was tried with him on charges of sedition and hanged. It has not been unusual in slave culture for slaves to be silent concerning extremely painful episodes in their lives. In any case Liele was released, perhaps because of the influence of important friends such as Col. Moses Kirkland, who introduced him to Governor Campbell, who then provided him with employment on his arrival in Jamaica. Baptist theologian Ernest Payne reminds us that "on his arrival in Kingston in 1783, Liele was employed for a while by the Governor of Jamaica. . . . Already in 1791 the need for a permanent building for the church was acute and an appeal for help was made. A number of white men, including Bryan Edwards, the Jamaican historian, responded generously, and in 1793 the first dissenting chapel in the island was built."[45] Perhaps it was Liele's ability to relate to both worlds, that of the master and enslaved, that saved him from being hanged.

Perhaps, the hanging of a fellow preacher served as an atoning sacrifice for his culpability, thereby satisfying the authorities.

Liele devised a plan while in jail to placate the ruling class. He assured the House of Assembly that unlike several Methodist churches, he would not take enslaved persons into the membership of his church without first obtaining permission from owners. Further, he would not take an offering from enslaved persons; and there were laws against that practice. Liele relied on donations from persons of means among the ruling class. Gates writes, "One of these was Stephen Cooke, a member of the Assembly, who, although he preferred the discipline of the Methodist Church, contributed to the building of Liele's sanctuary and later wrote to Dr. Rippon in London in order to help secure funds from English Baptists."[46] Undoubtedly, in prison Liele equivocated between the strong preaching of a gospel of salvation that led to physical liberation of enslaved persons under the brutality of the system of slavery in Jamaica. He would have had fond memories of how the gospel of a strong salvation worked for himself and his protégés in churches in Georgia and South Carolina. Now in prison in Jamaica, where his own life was threatened, if word may have been leaked to him that a fellow preacher, perhaps of his Baptist faith, was hanged, it was clear that Liele's choice was survival rather than emancipation. While in prison, Liele produced a church covenant that was sent to the Jamaica Assembly for approval and ratification, and one assumes it was also sent to his church to assure them he was negotiating a release from prison that would restore him to the congregation. The covenant was titled, "The Covenant of the Anabaptist Church, begun in America, December 1777 and in Jamaica, December 1783."

1. We are of the Anabaptist persuasion, because we believe it agreeable to the Scriptures. Proof: (Matt. iii. 1-3; 2 Cor. vi. 14-18.)

2. We hold to keep the Lord's Day throughout the year, in a place appointed for Public Worship, in singing psalms, hymns, and spiritual songs, and preaching the gospel of Jesus Christ. (Mark xvi. 2, 5, 6; Col. iii.16.)

3. We hold to be Baptized in a river, or in a place where there is much water, in the name of the Father, and the Son, and the Holy Ghost. (Matt. iii.13, 16, 17; Mark xvi. 15,16; Matt. xxviii. 19.)

4. We hold to receiving the Lord's Supper in obedience according to His commands. (Mark xiv. 22-24; John vi. 53-57.)

5. We hold to the ordinance of washing one another's feet. (John xiii. 2-17.)

6. We hold to receive and admit young children into the Church according to the Word of God. (Luke ii. 27-28; Mark x. 13-16)

7. We hold to pray over the sick, anointing them with oil in the name of the Lord. (James v. 14, 15)

8. We hold to laboring with another according to the Word of God. (Matt. xviii. 15-18.)

9. We hold to appoint Judges and such other Officers among us, to settle any matter according to the Word of God. (Acts. vi. 1-3.)

10. We hold not to the shedding of blood. (Genesis ix. 6; Matt. xxvi. 51-52.)

11. We are forbidden to go to law one with another before the unjust, but to settle any matter we have before the Saints. (1 Cor. vi. 1-3.)

12. We are forbidden to swear not at all (*sic*). (Matt. v. 33-37; Jas. v. 12)

13. We are forbidden to eat blood, for it is the life of a creature, and from things strangled, and from meat offered to idols. (Acts xv. 29.)

14. We are forbidden to wear any costly raiment, such as superfluity. (1 Peter iii. 3, 4; 1 Timothy ii. 9-10.)

15. We permit no slaves to join the Church without first having a few lines from their owners of their good behavior. (1 Peter ii. 13-16; 1 Thess. iii. 13.)

16. To avoid Fornication, we permit none to keep each other, except they be married according to the Word of God. (1 Cor. vii. 2; Heb. xiii.4.)

17. If a slave or servant misbehave to their owners they are to be dealt with according to the Word of God. (1 Tim. i. 6; Eph. vi. 5; 1 Peter ii. 18-22; Titus ii. 9-11.)

18. If any one of this Religion should transgress and walk disorderly, and not according to the Commands which we have received in this Covenant, he will be censured according to the Word of God. (Luke xii. 47-48.)

19. We hold, if a brother or sister should transgress any of these articles written in this Covenant so as to become a swearer, a fornicator, or adulterer; a covetous person, an idolater, a railer, a drunkard, an extortioner, or a whoremonger; or should commit any abominable sin, and do not give satisfaction to the Church, according to the Word of God, he or she, shall be put away from among us, not to keep company, nor to eat with him. (1 Cor. v. 11-13.)

20. We hold if a Brother or Sister should transgress , and abideth not in the doctrine of Christ, and he, or she, after being justly dealt with agreeable to the 8th article, and be put out of the Church, that they shall have no right or claim whatsoever to be interred into the Burying-ground during the time they are put out, should they depart life; but should they return in peace, and make a concession so as to give satisfaction, according to the word of God, they shall be received into the Church again and have all privileges as before granted. (2 John i. 9-10; Gal. vi. 1, 2; Luke xvii. 3, 4.)

21. We hold to all other Commandments, Articles, Covenants, and Ordinances, recorded in the Holy Scriptures as are set forth by our Lord and Master Jesus Christ and His Apostles, which are not written in this Covenant, and to live to them as nigh as we possibly can, agreeable to the Word of God. (John xv. 7-14.)

Chapter 1

Source: See Ernest A. Payne, "Baptist Work in Jamaica Before the Arrival of the Missionary," in *The Baptist Quarterly Incorporating the Transactions of the Baptist Historical Society*. New Series, Volume VII 1934-1935, 24-26. 20-26.

The covenant was important both for pastoral guidance to the congregation and as a tool to pacify the Jamaica Assembly, as a good-faith gesture that Liele would work within the system of slavery and not incite enslave people to rebellion or to run away from their masters, as the Maroons of Jamaica did.

Why would the membership of Liele's church embrace a covenant that in part supported the violence of masters against the enslaved community, curtailed their freedom of movement, and made them vow obedience to masters? There were sections of the covenant that read as if it was written by the masters, as Liele promised on their behalf to his congregation that they were against the shedding of blood and against challenging claims of freedom by the enslaved community. The membership of Liele's church would have understood that the covenant was written in a context of extreme oppression in which their pastor was on death row charged with plotting and planning sedition against the government of Jamaica. This would have amplified their angst if word had gotten to them that a fellow preacher of the gospel of Christ had been hanged because of his participation with Liele in preaching a hopeful gospel of salvation for the enslaved community. The covenant was read at church services when the sacrament of the Lord's supper was observed. In short, the membership of the church would understand that they had to do what was necessary for the survival of the church. The survival of Black churches was indeed a part of the legacy of enslaved persons. And Baptist churches had a special role as many of these churches were independent without the need for a parent organization to sponsor them.

However, Liele was in for a season of challenges. Shortly after the opening of his church he was imprisoned once again, this time for debt—he was unable to pay for erecting his church. Liele was thus imprisoned from 1797 to 1801. During the interim there were schisms in his church as his son Paul, who officiated during his father's absence, met strong resistance from Deacon Swigle, who often served as schoolmaster for the freed school and assistant pastor to Liele. Swigle broke away and formed his own church, taking more than half of Liele's membership with him. Rippon mentioned that by 1802, a year after Liele was released from jail, Swigle's congregation could boast a membership of five hundred.

To further make life difficult for dissenting congregations in Jamaica, the House of Assembly passed a law in 1806 forbidding teaching and preaching on plantations, and this law remained in force until 1814. Colonial governments throughout the Caribbean were extremely agitated in the wake of the Haitian Revolution that was in full force. With the overthrow of the colonial government in Haiti and masters fleeing to other countries, the colonial powers in Jamaica were agitated and viewed churches as centers and contexts where a gospel of freedom and equality could be dangerous and needed to be curtailed. The clergy of all dissenting churches were required to produce letters to the Honorable House of Assembly, from the leadership of their churches, usually in England, granting them permission to preach. The problem Liele had was that in a slave culture, he was not regarded as the head of his church. Further, the House of Assembly expected Liele and his church to relate to an authority such as the Baptist Missionary Society in England for authorization to lead his churches. Although Liele had a relationship with the British Baptists through the aegis of John Rippon, and friends who would offer financial and moral support in the building of his church and providing educational material for Liele and his membership, in the tradition of the independent Black Baptist churches in Georgia and South Carolina, Liele did not appeal to a central ecclesial authority for permission or counsel in matters of faith, polity, or doctrine. There was no parent church or organization; it was an independent church with Liele as chief pastor. This was not the case with the Methodist Church in Jamaica, to which Liele and his churches were compared. This became even more complicated for Liele, and his churches, in relation to the Honorable House of Assembly when Baptist missionaries from England came to Jamaica in 1814 and declared the Baptist Missionary Society as their sponsoring organization. What is of interest in the missionary presence of the English Baptists in Jamaica was they were not considered

CHAPTER 1

a part of Liele's church. Robert J. Stewart, in *Religion and Society in Post-Emancipation Jamaica*, illustrates Liele's dilemma:

> The Wesleyan-Methodist Missionary Society was born in the 1780's under Dr. Thomas Coke's directions. His visit to Jamaica in 1789 can be taken as the commencement of the society's connection with the island. The key terms of organization in the Methodist missionary structure were conference, district, district meeting, district chairman, and circuit. The Jamaican mission belonged to the British Conference, or in other words, to the Wesleyan-Methodist church in England.[47]

Liele was not commissioned as a missionary. He was the product of independent Baptist churches and was confronted with a new expectation by the House of Assembly to provide permission from an external denominational agency in order to preach and administer churches.

How could a Black man, a former slave who was in and out of jails, provide leadership for churches he administered, when he was expected to provide authorization from an ecclesial organization such as the Baptist Missionary Society of London? Maya Jasanoff states the problem that confronted Liele if he were to preach again in Jamaica, granted the explosion of fear engendered by the Haitian Revolution:

> But when the Caribbean blew up in a new revolution, Liele found himself staring into the authoritarian face of the British Empire. An empire of law and of liberty some might claim it to be, but this was still an empire that practiced mass enslavement, and Britain was still the world's preeminent slave-trading nation. . . . Liele's prosecution in 1794 was just part of a larger campaign against suspected dissidents. In 1802 the house of assembly passed a law banning "the preaching of ill-disposed, illiterate, or ignorant enthusiasts, to meetings of negroes and persons of color, chiefly slaves." Liele himself never returned to regular preaching after the 1790s.[48]

These were extremely difficult times for preachers from dissenting churches. Moses Baker, a fellow preacher who was baptized by Liele, was arrested for quoting the words of a Baptist hymn: "We will be slaves no more/Since Christ has made us free/Has nailed our tyrants to the cross/ And bought our liberty."

This challenge did not prevent Baker from finding ways to preach to his community. Liele, like generations of enslaved Africans both before and after his time in serving churches, would have found occasions to witness "down by the riverside" or as was a tradition among the Native Baptists, seek to meet the spirits in the forests at nights. Jasanoff also suggests that the persecution among the Baptists from the House of Assembly and the owners of plantations was so severe that she posits Liele did not leave Jamaica, in similar fashion as his mentee David George who migrated with enslaved persons to Nova Scotia for ten years and then to Freetown, Sierra Leone, in West Africa. Jasanoff suggests a dead end for Liele: "George Liele, though, stayed put in Jamaica, despite the persecution he faced as a free black and Baptist. If indeed he ever wished to leave, he may have found the cost of a passage to Britain or North America prohibitive."[49] But Jasanoff is wrong. Liele found a way. Black people and Black preachers often find a way. In the Black church they would sing about making a way out of no way. Liele traveled to England in 1822 in search of a letter of authorization that would satisfy the demands of the Jamaica House of Assembly. In similar fashion it is conceivable that Liele found ways of communicating the gospel to churches under his supervision. This was who he was at his core: a preacher of the word of God to the enslaved and oppressed communities.

LIELE IN ENGLAND

Liele took the bold step of traveling to England in 1822 in search of a letter of authorization from the Baptist Missionary Society that he could present to the Jamaica House of Assembly to grant him permission to preach in Jamaica. John Clark, a missionary colleague of Liele, stated:

> About 1822, Mr. Liele paid a visit to England, but soon returned, and a few years afterward died. Mr. William Knibb attended his funeral and believed him to be a God-fearing man. One of his daughters became a member of the Hanover Street Church, and two of his grandsons attended East Queen Street School; one of these afterwards became a

member of the House of Assembly and frequently showed good ability and love to his country.[50]

These claims by Missionary Clark are of first importance as his claim that Liele visited England is substantiated by the minutes of the Baptist Missionary Society of England. Further, Clark's observation that William Knibb attended Liele's funeral may be the only clue we have as to when Liele died and was funeralized. William Knibb arrived in Jamaica February 12, 1825, when Liele would have been seventy-five, so it is reasonable to place his death in 1825.

These were difficult times for the Native Baptists. Liele's Windward Road Chapel was in need of much repair. During Liele's visit to England, his congregation invited Missionary Tinson to serve as pastor during the interim. Tinson had arrived on the island a couple of months prior to Liele's departure. It is not likely that Liele met with any of the folks with whom he corresponded in England over the years, especially John Rippon. Horace Russell stated without evidence that Rippon invited Liele to England in 1822 to 1828. "When the numbers of freed Africans increased over time, John Rippon invited Liele to come to London to help him, which he did for six years (1822–1828). Liele's work in England remains an area of fruitful research."[51] The minutes of the British Baptist Missionary Society clear up any misunderstanding of the purpose of Liele's visit to England:

> Mr. Burls reported that he and the Secretary (Mr. Dyer) had seen and conversed with George Liele, a black minister from Jamaica, who had come to this country with a view to procure a license for preaching himself, or a minister to accompany him back to Jamaica, under the sanction of the Committee, on which it was "Resolved, that the Committee cannot sanction the application of Mr. Liele unless it be concurred in by those brethren in connection with us, who are already in the island."[52]

It is clear that Liele was not in good graces with members of the British Baptist Missionary Society General Committee. John Rippon shared with the wider community Liele's work in Jamaica and Savannah,

Georgia. But now Rippon was pastor of the famous Carter's Lane Baptist Church in London from 1771 to 1834. Rippon seems to have become unpopular as pastor as three deacons, Gilbert Blight, Thomas Evans, and Samuel Gayle, said they were "derelict in their duty of not asking the pastor to leave."[53]

Missionary Clark sums up Liele's contribution: "Mr. Liele appears to have been a good man and devoted to the work of the divine master. He baptized Moses Baker, was a light, in those dark days, shining in a dark place, and among dark people. He has been charged by many men who came to Jamaica long after his decease, with teaching false doctrine, and following superstitious practices."[54]

What may we make of Liele's contribution to church and state? It is clear Liele was a man of firsts. The first African American to be ordained to the Christian ministry, on May 20, 1775. The first Baptist missionary to take the gospel outside the American colonies, in 1782. Liele named his church the Ethiopian Baptist Church, and thereby made connections in Savannah, Georgia; Silver Bluff, South Carolina; Augusta, Georgia; New Providence, Bahamas; Kingston, Jamaica; Nova Scotia, Canada; and Sierra Leone, Africa. Several of these connections were made through his protégés David George, Amos Williams, Jesse Peters, Andrew Bryan, and Moses Baker. Liele was proactive in combining religion and education in his approach to the preaching and educational task. It is quite likely that Liele was the first to preach the gospel to enslaved persons in Jamaica. Although the Moravian Church was in Jamaica as early as 1754, they were not focused on sharing the gospel of Christ with enslaved persons. One reason for their lack of passion for the enslaved was they were invited to the island by plantation owners. This of course was also the case with some Baptist missionaries who came to Jamaica after 1814 from Great Britain.

Liele enjoyed a level of freedom that got him in trouble with the planter class and the House of Assembly, because he was not sponsored by any church or organization. In the end, Liele was forced to seek ecclesial sponsorship as the Jamaica House of Assembly created laws that made preachers accountable to external organizations such as the British Baptist Missionary Society. Liele had to come to grips with the reality that he was a former slave, Black, and without ecclesial sponsorship in Jamaica, a British colony. Liele's passion was to place the Bible in the hands of enslaved persons. He insisted on having literacy training in Native churches as he appointed schoolmasters in schools for both freed and enslaved persons. Deacon Swigle, Liele's assistant, was in charge of literacy in the Windward Road Church. In a letter to Rippon, Swigle pointed out that in Eastern and mid-island parishes, there was the tradition of often beginning the church in a schoolhouse. In a profound sense Liele conjoined salvation and education. Education was for liberation—the enabling of enslaved persons to read the Bible for themselves. Liele's tradition of combining church and education led to the formation of Calabar College for the training of native clergy in 1843.

Liele began Baptist work in Jamaica. In a letter to John Rippon in 1792, Liele pointed out that his Baptist Church was the only Baptist place of worship on the island. The British missionary John Rowe came to the western parish of St. James in 1814, thirty-two years after Liele had Baptist witness making a difference throughout Jamaica. It is of interest that Liele did not take the lead in inviting the British missionaries to Jamaica. It was Liele's protégé Moses Baker, who was baptized by Liele and under the employ of plantation owner Samuel Vaughn. It seems that what happened was Moses Baker through the instrumentality of Vaughn invited missionaries to the island. In any event what occurred was two Baptist churches began to emerge on the island: the Native Baptist church led by Afro-Jamaicans and the orthodox Baptist church led by missionaries. In the mind of enslaved persons these churches complemented each other, and the children of Africa brought a "both and" methodology rather than an "either or" approach to their understanding of Baptist churches. This is illustrated by the Baptist War of 1831 led by Baptist Deacon, who belonged both to Moses Baker's mission on the plantation and was referred to by all who knew him as "Daddy Sharpe" and at the same time Deacon Sharpe. At the missionary's church he was known as Deacon Sharpe and at Baker's he was known as Daddy Sharpe. The Baptist War signaled the beginning of the end of slavery in Jamaica. The struggle for freedom over the years took the form of enslaved persons running away—as was the case of the Maroons fleeing to the hills and organizing attacks against the British from time to time. The focus of the Baptist War was Black people organizing to withdraw their labor, and because of this the brunt of the attack was on the institutions of the plantations.

One hundred and twenty buildings were torched as Daddy Sharpe from the Native Baptist Church led a rebellion that insisted enslaved people were human beings. Slavery was partially abolished in 1834 in Jamaica, and complete emancipation arrived in 1838. Enslaved, and then free, Liele could dream of this day when the children of his ministry would ignite a flame of liberation and freedom in Jamaica—even if he were forced to make peace with survival and not liberation. Liele, with a hymnal in one hand and the Bible in the other, taught church and society "for freedom that Christ has set us free" (Galatians 5:1 RSV).

Notes

1. John Rippon, *Baptist Annual Register, for 1790, 1791, 1792, and Part of 1793, Including Sketches of the State of Religion among Different Denominations of Good Men at Home and Abroad*, volume 1 (London, 1793).

2. Robert G. Gardner, "Primary Sources in the Study of Eighteenth-Century Georgia Baptist History," *Viewpoints: Georgia Historical Society*, no. 7 (1980): 59–119, 103.

3. Rippon, *Baptist Annual Register*, 332–33.

4. Rippon, *Baptist Annual Register*, 334.

5. Edgar Garfield Thomas, *The First African Baptist Church of North America* (Savannah, GA: E. G. Thomas, 1925), 11. Cited by John Parmer Gates, "George Liele: A Pioneer Negro Preacher," *The Chronicle: A Baptist Historical Quarterly* 6, no. 3 (July 1943): 118–29, 120.

6. Rippon, *Baptist Annual Register*, 336.

7. Rippon, *Baptist Annual Register*, 336.

8. Milledge Galphin Murray, "Geographic and Socio-Economic Environment at Silver Bluff: George Galphin, Indian Trader and Plantation Owner," in *George Liele's Life and Legacy: An Unsung Hero*, ed. David T. Shannon, Julia Frazier White, and Deborah Van Broekhoven (Macon, GA: Mercer University Press, 2012), 18–19. The full text of David George's conversion and responsibilities as elder of the Silver Bluff Church as reported by John Rippon is reported in the *Baptist Annual Register*, 1790–1793, 473–80.

9. Walter H. Brooks, "The Priority of the Silver Bluff Church and Its Promoters," *Journal of Negro History* 7, no. 2 (1922): 172–73, 172–96.

10. Albert J. Raboteau, *Slave Religion: The "Invisible Institution" in the Antebellum South* (New York: Oxford University Press, 1978), 139.

11. Brooks, "The Priority of the Silver Bluff Church and Its Promoters," 176.

Chapter 1

12. Carter G. Woodson, *The History of the Negro Church* (Washington, DC: Associated Publishers, 1921), 43.
13. Brooks, "The Priority of the Silver Bluff Church and Its Promoters," 176.
14. John W. Davis, "George Liele and Andrew Bryan, Pioneer Negro Baptist Preachers," *Journal of Negro History* 3, no. 2 (1918): 120, 119–27.
15. Davis, "George Liele and Andrew Bryan, Pioneer Negro Baptist Preachers," 121–22. See also Rippon, *Baptist Annual Register, 1790–1793*, 340. Rippon affirms that Andrew Bryan was converted by Liele's preaching.
16. Brooks, "The Priority of the Silver Bluff Church and Its Promoters," 185.
17. Brooks, "The Priority of the Silver Bluff Church and Its Promoters," 185.
18. Rippon, *Baptist Annual Register, 1791*, 336.
19. Brooks, "The Priority of the Silver Bluff Church and Its Promoters," 189.
20. L. H. Whelchel Jr., *The History and Heritage of African American Churches: A Way Out of No Way* (St. Paul, MN: Paragon House, 2011), 106.
21. Alfred Lane Pugh, "The Great Awakening and Baptist Beginnings in Colonial Georgia, the Bahama Islands, and Jamaica (1739–1833)," *American Baptist Quarterly* 26, no. 4 (2007): 371.
22. Pugh, "The Great Awakening and Baptist Beginnings in Colonial Georgia, the Bahama Islands, and Jamaica (1739–1833)," 371–72.
23. Antonina Canzoneri, "The History of Bethel Baptist Church, Nassau," August 1994, No. 79698, Department of Archives, Bethel Baptist Church, Nassau. See also Colonial Office papers on microfilm in Public Archives, Nassau, Co 23/81 Folio 316 ff. 1826.
24. Jim Lawlor, "Shadrach Kerr: Priest and Missionary," *American Baptist Quarterly* 26, no. 4 (2007).
25. Maya Jasanoff, *Liberty's Exiles: American Loyalists in the Revolutionary World* (New York: Alfred A. Knoff, 2011), 149.
26. Jasanoff, *Liberty's Exiles*, 149–50.
27. John Clark, W. Dendy, and J. M. Phillippo, *The Voice of Jubilee: A Narrative of the Baptist Mission, Jamaica, from Its Commencement* (London: Paternoster Row, 1865), 30.
28. Clark, Dendy, and Phillippo, *The Voice of Jubilee*, 31.
29. Charles O. Walker, "Georgia's Religion in the Colonial Era, 1733–1790," *Viewpoints: Georgia Baptist Historical Society* 5 (1976): 17–44, 31.
30. Walker, "Georgia's Religion in the Colonial Era, 1733–1790," 31–32. See also B. Carlisle Driggers, "The Early Baptist Roots and Religious Environment of George Liele," in *George Liele's Life and Legacy: An Unsung Hero*.
31. Ernest Payne, "Baptist Work in Jamaica before the Arrival of the Missionaries," *Baptist Quarterly* 7 (1934–1935): 20–26, 21.
32. W. E. Burghardt Du Bois, *The Negro Church* (Atlanta, GA: Atlanta University Press, 1903), 5.
33. For a full discussion of the covenant, see Noel Leo Erskine, *Plantation Church: How African American Religion Was Born in Caribbean Slavery* (New York: Oxford University Press, 2014), 174–76.
34. John Rippon, *Baptist Annual Register, for 1790, 1791, 1792, and Part of 1793*, volume 1, 334.

35. James Mursell Phillippo, *Jamaica: Its Past and Present State* (London: John Snow, 1843; reprinted, Westport, CT: Negro University Press, 1970), 147–48.
36. Gates, "George Liele: A Pioneer Negro Preacher," 118–29, 123.
37. Philip Curtin, *Two Jamaicas* (New York: Atheneum, 1970), 33.
38. W. J. Gardner, *A History of Jamaica: From Its Discovery by Christopher Columbus to the Year 1872* (London: T. Fisher Unwin, 1909; first published 1873), 344.
39. Curtin, *Two Jamaicas*, 33.
40. Curtin, *Two Jamaicas*, 33–34.
41. Horace O. Russell, *Foundations and Anticipations: The Jamaica Baptist Story, 1783–1892* (Columbus, GA: Brentwood Christian Press, 1993), 9.
42. F. A. Cox, "The Jamaica Mission, from Its Commencement to the Period of Freedom," in *History of the Baptist Missionary Society. From 1792–1842*. Volume 2, part 3 (London: T. Ward, 1842), 182.
43. Christopher Brent Ballew, *The Impact of African American Antecedents on the Baptist Foreign Missionary Movement, 1782–1825* (Lewiston, NY: Edwin Mellen Press, 2004), 51.
44. Gates, "George Liele: A Pioneer Negro Preacher," 122.
45. Payne, "Baptist Work in Jamaica before the Arrival of the Missionaries," *Baptist Quarterly* 7 (1934–1935): 20–26, 21.
46. Gates, "George Liele: A Pioneer Negro Preacher," 125.
47. Robert J. Stewart, *Religion and Society in Post-Emancipation Jamaica* (Knoxville: University of Tennessee Press, 1992), 6.
48. Jasanoff, *Liberty's Exiles*, 271.
49. Jasanoff, *Liberty's Exiles*, 276.
50. John Clark, *Memorials of Baptist Missionaries in Jamaica, Including a Sketch of the Labours of Early Religious Instructors in Jamaica* (London: Yates and Alexander, 1869), 11.
51. Horace Russell, "Prologue," in *George Liele's Life and Legacy: An Unsung Hero*. A careful examination of the *General Minutes of Carters Lane Baptist Church, December 1830–October 1834* does not mention a Black presence in the congregation. Rippon became pastor of Carter's Lane Church in 1771. In October 21, 1822, the church celebrated the fiftieth anniversary of their pastor. The minutes indicate that several deacons wanted him gone. He left in 1834.
52. Baptist Missionary Society of England Committee Minutes, October 1819–July 1823. See Minutes for May 21, 1822. Pages 203–204.
53. *General Minutes of Carter's Lane Baptist Church*, August 28, 1808. Carter's Lane Baptist Church, London.
54. Clark, *Memorials of Baptist Missionaries in Jamaica*, 11.

Chapter 2

Theologian of Hope

James Melvin Washington, in his important text *Frustrated Fellowship: The Black Baptist Quest for Social Power*, gives us a flavor of the theological leanings of George Liele within Baptist traditions and the import of the evangelical awakening on the emergence of Black preachers, especially in the American South. In this chapter we will look at the emergence of George Liele along with his protégés under the impact of the revivalistic movements that swept the American South during the 1750s, especially under the aegis of evangelists George Whitfield and Freeborn Garrettson. Attention will also be given to the culture in which the revivalistic mission came to the fore and made possible what Carter G. Woodson termed the "The Dawn of a New Day."[1]

Washington divided Baptist doctrinal positions in the American South into three groups during the eighteenth century—the "General" Baptists, who were universalists in their theology and claimed that Christ died for all people and not only for a chosen elect. Over against the General Baptists were the "Particular" Baptists, who believed Christ did not die for all but for a chosen few. Washington claims this was a dominant theological position in eighteenth-century America among the British Baptists. They claimed a rigid dependence on divine providence that would support and sustain the elect of God in times of spiritual and material adversity. The powerful Philadelphia Baptist Association of churches was a primary factor in giving credence and prominence to this theological viewpoint, that Baptists were "a chosen people, a royal priesthood" (1 Peter 2:9 RSV).

In New England the Awakening produced the Separate Baptists. Numerous "New Light" (or revivalistic) Congregational Churches became Baptist. These Baptists may be characterized as revivalistic hyper-Particulars; in their wanderings they radically changed the religious demography of the South. . . . Some of these "New Light" or Separate Baptists, led by Shubal Stearns and Daniel Marshall migrated to Virginia in 1755. Soon afterward Stearns led a group to North Carolina, and Marshall around 1772 led another to Georgia. The Georgia group settled near Kiokee Creek, a tributary of the Savannah River. Undaunted by the successes of the fiery Separates, representatives of the Particular Baptist tradition . . . extended their version of the faith. They called themselves Regular Baptists as a rebuke to the Separate group, which they deemed "irregular." . . . Matthew Moore was one of several Regular pastors who responded to the Separate challenge by stepping up their own revival activity. Moore was pastor of the Buckhead Creek Church, which was probably formed shortly after George Liele, the first formally ordained black Baptist minister, was converted sometime in 1772.[2]

According to Washington the split between the Separate and Regular Baptists did not effect a profound theological difference in Georgia. This was attributed to the skill of Daniel Marshall of the Kiokee Baptist Church and his friend Edmund Botsford of the Charleston Association, the oldest Regular or Particular religious deliberative community in the American South. It is of interest that these southern preachers along with Marshall and Botsford were sympathetic to the cause of American independence from Britain, unlike Matthew Moore, pastor of Big Buckhead Creek Baptist church, under whose ministry Liele was baptized and ordained to the Christian ministry. Both Liele's pastor and his master, Henry Sharp, were pro-British and insisted on British ways of viewing the world. This worldview would have been adopted by Liele, certainly if he hoped to receive freedom from the hands of his master.

THE RISE OF INDEPENDENT BLACK CHURCHES
The rise of independent Black churches and preachers was a direct result of the evangelical revival of the 1740s, known as the Great

Awakening.[3] Woodson informs us that a change of heart seemed to occur among church leaders during this time. Although church leaders were not advocates of the liberation of enslaved persons, they began to use the Bible as their source as they became advocates for addressing the souls of Black people with an emphasis on spiritual salvation. John Leland, a Baptist from Virginia, frames the issue for us.

> The poor slaves under all their hardships, discover as great an inclination for religion as the free born do, when they engage in the service of God, they spare no pains. It is nothing strange for them to walk twenty miles on Sunday morning to meeting and back again at night. . . . They seem in general to put more confidence in their own color, than they do in white; when they attempt to preach, they seldom fail of being very zealous; their language is broken but they understand each other, and the white may gain their ideas. A few of them have undertaken to administer baptism, but it generally ends in confusion; they commonly are more noisy in time of preaching than whites.[4]

During this period many masters allowed the enslaved to attend revival services. Washington reminds us that most enslaved persons, including George Liele, would attend religious worship not for doctrinal purposes but because their needs were existential, and they found a new freedom in community with one another. Sermons of divine justice gave them confidence in God, who would be just in relationship with them. The vision of a just God who would punish all including the master provided a theology of hope for enslaved persons who had to deal on a daily basis with the inequities of the plantation ethos and world.

Prior to the dawn of the new day of opportunity occasioned by the preaching of George Whitfield and Freeborn Garrettson among others, the life of enslaved persons was guided by what may be appropriately referred to as plantation ethics and ethos.

> The story of independent black Baptist congregations begins in Virginia and Georgia, where some slaves who had answered the revivalist call for repentance during the Southern phase of the revivals of the 1750s covenanted to form their own churches. They believed that

spiritual bondage was a greater affliction than material bondage, and that freedom from one might lead to freedom of the other. They knew that their churches were chattel arrangements. But they stubbornly trusted in the promises of the Bible that God is a liberator.[5]

The claim of this text is that Liele was one of the first slaves affected by the missionary outreach of this revival that swept the Southern colonies in the 1750s onward.

There is often a temptation to judge too harshly enslaved persons who turn to the religion of their oppressors and in that turn embrace plantation ethics and ethos. Granted that an aspect of the genius of the plantation preacher, or in another iteration, the medicine man or woman, was an uncanny ability to merge their African ways of understanding the world with Christian worldviews. Undoubtedly, this was one reason the master class did not win its fierce attempts to subjugate the will and destroy the soul of Black folk. It is of interest that one response of Liele's master to the reality of Liele's baptism and membership in the Baptist church that both Liele and his master attended was to commission Liele to share verses of hymns with fellow enslaved persons on plantations owned by the master and, as a signal that the master was pleased with Liele's work in that regard, Liele was able to include other plantations in the Savannah area.

> As to his religious life Liele relates, "I always had a natural fear of God from my youth," which had the effect of "barring me from many sins and bad company." In about the year 1773, while listening one sabbath afternoon to Matthew Moore, pastor of the Kiokee church, he became convinced that he was "not in the way to heaven, but in the way to hell." . . . He was baptized by Moore and admitted into the fellowship of the church. It was not long until it became evident that Liele was "possessed of ministerial gifts" and was permitted by his master to "instruct" the colored people on his estate. The privilege was later extended to include other plantations along the Savannah River. His method at first, according to Rippon, was to read hymns to his fellow slaves, encouraging them to sing and then to explain the "most striking parts of them." Soon he was given the opportunity to preach for the

congregation at Kiokee whereupon they granted him a license to preach as a probationer. . . . He was finally ordained, May 20, 1775.[6]

Liele's master allowing him to interact with fellow enslaved persons on his plantations to share hymns and possibly verses of the Bible was within the purview of plantation ethics and culture. There were strict rules concerning social intercourse, as slaves were often required to limit social meetings and exchanges to folks on their own plantation. There was a sense of dis-ease that the enslaved community would become restless believing "the grass to be greener on the other side." Liele's sharing verses of hymns with the enslaved and perhaps even singing for them was undoubtedly a gesture in the direction of social control of the enslaved class. Plantation ethics required outer expressions of happiness and laughter. Africans in the New World trapped on plantations were obligated to obey and perform their duties cheerfully. A happy and cheerful slave witnessed the generosity of the master and would result, so it was argued, in a more humane master. Failure of the enslaved to work hard would trigger the brutality of the master. It was incumbent on the enslaved to work hard and to perform these duties cheerfully. Frederick Douglass captures important elements of plantation ethics:

> Does a slave look dissatisfied? It is said, he has the devil in him, and it must be whipped out. Does he speak loudly when spoken to by his master? Then he is getting high minded, and should be taken down a button-hole lower. Does he forget to pull off his hat at the approach of a white person? Then he is wanting in reverence and should be whipped for it. Does he venture to vindicate his conduct when censured for it? Then he is guilty of impudence,—one of the greatest crimes of which a slave can be guilty. Does he ever venture to suggest a different mode of doing things from pointed out by his master? He is indeed presumptuous, and getting above himself; and nothing less than a flogging will do for him.[7]

Liele was born into slavery and spent most of his years as an enslaved person with Henry Sharp, whose sister was married to Matthew Moore, the pastor of Big Buckhead Creek Baptist church, where Liele was baptized. Liele knew very well the demands and expectations of slave etiquette and culture. And yet it seems that, in his practice of ministry and in his sharing of clues in terms of where he wanted to go as an evangelist and pastor, he did not explicitly combine themes of survival and liberation. However, there were times when he called slave culture and etiquette into question. In the narration of his conversion experience to John Rippon, Liele, in a letter dated 18 December 1791, from Kingston, Jamaica, stated: "I saw my condemnation in my own heart, and I found no way wherein I could escape the damnation of hell, only through the merits of my dying Lord and Savior Jesus Christ; which caused me to make intercession with Christ, for the salvation of my poor immortal soul; and I full well recollect, I requested of my Lord and Master to give me a work, I did not care how mean it was, only to see how well I would do it."[8]

There is clearly a Christological point of departure in Liele's acknowledgment of feelings of condemnation and notions of being sentenced to hell. But there was an answer to the problem of unworthiness and a sense that he deserved hell as his own heart condemned him. The answer was his sense of solidarity with the suffering and dying Christ, who would intercede on his behalf and save his poor immortal soul. It becomes clear that Liele identified with the suffering Jesus. There emerges in these lines a unique relationship between Jesus and Liele—a relationship that transcends the relationship between Liele and his master. Not only does Jesus, the Lord and Master, who is unlike the earthly master, offer salvation in the midst of condemnation and damnation, but in the end Liele appeals to Jesus to provide work for him. He does not care how menial this work may be; all he asks is the strength to do it well. This new relationship opened the door to possibilities to love fellow enslaved persons and to claim equality before God with the master class, in his search for freedom.

Washington points out that it is quite clear that George Liele believed in a literal "heaven" and "hell." Evangelists Edwards and Whitfield were militant in their emphasis that the righteousness of God demanded that sin could not go unrequited, and the judgment of God required punishment outside of repentance. It is of first importance to note that the punishment proffered was eternal torment in hell. The notion of eternal punishment was often portrayed with graphic and descriptive language, which occasioned immense anxiety among Protestants. Liele in his description of his own conversion informed us that he discovered he was not on the way to heaven but on the way to hell. Hell was not only a symbol of divine displeasure but of "everlasting burning." Liele's torment was existential as he spent several months in anguish and anxiety until deliverance was granted to him through the mercies of Christ, who died on his behalf. Washington gives us a flavor of one of evangelist Whitfield's sermons, *Eternity of Hell Torments*.

> Probably during Whitfield's first visit to North American colonies in 1738, he preached a sermon in Savannah, Georgia, on the *Eternity of Hell Torments*, which was palpably a defense of the doctrine of eternal punishment. He spoke with enormous power.

> "Come, then, all ye self-deluding, self-deluded Sinners, and imagine yourselves for once in the Place of the truly wretched Man [Dives] I have been describing. Think, I beseech you by the Mercies of God in Christ Jesus, think with yourselves, how racking, how unsupportable the never dying Worm of a self-condemning Conscience will hereafter be to you—Think how impossible it will be for you to *dwell with everlasting burning*."[9]

What was at stake was the gospel mandate to salvation through the mode of fear. If fear was the vehicle to induce conversion and ultimately salvation as it was in the case of Liele and Richard Allen, then it was worth the price of salvation. It is worth noting that the call to conversion and salvation mostly ignored the social situation in which oppressed persons languished for healing and the restoration of their humanity. Washington wagers that it must have been difficult for Black people caught in the inferno of New World slavery to use religion as an escape hatch in the face of their toils and the desecration of their humanity. Injustice was always around the corner. Their hearts were always in search of freedom. This meant they could not for long ignore the moral and social responsibilities to press for their own survival and liberation.

But almost incessant toil numbed their bodies and often their spirits. It is one thing to want deliverance from oppression; it is quite another task to develop effective strategies, means, and energies to achieve such a worthy end. Such difficulties did not necessarily compel black Christians to enshroud themselves with "otherworldliness." It must have been quite difficult for Black Christians to use religion as an escape: the toils and humiliations of the next day always served to remind them of the reality of their oppression. Neither their personhood nor their religion can be solely defined in sociopolitical terms. . . . The right to imagine or believe that the Lord of Creation would vindicate all wrong saved many Black Christians from committing the same suicide other blacks committed out of the despair induced by subjugation and humiliation told and untold.[10]

It is quite reasonable to infer that emotional and evangelical religion may not be simply dismissed as escapist as often the following day one returns to the problems in the sociological context. For Liele and fellow enslaved persons in the Georgia context, slavery, racism, and one's location in the world of plantation slavery do not disappear with an acknowledgment that one identifies with the dying of Jesus, as Liele claimed in his account of his conversion. And yet their hope in a God who will never leave or forsake them even in the teeth of the violence engendered by slavery provided the energy to hope against hope as they worked for the removal of the self from the throes of slavery.

It was noted above that it was during the American Revolution that Black people in the Southern colonies made their first steps toward freedom and progress in American society. "In colonial times he [the Black person] was subjected to the most harsh regulations and was never in any sense regarded as a potential citizen. There were a few voices both in England and America before the conflict who were attacking the evils of the slave trade, but it was not until their masters were struggling to free themselves from British imperialism that the Negro's time for betterment had come."[11] Gates suggests that enslaved persons in Georgia and in South Carolina concluded that American views regarding the situation of enslaved persons in relationship to Black freedom were confused. Thousands of Blacks, including George Liele, seized the initiative to side with the British in what they perceived to be the side of freedom, and the British were explicit in promising the enslaved freedom if they won against the Americans. Even in the face of imprisonment, Liele and his peers refused to lose confidence in the moral power of Black faith's ability to transcend the situation of rabid oppression at the hands of their enslavers. Liele and later Andrew Bryan and his wife, Hannah, who were baptized by Liele shortly before Liele left for Jamaica in 1782, exhibited a faith that was rooted in the sovereignty of a righteous God who would ultimately make all things right.

> Liele obviously believed that eternal punishment for sin by being cast into a lake of fire and brimstone was a worse fate than either the few mortal (and possible immoral) pleasures available to a slave such as sexual license, or the agonies of slave life itself. He hurriedly began to share the peace of knowing that heaven can be the home of every truly converted believer with his fellow oppressed black sisters and brothers. The power of Liele's discovery was matched only by the magnitude of his influence upon the development of the Black Baptist movement. Liele's subsequent career demonstrates that he felt that his major mission was to save black folk.[12]

Washington points out that although many Black preachers who responded to the call to preach the gospel of Christ saw their primary community as oppressed Black persons, this was rather natural as the social construct of slave culture and society made fellow slaves readily available as a community to be evangelized. It was clear Liele's commitment to Africa and the people of Africa took precedence over his relationships with the white community. Other Black preachers such as Andrew Bryan, Harry Hosier, Josiah Bishop, and Lemuel Haynes were able to preach to congregations including both white and Black persons. This was also true of Liele during his early years as a preacher in the United States, where his home church was pastored by Matthew Moore, who was white and provided the community for Liele's license to preach as a probationer and ultimately his ordination in May 1775. However, in Liele's subsequent ministry in Jamaica, his primary mission was to the enslaved and freed Black community. This was the pattern of his protégés such as David George, who established the first Black Baptist church in Free Town, Sierra Leone, Africa. The same was true of Jesse Peters, who, after the revolution when the Americans recaptured Savannah, returned to Silver Bluff along with about sixty folks from that community. They reestablished the Silver Bluff Church there prior to relocation of that church in Augusta, Georgia, as the Augusta Institute, which ultimately became renamed Springfield African Baptist Church, in whose basement Morehouse College was formed. We should not forget Brother Amos, who was the founder of Bethel Baptist Church in Providence, Bahamas. Like Liele, these preachers took Psalm 68:31, "Let bronze be brought from Egypt; let Ethiopia hasten to stretch out her hands to God," as a call to embrace Africa. It is of interest that Liele named his church in Jamaica "The Ethiopian Baptist Church" and interpreted the term Ethiopian broadly as African. The community that migrated with Liele to Jamaica referred to one another as Ethiopians, and therefore it was logical to call one's church African or Ethiopian.

> The naming of Black churches point to a time when Africa (Ethiopia) as a central element in the identity of enslaved persons was of first importance. Some of the early Black churches were explicit in including Africa in their identities: First African Baptist Church of Savannah, Georgia (1788); African Baptist Church, Lexington, Kentucky (1790); Abyssinian Baptist Church, New York City, (1800); Free African Meeting House, Boston (1805); First African Presbyterian Church, Philadelphia (1807); Union Church of Africans, Wilmington (1813); First African Baptist Church, New Orleans (1826); First African Baptist Church, Richmond, Virginia (1841).[13]

The church that Liele formed in the Savannah area during the American Revolution in 1778–1782 was named First African Baptist Church by his protégé Andrew Bryan. James Washington points out that Liele began the tradition that resulted in the naming of churches that reflected an African identity. "Before finally embarking to Jamaica in 1783, Liele, who had been freed in 1778, baptized Andrew Bryan and his wife Hannah from the revivalistic Presbyterianism of Jonathan Bryan, their master, to Baptist antipedobaptism and strict congregationalism. These black

Baptist slaves, along with others, established the first permanent black (and black Baptist) congregation in North America."[14] In a profound sense this trail that affirmed the identity of churches with an African identity began with Liele in the Savannah area, and in Jamaica he named his church the Ethiopian Baptist Church.

THE SEARCH FOR FREEDOM

The distinction in Liele's approach to the survival and liberation of African churches and communities may be contrasted to the approach of Denmark Vesey, a leader in an African church in 1822 in Charleston, South Carolina. Like Liele, Vesey had been a faithful slave to his master, Captain Vesey, and a careful student of the Bible. It is reported that Vesey was preoccupied with the Bible, believing like Liele in the power of the Bible to transform lives. Vesey believed that African people and people of African descent were meant for freedom and that the world of slavery was impeding the spiritual growth of African peoples. In South Carolina, Vesey lived among Africans who were steeped in African expressions of worship and religion. "There an essentially African religion was being practiced, with blacks, slave and free, gathering to worship. Since the majority of Blacks in South Carolina came from regions of Africa, like Congo-Angola and the western slave coast, in which the ring ceremony was prominent, the shout could hardly have been practiced less fervently there in the 1820s than in the 1860s, the decade in which New Englanders entered the state to find it performed on innumerable occasions, day and night."[15]

Vesey was purchased on one of Captain Vesey's voyages to the Caribbean at age fourteen. Vesey reminds us here of Liele, who was taken to New Georgia at age fourteen and was a most faithful slave to his master, Sharp.

> He [Vesey] was "for 20 years a most faithful slave," during which time he accompanied his master, as a cabin boy, to the West Indies, which once again provided him with the opportunity to observe Africans from many parts of Africa and to relate to the variegated sweep of their ethnicity.... Indeed he lived among men and women in South Carolina

and the West Indies who had experienced the Middle Passage and retained memories of the complexities of African culture.[16]

In similar fashion as Liele, Denmark Vesey had the confidence of his master, and this meant he had more latitude than others to plot and plan a rebellion against the establishment without being easily noticed. It is worth noting, however, that one advantage Vesey had over Liele was that in the South Carolina context Vesey would have been among the minority and therefore the threat factor would not have been as high as in the Jamaican context for Liele. In the Jamaican context where Liele was when Vesey hatched his plot to pattern the revolution that took place in Haiti, Liele already had departed Savannah for Jamaica, where people of African descent—the enslaved community, were in the majority. Jamaicans with the legacy of the Maroons, who fled to the hills when the British captured Jamaica from Spain in 1655 and would launch surprise attacks from the forests against the British, made the master class live with a sense of precarity and insecurity, as they were always on the lookout for attacks. Liele would have known that an attack against the British would not have survived. We will note in later chapters that Liele's legacy includes leaders from the Baptist church he planted in Jamaica in 1784 raising dark hands of rebellion against the British, first in the quest for emancipation in 1831 and again in 1865 pressing for societal changes to improve the quality of life for Jamaicans who had recently survived slavery.

Vesey was ideally suited to provide leadership for a rebellion in South Carolina as he was not only close to Captain Vesey the enslaver, but an ardent member of the African Methodist Church, where the Bible coupled with African ways of thinking provided the impetus for his passion for liberation of Africans from the bondage of slavery.

It becomes clear that whereas George Liele envisioned coexistence with the master class and, like George Whitfield, whose approach to salvation Liele seemed to have endorsed, gestured in the direction of the sovereignty of God who in the end would bring the unrepentant to justice, Vesey, on the other hand, wanted to effect divine justice in the here and now. Vesey was preoccupied with the study of the Bible, believing in its liberatory power to break the chains of bondage and set the enslaved persons free. The Bible was not merely in the service of enlightenment or edification but for liberation. There was a liberation hermeneutic that propelled him to want to set aside the house of bondage that kept Africa's children in slavery. It is not surprising then, that Vesey gave particular attention to the Biblical story of the children of Israel in Egypt and their cry to God for liberation and freedom. In his study of the Bible, he highlighted Joshua 6:21: "Then they utterly destroyed all in the city, both men and women, young and old, oxen, sheep, and asses, with the edge of the sword" (RSV).

Vesey received much help from Gullah Jack, one of the leaders of the African Methodist Church and who preached the conjurer's doctrine of invincibility and gave courage and confidence to all who would participate in the revolt. However, the plot was betrayed to slave masters. "William, 'a Negro man belonging to Mr. John Paul,' testified against Gullah Jack, saying that 'all those belonging to the African Church are involved in the insurrection from the country to the town—that there is a little man amongst them who can't be shot, killed or caught.' . . . Secrecy shrouded the services of the African Church and the religion of the two churches of the African Association, secrecy born of the exigencies of planned revolt, secrecy natural to slaves worshipping in a town like Charleston."[17]

Vesey used the Bible and the African traditions taught by Gullah Jack, an African priest, in his search for liberation. What was clear for Vesey and Prosser and Nat Turner, fellow liberationists, was that unlike Liele, violence was an option. Liele's confidence in the sovereignty of God, the power of prayer and the Bible, coupled with the power of literacy, and to some measure accepting the social arrangement of society, Liele believed that if he were faithful in teaching the word of God through hymns, songs, literacy, and the study of the Bible, a breakthrough would come in God's time. This perhaps was the promise and the setback from his posture as a Regular-Particular Baptist who placed much confidence in divine providence and notions that as children of the heavenly king, God would stand with them and eventually make all things right. E. Brooks Holifield, in his text *Theology in America: Christian Thought from the Age of the Puritans to the Civil War*, wagers that Calvinist theology in the Black community had its deepest roots in the Baptist church and leads one to speak of an "Afro-Baptist Sacred Cosmos" that draws on both African and Christian worldviews. African preachers both in the eighteenth and nineteenth centuries combined both African and Christian ways of viewing the world in their approach to survival and liberation as they sought to dismantle the house of bondage in which they lived. This Afro-Baptist sacred cosmos was expressed not only in the rebellion led by Gullah Jack in the African Methodist Episcopal Church in Charleston, South Carolina, in 1822 but also by George Liele in his solidarity with refugees in Tybee Island during the American Revolution in Georgia from 1778 to 1782. "Rev. George Liele. Although not a runaway slave, appears to have some liking for the Tybee River, as a place of abode, and it is probable that when he could no longer visit Silver Bluff, . . . he resorted to Tybee Island to preach the Gospel of Christ to the refugees there assembled."[18] Holifield called attention to Liele's witness to what perhaps was the kernel of his Calvinistic faith: "I agree to election, redemption, the fall of Adam, regeneration, and perseverance, knowing that the promise is that all who endure, in grace, faith, and good works to the end shall be saved."[19] In this short synopsis of his theological position, Liele touches on doctrines of election, redemption, the fall of Adam, regeneration, grace to persevere, and faith in the divine promises. It should be noted that Liele did not dwell on doctrine. It will be observed in this chapter that when Liele deals with how Christians within his congregation must comport themselves, he is quite comfortable in summing up what ought to be their conduct in the context of slavery, racism, and colonialism, by pointing them to the Biblical injunctions, sometimes referenced to two or three biblical citations.

Liele would sum up his understanding of doctrine with his understanding of the teaching of the church informed by the Bible and the saving work of the suffering Christ with whom he and his people identify. His short description of church teaching-doctrine oscillates between the human situation of the fall of Adam—human beings turning from God and against each other—and the divine answer through redemption and regeneration made possible through the suffering and dying of Christ. What is of interest here is when we look at testimonies from the persons

Liele baptized and their short summaries of his sermons, whether in the cornfield when he counseled David George, encouraging him to pray and share his testimony with confidence in the divine presence, or in the case of Andrew Bryan and his wife, Hagar, who he immersed in the waters of baptism shortly before he left for Jamaica, after preaching on the theme, "Ye must be born again," Liele does not directly address the social sin of slavery and the tyranny of the house of bondage erected by slave masters. Perhaps this is one of the shortcomings of the Baptist approach to sin and Liele's focus on salvation as survival rather than liberation. This will be made quite clear when we take a close look at the church covenant produced by Liele as a statement of compromise with the Jamaica House of Assembly as a guarantee that he would not incite enslaved people to insurrection. It was observed earlier in this chapter that Liele believed as evidenced in his statement at his conversion to the Christian faith that salvation that provided a way to bypass eternal fire in hell was of first importance and this was what regeneration and redemption was all about, ensuring that the trials and travails of this earthly life did not detour those who embraced the Afro-Baptist faith from the promises of an eternal relationship with Christ.

There was a Christological point of departure at the core of Liele's theology, as Christ the master who is above all masters reverses the damnation and bondage that Adam's children deserve, and in its place guarantees salvation at the end of the journey called life. It would be unbearable to suffer at the hands of the master destruction of the body and to live in a culture and space where one's children are prevented from offering respect and love to parents only to be followed in a context where the reward is eternal fire in hell. Another hermeneutical principle for Liele highlights eschatology that is linked to Christology. This means that the promise of Christ for deliverance from sin, signified by his own suffering and dying, guarantees eternal life and felicity with Christ for all who endure to the end. The vision of the end—being with Christ and all who endure to the end, provided the courage to endure even the house of bondage fired by the promise that God is faithful and will keep his promise to Adam's children who through grace endure to the end. Therefore Afro-Baptist faith must provide a way for Adam's children, who have a proclivity to sin, to claim their election, their chosen-ness to overcome the cruelty and savagery of the master whose practice of brutality is aimed at their missing the rewards provided for them with Christ. Faith rooted in grace has an in-spite-of quality. According to Liele, in spite of the violence of plantation life, violence against the Black family and the Black body, Liele promises hope in the next life. He gestures in the direction of St. Paul in 1 Corinthians 15: "For as in Adam all die, so also in Christ shall all be made alive." In Liele's theological worldview there was an eschatological horizon that provided energy for the journey and the courage to make it to the end. Liele sums up the call to duty that overrides the call to morality: "Knowing that the promise is to all who endure, in grace, faith and good works to the end shall be saved."[20]

STRATEGIES TO SURVIVAL

It was clear that Liele's passion was singing hymns, praying, preaching, and founding churches that included an emphasis on literacy. Liele combined his passion for preaching by providing settings in which salvation of souls was conjoined with liberation and survival through education. In Jamaica he appointed a schoolmaster at his church, and as he formed a circuit of churches, often classes in literacy preceded space for preaching. The bottom line for Liele was to vanquish ignorance about the Bible as he gave enslaved persons the ability to read the Bible and hymnal.

Philip Sherlock and Hazel Bennett, in their text, *The Story of the Jamaican People*, illustrate the context into which George Liele arrived in 1783 on his voyage from Savannah, Georgia, to his new home in Kingston, Jamaica. "The nineteenth century dawned to the cannonade and battle cries of the Napoleonic war (1802–15), to the flames and carnage of the Haitian revolution and, in Jamaica, to terrifying rumors that the slaves brought from St. Domingue by fugitive French planters were planning an uprising. More than 1,000 were transported. There followed conspiracies in Kingston in 1803, and in 1808 a mutiny of 50 African Chambas and Coromantis."[21] Sherlock and Bennett claim that by the turn of the century there were rumblings that freedom for Afro-Jamaicans seemed a real possibility and this was linked in part to the presence of Afro-Baptist preachers who were freed by their masters and traveled to Jamaica. Sherlock and Bennett mention George Liele and Moses Baker had a profound influence on the enslaved population. W. J. Gardner in his important book on the history of Jamaica points out that Baker, who was a barber by trade in New York and came to Jamaica along with his wife, practiced his trade as a barber in Jamaica. According to Gardner, "for four years (1783–1787) Baker lived in utter disregard of religion."[22] It was widely acknowledged that Baker was steeped in African religion that was later transformed with the help of George Liele to an Afro-Baptist faith. It was under Liele's teaching and preaching that Baker was converted and became a member of Liele's team, with Baker at first serving as chaplain on a plantation in one of the western parishes, St. James, and later as pastor at the famous Salters Hill Baptist Church. He is honored with a statue in his memory in the center of the village of Lottery, in St. James, Jamaica, not far from the church where Baker served as pastor. However, after his baptism by Liele and his ministry to enslaved persons at the Adelphi plantation, it was reported, "The followers of Baker and Gibb were required to be possessed of 'the spirit' before baptism was administered. This meant the spirit had to descend on the applicant in a dream, which was then described to the leader. . . . There evolved a regular technique and ceremonial for bringing on spirit-possession, which included a fast according to a set canon followed by a trip to the bush alone at night to wait for the spirit to descend."[23] An Afro-Baptist faith was clearly at work in this context as Liele and Baker related their version of the Christian faith to the existential situation in which Afro-Jamaicans were paying attention for the first time to missionaries—albeit Afro-Baptist missionaries providing an approach to graft Baptist faith to African ways of understanding the world. An important index of their faith on both sides—whether Black missionaries from the United States or Africans in Jamaica—was to find ways of maintaining the integrity of their religious beliefs while at the same time being open to the new ideas that the sociological and theological environment offered to them. Sherlock and Bennett explain:

> The Bible reached the African-Jamaican people in the 1790s when two black Baptist preachers who had been freed by their masters came to

Jamaica, George Liele and Moses Baker. They built up large followings, Liele in Kingston and Baker in Western Jamaica. Their congregations grew rapidly, and they appealed to the newly-founded Baptist Missionary Society in England for help.... Never before had the enslaved people held a book in their hands, and certainly not the Bible, for it was not regarded with favor on the Jamaican sugar-and-slave plantation. All school doors were closed to African-Jamaicans, so they could not read. Church doors were closed to them, for in the eyes of the plantocracy God was white and there was a color line. The African-Jamaicans, a very religious people, sought what comfort they could find in communion with Obi, Myalism, Cumina, in Haiti with Vodum, in Trinidad in a later period with Shango. Barred from the Church, the school and any form of marriage, the African-Jamaicans were derided as being superstitious, stupid and immoral.[24]

According to Sherlock and Bennett, when Liele and later his protégé Moses Baker began work among the enslaved population in Jamaica, many doors were closed to enslaved persons. School doors were closed, church doors were closed, and the enslaved were not allowed to marry. One reason why enslaved Jamaicans preferred African American and later Afro-Jamaican preachers was that through the coming together of community, they were able to connect to their historical myths and religious practices of their native lands. In a profound sense the teaching and ministry of Black Americans was merged with African beliefs. There was a sense in which the slave and sugar plantation disconnected Afro-Jamaicans from their historical past as labor lost its traditional meaning as a communal endeavor. Survival and decolonization resided in adaptation to a new environment with the master's book, the Bible, which Liele introduced to the enslaved class as a means of survival and social organization in an alien land. The plantation was designed to teach the Black person his or her place at the bottom of the society. The danger here was, could enslaved persons transform their world with tools granted to them by the master class? As we will note throughout this chapter, the Bible provided a double-edged sword, for even with good intentions by Liele and Baker, Afro-Jamaicans began to learn through Black missionaries that they were not the only ones who have been slaves.

They now had an association with slaves in Egypt who were guided by Moses toward the promised land.

> Now, with [Black] missionaries as their teachers in Sunday School, the Bible became their holy book that contained the word of God, their comforter and beloved companion in the Valley of the Shadow of Death. It was their certificate of identity which confirmed their status as God the Father's children, their guarantee of a future in the Father's company and above all their blessed assurance that each one was a worthwhile some-body for whom Massa God gave his only son. They were no longer the only ones who had been slaves. They shared the Jewish experience of having been an oppressed people. In the prophets, patriarchs, psalmists they found comfort and hope. The Jewish story had for them an almost unbearable, piercing relevance.[25]

Liele in concert with Moses Baker provided a context for faith and worship in the Afro-Baptist Jamaican setting that did not occur in either the Moravian or Methodist expression of faith. In a profound sense neither the Moravians, Methodists, or Presbyterians could have made this happen as they could not tap into the Afro-Jamaican experience in similar fashion as Liele and Baker, who brought with them from the United States the evangelical experience of the Great Awakening filtered through the black experience.

> Liele and Baker have a place of honor in the story of Jamaican people. They did things that neither the Moravians nor the English Baptists and Methodist missionaries who came after them, could have done. They planted the seed of an indigenous evangelical movement amongst the people, blending the Christian message with traditional African modes of worship, including spirit possession dancing, the clapping of hands and swaying of the body. Like Africans, African-Jamaicans are deeply religious. No aspect of their story is more important than their religion, folk beliefs, native churches. . . . Liele and Baker established a religious movement though itinerant preachers, "Daddys" or deacons, and warners, men and women who felt called "to go through the villages and fields for to warn them."[26]

CHAPTER 2

Perhaps, because George Liele and his protégé Moses Baker were enslaved, they had a special passion to relate to and empower enslaved persons not only by placing two books, the Bible and the hymnal, in the hands of the enslaved but also by assiduously teaching them to read the Bible and the hymnal. An amazing index of the passion with which Afro-Jamaicans revered and loved these two books was their memorization of large parts of the Bible and many songs in the hymnal. One approach that Liele and Baker perfected was while Liele concentrated on the eastern part of the island, Baker focused on the western parishes. Further they could raise churches across the island that were administered by itinerant leaders, called deacons, "Daddys" and later "Mothers." One of the organizational principles that made this possible for Liele and Baker was the autonomy of the local church. Each local church could choose leaders without having Liele or Baker approve the selection as there was no central organizational basis for the Baptist church structure.

> The use of assistant preachers was in itself a significant development. It was a "ranking" of the slaves by blacks and not by white owners, masters, overseers; an appointment of slaves by the preachers to guide, counsel and convert, not to act as drivers whose symbol of authority was the whip. Their symbol was a sacred book that contained messages of brotherhood and love. Through their preaching George Liele and Moses Baker defined the mission of the Christian Church in Jamaica and gave it a system of organization based on small chapels and deacons. They brought within the reach of the people two books that soon became the treasured library of the African-Jamaican people, the Bible and the Hymn Book.[27]

During the Liele and Baker era, most church buildings started as meeting places where there would be Bible study and a great deal of singing inspired from a hymnal imported from England. One wonders how much of this focus on singing in Jamaica was encouraged by the fact that John Rippon, of the British Baptist Missionary Society, was himself compiling a Baptist Church hymnal with hymns with a Trans-Atlantic flavor. However, it is also clear that the root of this passion of Liele to guide Afro-Baptist churches in Jamaica to engage the hymnal was also inspired by his first activity as an enslaved person in Georgia belonging to Master Sharp, who set him aside to share hymns with fellow enslaved persons on plantations in the Savannah area. On the downside of looking to a hymnal for songs to sing at worship or in church fellowships, the danger was that one became dependent on the hymnal from a metropolitan center, such as London, where in the era of Liele and Baker, Jamaicans at worship over the years received their hymns, and included in these hymnals were prayers. In the Jamaican-Caribbean context, congregations, from Baptists to the Church of England, disparaged the local expressions of songs that emerged from local culture, as in the tradition of Liele the churches looked outside for songs and prayers.

> I find it interesting that one of the oldest Christian churches in Jamaica, [the Church of England] the Anglican Church, adopted for inclusion in its hymnal two songs of well-known Rastafarians, Bob Marley's "One Love" and Peter Tosh's version of Psalm 27. The rector of St. Mary the Virgin, the Revd. Canon Ernie Gordon, made the announcement and noted that "One Love" was used in an ordination service for St. Andrew Parish Church two years ago. "I don't live in England," he stated, "I live here, [in Jamaica] so my theology and how I think must reflect my cultural morals. You have to interpret the Bible according to where you are. The Church in Jamaica is out of date."[28]

Influenced by British hymnody, Baptist ecclesiology made a separation between the sacred and the secular, observing that if the songs and prayers came from outside of Jamaica, they were likely to be sacred, and if the origin hailed from the Jamaican context, then they were most likely secular. This has begun to change in recent years, as Cannon Ernie Gordon made clear as he pivoted to the music of Bob Marley. This was in keeping with African traditional music coupled with the advent of Pentecostalism. A good test for its authenticity as Cannon Gordon stated was its need to emerge from the context and culture in which Afro-Jamaicans live and find its inspiration from the good book the Bible.

James Washington reminds us that a discussion of Liele's engagement as a minister to fellow enslaved persons highlights the presence of racism, legacies of slavery and colonialism. Oppressed people whether in the American colonies or in the Caribbean understood that Christian churches were not always on their side. Enslaved communities discovered early that churches were often in harmony with the planter class, and in many cases, missionaries were paid by the planter. The Great Awakening placed as a central question, "Can one be slave and Christian?" Another form of this question was "Can one be Black and Christian?" According to George Whitfield, the answer was yes. And to those who embraced the ethos and teachings of the Regular Baptists, the answer was also yes. The problem here was that most evangelists and preachers, including George Liele, did not adopt the belief that slave and Christian were antithetical. "Whitfield in Georgia advocated the introduction of slaves and rum for the economic improvement of the colony. He even owned slaves himself, although Wesley, Coke and Asbury opposed the institution and advocated emancipation as a means to thorough evangelization."[29]

But if we bracket the zeal of Whitfield to use enslaved persons to increase the economic standing of Georgia, Carter G. Woodson would wager that Methodists like Freeborn Garrettson and Bishop Asbury were traveling evangelists like the apostles of old in their ministry and mission to the master class in the interest of enslaved Blacks.

The dilemma Liele had was that in much of his life in Georgia he was known as a slave, and he could not disguise the color of his skin. James Washington is compelling in his claim that at his core Liele was for the redemption of Africa and all Black people. But the problem of race in the context of slavery was the planter class and the brokers of power in the society did not trust preachers and their doctrine of the fairness and justice of God in relation to Black people. As was mentioned earlier, Liele lived with a sense of the precarity of his situation as a Black preacher who for most of his life in Georgia was a slave. During the American Revolution when Britain occupied Savannah, Liele was found most of the time on Tybee Island preaching to refugees and no doubt hoping that Americans and British, Patriots and Britons would grant the freedom for which they fought. Even in the Jamaican situation Liele's hands were tied, as for the first couple years in that context, he was indentured to Moses Kirkland, the chief officer of the British armed forces in

Savannah, who loaned him the fare to take his family along when he left Savannah to live in Jamaica.

We noted in chapter 1 that at the opening of his church in Jamaica, the Ethiopian Baptist Church, Liele was imprisoned for preaching a sermon that was understood by the Jamaica Assembly "as inciting the people to rebellion," in preaching from Romans 10:1: "Brethren my heart's desire for Israel is that they may be saved." Liele was placed on death row, with feet and hands in stocks, and his family forbidden to visit him. He was freed through the advocacy of friends and his producing a church covenant in which he informed both the membership of his church and members of the Jamaica Assembly that he would insist on prospective members of his church providing a note from their owners granting permission for them to become members of the church. Viewing the world from the vantage point of death row would remind Liele that racism was more vicious in Jamaica, as enslaved persons were in the majority, and the ethos of the society was informed by the rebellion in Haiti and the overthrow of that government by enslaved persons.

In clever ways Liele would join the theological and the political spheres as baptism and church membership were at their core about freedom from work that was enforced by the plantation system and the journey toward equality with whites, for themselves and their children.

In the American context the cross for Liele was at the center of his faith. Being a member of a minority group, he would not have felt as personally threatened for his own life as he did in Jamaica where the reverse was the case. In the Jamaican context his life was threatened as he was placed on death row on the charge that he preached sedition, in a sermon from Romans 10:10 in which he declared that it was God's will for the oppressed to go free.

LIELE IN PRISON FOR HIS FAITH

Earlier in this chapter we noted the claim by church historian James Washington in his text *Frustrated Fellowship: The Black Baptist Quest for Social Power* that Liele as a Particular or Regular Black Baptist subscribed to a Calvinistic creed that gave ultimate credence to the sovereignty of God and an eschatology that proffered an eternity in hell for persons who failed to turn to God in repentance, regeneration, and salvation in the journey toward peace with God. This was especially poignant for enslaved Black Americans and Afro-Jamaicans who had to experience the torture of plantation slavery in which they were often whipped to offer forced labor to produce a crop or to build cities and towns at the behest of the master class. The logic that fired Liele's passion to witness to Africans and people of African descent was that although enslaved persons of African descent had to live in the valley of oppression and torture while in the custody of the oppressor, that was inconsequential as compared to eternity in hell.

In the Jamaican context the emphasis seems to change for Liele from an otherworldly emphasis on heaven and hell to an existential-contextual framework that points to survival and dignity for his family and the people he served. John Clark, a missionary to Jamaica, writes of the witness of George Liele in Jamaica.

> Mr. Liele labored without a fee or reward. Supporting himself by work of his own hands. He also employed a teacher to instruct the children of free parents and slave. In little more than seven years he had the happiness of baptizing five hundred persons, of whom, after deducting deaths, exclusions, etc., there were in church-fellowship three hundred and fifty persons. The first chapel was erected in 1793, the first dissenting chapel in Jamaica.[30]

According to Missionary John Clark, when Liele arrived in Kingston and saw the enslaved condition of Afro-Jamaicans living in ignorance and without hope, he was moved with compassion and took his stand at the Race Course, a public park in Kingston, where he preached regularly. Afro-Jamaicans had never witnessed someone of their own race preaching the gospel of Christ. Liele the theologian of hope was off to a good start.

Notes

1. Carter G. Woodson, *The History of the Negro Church* (Washington, DC: Associated Publishers, 1921), 23–39.

2. James Melvin Washington, *Frustrated Fellowship: The Black Baptist Quest for Social Power* (Macon, GA: Mercer University Press, 1990, second printing), 6.
3. Woodson, *The History of the Negro Church*.
4. Herbert S. Klein, *Slavery in the Americas* (Chicago: Quadrangle Books, 1971), 120.
5. Washington, *Frustrated Fellowship*, 8.
6. John Parmer Gates, "George Liele: A Pioneer Negro Preacher," *The Chronicle: A Baptist Historical Quarterly* 6, no. 3 (July 1943): 118–29, 120.
7. Frederick Douglass, "Slaveholding Religion and the Christianity of Christ," in *Afro-American Religious History: A Documentary Witness*, ed. Milton C. Sernett (Durham, NC: Duke University Press, 1985), 101–102.
8. John Rippon, *The Baptist Annual Register for 1790, 1791, 1792, and part of 1793*, volume 1 (n.d.), 332–33.
9. *The Eternity of Hell Torments: A Sermon Preached in Savannah Georgia*. (London: n.p., 1738), 2021. Cited in James M. Washington, "The Origins of Black Evangelism and the Ethical Function of Evangelical Cosmology," *Union Seminary Quarterly Review* 32, no. 2 (1977).
10. Washington, "The Origins of Black Evangelism and the Ethical Function of Evangelical Cosmology," 109.
11. Gates, "George Liele: A Pioneer Negro Preacher," 119–29, 118–19.
12. Washington, "The Origins of Black Evangelicalism and the Ethical Function of Evangelical Cosmology," 110–11.
13. St. Clair Drake, *The Redemption of Africa and Black Religion* (Chicago: Third World Press, 1970), 26.
14. Washington, "The Origins of Black Evangelicalism and the Ethical Function of Evangelical Cosmology," 110.
15. Sterling Stuckey, *Slave Culture* (New York: Oxford University Press, 1987), 43.
16. Stuckey, *Slave Culture*, 44.
17. Gayraud S. Wilmore, *Black Religion and Black Radicalism* (Garden City, NY: Doubleday, 1972), 82.
18. Walter H. Brooks, *The Silver Bluff Church: A History of Negro Baptist Churches in America* (Washington, DC: Press of R. L. Pendleton, 1910), 2.
19. E. Brooks Holifield, *Theology in America: Christian Thought from the Age of the Puritans to the Civil War* (New Haven, CT: Yale University Press, 2003), 310. See Also John Rippon, *The Baptist Annual Register for 1790, 1791, 1792, and Part of 1793*, volume 1 (n.d.): 336.
20. Holifield, *Theology in America*, 310.
21. Philip Sherlock and Hazel Bennett, *The Story of the Jamaican People* (Kingston, Jamaica: Ian Randle Publishers, 1998), 200.
22. W. J. Gardner, *A History of Jamaica: From Its Discovery by Christopher Columbus to the Year 1872* (London: T. Fisher Unwin, 1909; first published 1873), 344.
23. Philip D. Curtin, *Two Jamaicas* (New York: Atheneum, 1970), 33–34.
24. Sherlock and Bennett, *The Story of the Jamaican People*, 39.
25. Sherlock and Bennett, *The Story of the Jamaican People*, 39.
26. Sherlock and Bennett, *The Story of the Jamaican People*, 180–81.

27. Sherlock and Bennett, *The Story of the Jamaican People*, 181.

28. Noel Leo Erskine, "Black Theology in Jamaica," in Dwight N. Hopkins and Edward P. Antonio, *The Cambridge Companion to Black Theology* (New York: Cambridge University Press, 2012), 267. See also *Daily Observer* 13, 201, August 2, 2007, Jamaica edition, 1.

29. Woodson, *History of the Negro Church*, 26.

30. John Clark, W. Dendy, and J. M. Phillippo, *The Voice of Jubilee: A Narrative of the Baptist Mission, Jamaica, from Its Commencement: With Biographical Notices of Its Fathers and Founders* (London: John Snow, Paternoster Row, 1865), 31.

CHAPTER 3

Patriarch of the Native Baptist Movement

WE NOTED EARLIER THAT THE EVANGELICAL MOVEMENT LED BY George Whitfield and Jonathan Edwards swept the American landscape and impacted George Liele in the context of his balancing act between embracing the Regular-Particular Baptists and the Separate Baptists, who were largely influenced by George Whitfield. In a close look at "The Covenant of the Anabaptist Church" presented by Liele to the Jamaica Assembly and to his parishioners, he gestures in the direction of the role of the sociological context to shape his understanding of doctrine and church polity. Theologian Devon Dick in his important text, *The Cross and the Machete: Native Baptists of Jamaica*, calls attention to Liele's protégé and assistant Moses Baker, who amended sections in Liele's covenant to bring it in harmony with his pastoral theology and practice.[1] Liele was at his core a contextualist and since Baptist polity and practice is centered on the autonomy of the local church, it is quite understandable that Baker, in conversation with his congregations and perhaps with Liele, had authority to make changes to Liele's covenant.

> The Evangelical Movement exerted a powerful influence in Jamaica through two black preachers, George Liele and Moses Baker. Towards the end of the War of Independence in 1782, a number of loyalist families moved from the United States with their slaves to Canada, the Bahamas and Jamaica. Among those who came to Jamaica were two black ex-slaves, George Liele and Moses Baker, who founded there the Native Baptist Church. . . . They did two things that neither the

Moravians nor English Baptists or Methodists who came after them could have done. They planted the seeds of an indigenous evangelical movement among the people, blending the Christian message with traditional modes of worship, including spirit possession dancing, the clapping of hands and the swaying of the body. Like Africans, African-Jamaicans are deeply religious. No aspect of their story is more important than their religion, folk beliefs, native churches.[2]

Richard Burton, in *Afro-Creole: Power, Opposition and Play in the Caribbean*, points out that in the Jamaican context in which Liele and his fellow preachers, who had also emigrated with him to Jamaica at the end of the War of Independence in the United States, sought to meld their Christian faith with the indigenous culture and religion; there were at least three cultural foci that shaped the sociological environment. With the arrival of the large African American contingent of refugees coupled with an emergent creole population in Jamaica, there was much conflict between the slaveholding class and the non-conformist missionaries, who, "since the 1790's, had been proselytizing in earnest among the nonwhite population, slave and free alike."[3] Second, there was also conflict between the slaveholding class and enslaved persons concerning the future of slavery. Burton indicates that sitting on the fence concerning the question of the future of slavery were the free coloreds who were mostly ambivalent. Finally, there was a conflict between white missionaries and the enslaved class, and Burton adds that the conflict most likely affected the relationships among enslaved persons. According to Burton, at the heart of the conflict between the missionaries and the enslaved class, the slave-owning class and slaves, was which expression of Christianity the enslaved class should follow. "[T]he moralistic, British-style nonconformism taught by the missionaries or the turbulent, charismatic Afro-Christianity autonomously created and espoused by the slaves. . . . Even the . . . conflict between missionaries and slaves—was other, or more than a conflict between 'Europeans' and 'Africans,' since the slaves the missionaries proselytized were often significantly creolized before Christianization."[4] Most students of George Liele's work as pastor and evangelist acknowledge that Liele's ministry in Jamaica preceded that of the Methodists and English Baptists. He was the most successful in the evangelization of Afro-Jamaicans. Liele and his family arrived in Jamaica as early as January 1783. Afro-Jamaicans, many of whom had come directly from countries in Africa, must have had a sense of nostalgia in hearing Liele preach in the open air at the Race Course Park in Kingston, Jamaica. In earlier chapters, we noted how Liele after boating along the Savannah River to Silver Bluff, South Carolina, preached to David George in a cornfield, which resulted in David George's conversion to the Christian faith. Prior to his departure to Jamaica, Liele preached to Andrew Bryan and his wife, Hagar, at the sea in Savannah, from the text in John 3:5–7: "You must be born again." This text was pivotal in Afro-Baptist faith, especially among enslaved persons, who after being soiled by the vagaries and indecency of slavery had a need to start their lives over and be born again.

> Both Black Baptists and White Wesleyan Methodists trained black and colored lay preachers for future proselytizing, but it seems clear from the outset there was a split in style, form, manner, and church organization between the "Euro-Christianity" taught by the Whites and their nonwhite trainees and the "Afro-Christianity" taught by the Black Baptists.... Even though in the eyes of the planter both groups were equally suspect there can be little doubt that it was the Black Baptist preachers who urged slaves to seek immediate freedom.... The Black Baptist preachers and their congregations split off to follow their own style of worship, which, giving a Christian form to long-established Myalist practices, emphasized music and dancing, "spirit possession," prophecy, and speaking in tongues.[5]

We are informed that there was a marked distinction between the Euro-Christianity approach advocated by white missionaries—principally the Methodists and the "Creo-Christianity" of the white-led Baptist churches—and the black-led Afro-Christianity of the slave masses. Burton contends that by 1813–1814 the creolization of the culture affected all these variations among the different religious organizations. Perhaps, only the Church of England represented a strict European version of Christianity; all the others represented a variation Creo-Christianity

CHAPTER 3

with the Native Baptist–Black Baptist the closest to variant forms of Myalism, Obeah, Revival Zion, and Kumina.

Dianne Stewart points out how careful Liele had to become in the Jamaican context in navigating the boundaries between the enslaved population in Jamaica, having been a slave himself in Georgia, coupled with his status in Jamaica for the first couple of years as an indentured servant to Col. Moses Kirkland, and his relating an Afro-Baptist faith to an enslaved community who in terms of sheer numbers would have memories of freedom in Africa. Undoubtedly, this was complicated in the emergent creole class in Jamaica who understood freedom as a right for themselves and their progeny. According to Stewart the bottom line was the master class did not trust missionaries, white or Black, preaching to an enslaved community. Stewart states:

> Although the nature of Liele's ministry is shrouded by ambiguities, Liele's work among enslaved Africans was viewed as a threat by the planters and even landed him in a prison on several occasions. It appears overall though that Liele and other African-American Baptist missionaries were cautiously appropriate under the scrutinizing gaze of local White authorities, canceling many of their doubts or fears. The numbers of Black preachers trickling in from the United States, Cuba, the Bahamas, Santo Domingo, and the newly liberated Haitian Republic, however, were more than discomforting to colonial authorities and White residents across the island. They, along with the African Jamaicans who came under their influence, became a force so fluid, widespread, and decentralized that they more easily escaped the White gaze and were less monitored, if at all by White officials. In one sense then, we can envision the Native Baptists at one extreme, patterning themselves after White congregations, as much as cultural and experiential limitations allowed, and preaching basic Christian doctrines. At the other extreme, we see a flexible and open tradition, capable of absorbing the Myal-Obeah religious culture and its political aspirations.[6]

Stewart reminds us of how difficult and bordering impossible it would be for the British missionary and expatriate to keep in sight Afro-Jamaicans, many of whom according to Liele lived in the hills of

Jamaica, outside the gaze of the colonizer, as Afro-Jamaicans sought often in secret to practice the Myal-Obeah religion. In the tradition of African expressions of religion, the hills, rivers, and forests would shield Afro-Jamaicans from the gaze of the missionary and the colonizer in the practice of their religion. No wonder dreams and visions as modes of worship were often down by the riverside. The precedent was set by the Maroons of Jamaica—Africans who fled to the hills—when the British captured Jamaica from the Spanish in 1655. Much of Myal and Obeah expressions of religion included spiritual meetings in the woods, in the forests, as time in the forests was an important aspect of engaging and claiming spiritual power.

In this chapter I refer to George Liele as patriarch, elder brother. It will become clear why when we note how his assistants fanned out across Jamaica in relating their understanding of the Christian faith to African spirituality, which they encountered in "slave religion" throughout Jamaica. Liele was focused on the eastern part of the island, primarily Kingston and Spanish Town, while George Gibb and George Lewis focused on the middle sections of the island. Moses Baker lived in the western section of Jamaica and worked primarily in St. James. With this in mind Stewart's observation is quite appropriate in asking how much leeway did Liele's people have, and how far did they go in blending African expressions of religion extant in Jamaica with their preaching of Christianity. Stewart opines:

> It is possible that Liele and his assistants persuaded their Myal converts to abandon the practice of holding spiritual meetings around silk cotton trees while other Native Baptist leaders may have invited their followers to hold services around cotton trees. It is difficult to know with certainty all that took place. What is certain is that the Native Baptist tradition was diverse across communities and penetrable with regard to Myal religious influence. Undoubtedly, Myal converts learned soul salvation through faith in Jesus Christ, yet, as Native Baptists, they uniformly attached more ritual significance to and displayed more reverence for the biblical figure John the Baptist who baptized Jesus before he began his ministry.[7]

Earlier Stewart mentioned that it is quite likely that Liele and his assistants preached tenets of the Christian faith that made cultural and practical connections to Afro-Jamaicans who lived in a world in which plantation slavery challenged their existence in a strange land, "a long ways from home."

INDIGENIZATION AND AFRO-BAPTIST FAITH

Yet on the other hand, their identity as Africans would suggest that their openness to African indigenous religions opened the door to the practice of Myal-Obeah religions, in the context of Jamaica. At the core of Stewart's highlighting of tenets of African religions extant in the Jamaica to which Liele and his assistants sought to make sense was the African proclivity to practice and embrace a "both and" approach to religion and life rather than an "either or" approach to questions of religion and life. In chapter 1 we raised the question of why would Africans trapped in the inferno of plantation slavery turn to the gods of their oppressors? It was suggested that one answer was Africans have always embraced a "both and" approach to life and religion rather than an "either or" approach that their masters practiced. It was this openness to the *novum* in history that allowed Liele and his assistants, on the one hand, to be open to the new in the sociological context of Afro-Jamaicans trapped in slave-sugar plantations of Jamaica. While enslaved Africans took elements of their indigenous faith seriously, such as dreams, the discovery of spirits associated with "cotton trees" in Jamaica, the presence and power of spirits, the language of drums, and speaking in tongues, they were at the same time open to the example of Jesus and saw a correlation between his suffering and theirs.

There were often tensions and disagreement between Baptists from Britain and the community to which Liele reached out as to whether or not their embrace of Afro-Baptist faith was in keeping with Baptist orthodoxy. Robert Stewart, in *Religion and Society in Post-Emancipation Jamaica*, gives us a flavor of the unease among the missionary class from Britain as to whether or not indigenous expression of the faith as embraced by Afro-Jamaicans was passing for Baptist orthodoxy. Stewart points out that Baptists in Jamaica who owe their ecclesial existence to

George Liele and his assistants complained that they were not being given enough credit for their ability to do church on their own terms in the context of the class meeting they were allowed to lead and structure in their neighborhoods, quite often in the hills, a distance from the church building. "They resented any interference with the size of their classes, any questioning of their reports on members' conduct, and their meetings with the missionary tended to be quarrelsome and aggressive"[8] This was a result of Liele's strategy and organization of empowering enslaved persons as class leaders, deacons, daddies, and assistants, who could act in his place, at a class house or meeting space often in the hills, or in other settings away from the church. Robert Stewart points out that this dis-ease with slaves choosing the members of their classes or meetinghouses and on occasion preaching in the absence of Liele or one of his assistants elicited the stern rebuttal from missionaries who were jealous that Liele's empowering of the Afro-Baptist community resulted in large memberships in Baptist churches.

> [A]ll the Negroes in Jamaica now call themselves "Christians"—generally "Baptists," though their religion differs little from their old African superstitions. The bulk of them are enrolled in Classes under some black Teacher as ignorant as themselves; and they are connected by the purchase of a ticket with the Baptist congregation in the nearest Town, where they go, and receive the sacrament once per month, or once a Quarter; but they are utterly ignorant of the simplest and plainest of God's commandment. They are too ignorant to understand and profit by the Public Preaching on the Sabbath; and they never see the missionary at any other time; for they live far away from him and he has thousands attending him whom he does not know. They are perishing in their sins, and stand in need of instruction as the Zooloos![9]

Missionary John Clark, of the Browns Town mission and a contemporary of George Liele, mentions that the Baptists practiced their ticket and leader system provided it ensured them large gatherings. Clark acknowledges that Baptists were not abashed in encouraging their leaders "to form their own prayer and worship groups with their own leaders, with no interference from the missionary."[10] According to Missionary

Clark, white missionaries adopted some of the practices of Liele and his group that allowed leaders in classes and meetinghouses, which were often some distance from the formal church that met for regular worship on Sundays and sacrament once per month, to allow Afro-Baptists to choose their leaders within the meetinghouses and in the absence of the pastor to lead and preach. It is in this sense, especially from the Baptist perspective, we can begin to see the emergence of Afro-Baptists belonging to two churches, the formal church service that would observe worship and sacraments on Sundays and the worship and organizational meetings that occurred during the week, in their meeting spaces out of sight of both Black and white missionaries, by folks as the missionaries stated who had no training and in many cases were unable to read and write. The ticket system that Liele and his assistants employed, even if it did not originate with them, continues to hold currency in Baptist churches in Jamaica.

Class Leader and Ticket System

The roots of the class leader and ticket system, although popularized in Jamaica by George Liele and his assistants, had its roots in the Wesleyan tradition and is reputed to have had the blessing and supervision of John Wesley at its inception.

> The lay class-leader and ticket system, for which the Baptists became notorious in Jamaica, was actually the invention of John Wesley. The ticket system came first . . . each society member was issued a ticket which was renewed periodically upon spiritual and moral reexamination. Later, Methodist groups were organized into classes of twelve with a lay leader. . . . The system was carried over into Jamaica, but in a more limited and tightly controlled way than that employed by the Baptists. . . . Baptist congregational procedure, however, allowed for the independence of individual congregations in the mission territory.[11]

The Baptists led by their patriarch George Liele were so successful in employing the ticket and leader system that several congregations outside the Baptist church thought the concept and practice were created by Baptists. "Often headmen on estates, but also laborers or tradesmen in the towns, the leaders, commonly called 'daddies,' were responsible for weeknight prayer meetings in class-houses on estates or in the villages, for the day-to-day spiritual oversight of class members, and for the collection of money for special purposes."[12] It was mentioned earlier that it was quite popular for Afro-Baptists to form their own classes and select their leaders without interference or directives from the missionaries, a custom that was never practiced or adopted by the Methodists. This custom and practice among Afro-Baptists allowed their congregations to grow exponentially, as it were, from the bottom up. Class leaders emerged as spiritual guides who kept their fingers on the spiritual pulse of the church and community. From the perspective of the Native Baptists, it was an ideal structure for Liele, who could serve as patriarch [bishop!] in Native Baptist churches throughout the island without having to be physically present.

Class leaders had power to refuse applicants for baptism, and at times even expel members. One way in which the Native Baptists grew throughout Jamaica was for the class-house to serve as the foundation for growing churches, where class leaders became itinerant preachers. This may be another organizational skill that the Baptists learned from the Methodists. In Jamaica churches were often linked into a circuit of churches under the leadership of a single pastor who was supported by deacons, "daddies," and church mothers. There were times when a couple of churches in a circuit would become a basis for growing other churches as deacons and lay leaders would be promoted to pastors. This happened with Liele, as Moses Baker, whom he baptized, and later the first creole Jamaican deacon and schoolmaster, Deacon Swigle, left Liele's church and formed their own. The loose structure of the Baptist church quite often allowed lay leaders and deacons to leave a particular church and form their own. Often, they left with a substantial number of the members as was the case with Deacon Swigle, who left with a sizable number of Liele's members and formed his own church not far from Liele's, Windward Road Chapel.

Mary Turner, in *Slaves and Missionaries: The Disintegration of Jamaican Slave Society, 1787–1834*, reminds us that prior to the advent of George Liele and his assistants on the Jamaican scene as Black missionaries, there was no advocacy from the planter class to influence and shape enslaved people's worldviews and ideas of the universe. "The slaves, however, stripped of country and family, had to exercise some form of control over their environment. They adapted the techniques developed in their homeland to serve their new needs."[13] Turner reminds us that Afro-Jamaicans did not abandon their religious worldviews but sought to blend them and make them relevant to Christian practices, which were gestured to in the leader and ticket system that was popularized by Liele and his assistants in Afro-Baptist faith. There were practices in slave culture that reminded Afro-Jamaicans of their own practices and stories back home in Africa. When Liele and his assistants preached about eternal salvation with Jesus and spending an eternity with friends in heaven, many Afro-Jamaicans interpreted heaven as traveling across the oceans back to Africa to join the ancestors.[14] Pocket crosses that masters would wear were understood as charms that would keep evil spirits at bay. Jesus was understood as a healer similar to the medicine man or woman in Africa, and the Bible was a storybook, not unlike many of the stories with which they were familiar, such as the woman going to the well to draw water, a chief having many wives, and the importance of sacrifice and burnt offerings.

Both Black and white missionaries attacked concubinage, and Liele in his Anabaptist covenant gestured in this direction in article xvi: "To avoid fornication, we permit none to keep each other, except they be married according to the Word of God" (1 Cor. vii. 2; Heb. xiii. 4). The Rev. F. A. Cox, in *History of the Baptist Missionary Society*, illuminates the problem:

> The denomination called Native Baptists, are under the teaching of black and colored men, who were once leaders in other congregations, but have broken off, and set up as ministers for themselves. Speaking of a visit he paid to a Negro Village to meet some of these people, he says "They profess to be Baptists in alliance or connection with a black Baptist teacher in Kingston, which city, twenty-five miles off, they sometimes visit; and after paying their money towards the support of himself and the chapel, receive a ticket of continued membership, which they seem to highly value. They are in a dark state of mind, living many of

them according to their own confession in a very immoral manner but this is no hindrance to church membership, if the leader choose to recommend them as candidates for baptism. It is to be apprehended, that, practically, if not theoretically, there is much of antinomianism among them."[15]

This description of the state of Native Baptists directly locates Liele as the patriarch of the Native Baptists. According to Missionary Cox, many of the Native Baptist congregations would break away from older congregations such as so-called orthodox (Particular) Baptists when conflicts ensued with British Baptists who sought to dictate doctrinal or organizational terms to deacons, itinerant preachers, and daddies who when under Liele's leadership were given leadership privileges. Before we turn our gaze to the Native Baptist view of Christian marriage, it is important to underscore the witness to Liele's church practice of the leader and ticket system and the obvious reference to Liele as the Black Baptist teacher in Kingston from whom they renew their ticket, which seems to function as a charm, and their location of their leader at the chapel—in Kingston. It is worth recalling that Liele referred to his church also as the Windward Road Chapel. Liele seems to have had several ways of speaking of his church. He refers to the building and congregation as the Ethiopian Baptist Church, and one reason for this appellation was that the group of African Americans who traveled from the United States with Liele referred to each other as "Ethiopians." We may recall Liele in 1784 began his church with four persons, all from the United States. As the church grew, there were many Afro-Jamaicans who joined, and Deacon Swigle, who was born in Jamaica, had a central role to play as deacon and the one who was schoolmaster of the school for freed and enslaved persons.

LIELE AS THE PATRIARCH OF NATIVE BAPTISTS

In his important text *The Cross and the Machete*, Devon Dick contends that whereas Liele was a Baptist and founder of Baptist work in Jamaica, he did not specifically identify as a Native Baptist and should not be restricted to this title. Reverend Dick states, "Native Baptists and Independent Baptists called Liele the founder of the Baptists and not founder of either the Native Baptists or the Independent Baptists. . . . The term 'Original Baptists' will be used to describe the Liele group, since they were the first Baptists to start a mission to Jamaica."[16] This is an interesting distinction that Dick makes as he seeks to locate Liele and his work in the Jamaican context. This is clearly not a distinction that Liele makes concerning his own work. According to testimonies given by members of Liele's congregation, such as the persons who traveled to Kingston to renew their tickets and give an offering to "The Black Baptist teacher in Kingston," it is clear that Liele did not have to differentiate his work from other Baptists until the British missionaries came to Jamaica in 1814 in the person of Missionary Rowe. Scholars of Baptist work in Jamaica attest to the fact that the missionaries did not make any significant impact on the Afro-Jamaican enslaved community until 1824 when Missionary Thomas Burchell arrived, having been invited to the island not by George Liele but by Moses Baker. Although Liele appealed to the British Baptists for help in erecting his Windward Road Chapel and was in correspondence with John Rippon of the British Baptist Missionary Society, Liele did not appeal to him for help with missionaries. Liele, who was enslaved for most of his life in the United States and was imprisoned both in the United States and in Jamaica twice, was clear that his commitment as a preacher and patriarch of the Native Baptists was to Afro-Jamaicans both freed and enslaved, as this was made clear in his exegesis of the text of Romans 10:1 for which he was imprisoned and tried for his life.

Liele informed us that most of the people who attended his church could neither read nor write, and so it was hardly likely that Liele would have spent much time equivocating or quibbling about the name of the church. It was clear that Liele was in solidarity with the enslaved and those who like the Christ he served were crucified on the plantations in Jamaica. I do agree with Reverend Dick that the popularizing of the name Native Baptists would have gained currency perhaps after Liele's death in 1825. The term gained currency when Afro-Baptists were forced to differentiate the practice of their faith in contradistinction from that of British Baptist missionaries who did not understand or appreciate the distinctions between the Afro-Baptist faith that was indigenous to

Jamaica and the imported version articulated and highlighted by the British.

Dick points out that "in 1838, there were 11 congregations with six 'Native Baptist Preachers.' The six preachers were William Killick, John Duff, John Davis, William Duggan, George Trueman and George Lyon."[17] In a letter that was apparently rushed to the British Baptist Missionary Society in 1836 by William Duggan, one of the pastors of the Native Baptist Church, Duggan titles the letter: "The First Annual Report of the Jamaica Native Baptist Missionary Society. Spanish Town. Signed Rev. WM. Duggan. 1836." Reverend Duggan must have been in a hurry because he did not date his letter except to state the year. However, the text of his letter may give us some clues as to when the letter was written. Reverend Duggan writes:

> The Church in this place may be said to have been formed in consequence of the Rev. J. Phillippo wishing me to relinquish my business, and wholly to devote my time to the work of the ministry, but his not offering me anything adequate to bear my travelling expenses, and support a wife and three children, I declined his proposal. I was after this severely rebuked by him for standing up to instruct my class people, and in various other ways, endured much misrepresentation and slander, which so wounded my spirit, that after seeking divine direction, and with advise of many of my Christian brethren, came to the determination of separating from a church, with whom I could not walk in peace.
> ... We have recently purchased a large dwelling for three thousand pounds, which is converted into a house of worship.[18]

In 1836, when Rev. William Duggan would have penned this, the first annual report of the Jamaica Native Baptist Missionary Society, it is interesting to see how his response to Missionary James Phillippo approximated that of Patriarch George Liele. First Duggan insisted to Phillippo that he had to provide for a wife and three children and that he needed to work beyond his activities in a church that was pastored by Phillippo. This would have been modeled for him by Liele, who worked for the city of Kingston collecting spent cartridges and additionally had a farm where he provided for the needs of his family. Also note the conflict between Reverend Duggan and Phillippo concerning the way Duggan insisted that the people he instructed in the class meeting were his people. This is of first importance because in a real sense Duggan suggested that he belonged to two churches—the church in which he had a conflict with Phillippo—the missionary church, and his church, the class meeting where he referred to "my people." Reverend Duggan left the missionary church and gave full time to a church he founded, which he called Native Baptist. Duggan differentiated his church from that of the missionary. The term Native Baptist may not have been in popular usage until after 1836, the year Reverend Duggan penned "The First Annual Report of Jamaica Native Baptist Missionary Society" to the Baptist Missionary Society of London. It is of interest that Reverend Dick lists a table of congregations that were members of the Jamaica Native Baptist Missionary Society in 1841. The largest membership belonged to George Liele's church known among the membership as Windward Road Chapel. The membership was the largest at 3,700. Liele had been gone for some time, having died in 1825.

Enculturation of the Faith

In an address at the Baptist chapel in Falmouth, Jamaica, Missionary James Phillippo in 1864 reminded his congregation that Baptist work in Jamaica owed its genesis to Black missionaries who hailed from the United States of America. Missionary Phillippo stated:

> How remarkable the manner in which the Baptist Mission in Jamaica was begun. Christian missionaries from England were not the first to commence the work. When John Rowe landed in 1814, George Liele and John Lewis and George Gibbs, and Moses Baker—men of your own color and your own descent; black men, who had received the gospel in America—had already been engaged in preaching it; and God had already given many seals to their ministry and souls for their hire.[19]

Phillippo also acknowledged that when Missionary James Coultart arrived in Kingston, Jamaica, the center of Liele's work as a missionary and pastor in 1816, "Crowds of people flocked him, calling themselves

Baptist—many had already made a Christian profession of faith; but their notions of Christianity were very often associated with the most absurd superstitions, partly from the imperfect character of the teaching under which they had been brought."[20] If on the one hand, Missionary Phillippo offers praise to the early Black missionaries, George Liele, George Gibb, Moses Baker, and John Lewis, for their formative work in caring for the souls of Afro-Jamaicans prior to the arrival of missionaries from England, on the other hand he attributes the rabid superstitions and lack of any responsible grasp of Baptist faith and polity to bad teaching from these missionaries. It is reasonable to affirm that Liele and his assistants arrived some thirty-one years before the first Baptist missionary from Britain set foot on Jamaican soil; scholars of Jamaican missiology point out that it was not until 1824 with the arrival of Thomas Burchell that any serious advocacy and teaching from the British Baptists took place on the island. This would mean that Liele and his assistants were without Baptist orthodoxy for forty-one years prior to the arrival of Thomas Burchell, who served in the western parishes of Jamaica.

It will be helpful to look at the religious context into which Liele and his assistants sought to do Christian witness in Jamaica and note the presence of what Dr. Du Bois refers to as the African Church. W. E. B. Du Bois, in his celebrated work *The Negro Church*, points out that in spite of the failure of the Christian church to protect enslaved persons in the New World from chattel slavery and colonization, and to compound the problem in several cases missionaries and evangelists also owned slaves and used Christianity as a weapon against the enslaved, it is a very sad situation that George Liele and several of the British Baptist missionaries also owned slaves. Black people had to use any means necessary as they sought to structure possibilities of their own liberation. It is at this point and in critique of a compromised Christianity that proclaimed freedom of the soul and at the same time kept the human body in bondage that Du Bois informs us that what endured and what saved enslaved persons from falling into the abyss of depression and extinction was what he termed the African Church. The African Church was not at first a Christian church. Du Bois claimed it took about two centuries for African religious practices to become Christian, and even then, Du Bois

CHAPTER 3

does not believe Africans in the New World ever became Christian. It was the missionary interference with these religious practices that gave these rites the feel of Christian faith. According to Du Bois, the marks of the African Church are strong respect for nature worship and proclivities toward witchcraft. An important key for Du Bois was the presence of African priests who saw and understood the need for equilibrium in the culture and in the practice of the art of religion—Obeah and Myal. Du Bois cites at length a comment by Jamaican historian Bryan Edwards. It is of interest to note that Bryan Edwards was one of the financial contributors to the building of the Windward Road Chapel in which Liele served as pastor.

> As far as we are able to decide from our own experience and information when we lived in the island, and from the current testimony of all the Negroes we have ever conversed with on the subject, the professors of Obi are, and always were, natives of Africa, and none other, they have brought the science with them from thence to Jamaica, where it is so universally practiced, that we believe there are few of the large estates possessing native Africans, which have not one or more of them. The oldest and most crafty are those who usually attract the greatest devotion and confidence; those whose hoary heads, and a somewhat peculiarly harsh and forbidding aspect, together with some skill in plants of the medical and poisonous species, having qualified them for successful imposition upon the weak and credulous. The Negro in general, whether African or Creoles, revere, consult and fear them. To these oracles they resort, and with the most implicit faith, upon all occasions, whether for the cure of disorders, the obtaining revenge for injuries or insults, the conciliating of favor, the discovery and punishment of the thief or adulterer, and the prediction of future events.... A veil of mystery is studiously thrown over their incantations, to which the midnight hours are allotted, and every precaution is to conceal them from the knowledge and discovery of White people.[21]

Dr. Du Bois was correct in highlighting the mischievous character of Obeah as he reminded us that in the context of the New World, and especially in Jamaica, the practitioners of Obeah were usually older

Africans. However, Du Bois seems to be unsure that Obeah as a religion practiced within the African Church provided equilibrium for society and social cohesion for enslaved persons in an alien land, "a long ways from home." In *The Negro Church*, Du Bois missed the significance of Obeah in Jamaica as the attempt of Afro-Jamaicans to adapt practices of the African Church to their enslaved condition and to use Obeah as a religious tool to dismantle the house of bondage created for them by the oppressor. There were few tools Afro-Jamaicans had to fight their oppressor in slavery, and one such tool was Obeah as a religion. Obeah flourished in Jamaica during the ministry of George Liele and his assistants. It is of interest that Liele was quiet in regard to what Du Bois referred to as the existence of the African Church. The records indicate that Moses Baker, one of Liele's assistants, was steeped in Obeah prior to his baptism by Liele. Liele himself never spoke about the presence or dangers of Obeah. He spoke with immense feeling about the precarity of the enslaved condition but refrained from engaging in a negative anthropology or discussing the indigenous expressions of religion. On the other hand, Baptist missionary John Clark, a contemporary of Liele, speaks of the condition of Afro-Jamaicans to whom Liele and his assistants sought to minister: "The condition of the greater part of the surviving slaves was wretched to the extreme. They were treated as beasts of burden, bought, sold, branded, driven by the whip. And compelled to labor to the utmost extent of endurance; debarred from self-improvement."[22] It was in this context that Missionary Clark spoke of Liele's compassion and of a sense that Liele preached as if the answer to the plight and precarious condition of the enslaved Afro-Jamaicans was the antidote of the gospel of Christ. Clark had this to say, "When Liele arrived in Kingston, and saw the wretched state of enslaved brethren living in ignorance and vice, without God, and without hope in the world, his heart was filled with compassion for their souls. He took his stand at the Race Course and boldly proclaimed the truth as it is in Jesus."[23] Afro-Jamaicans heard Liele and his assistants and as they merged their indigenous faith in spirits and their confidence in herbal medicine, Jesus became one of the spirits. For some of these people Jesus even became their favorite spirit, but if Jesus failed to provide healing or address their existential needs in a timely way, then other spirits were approached to meet the required need. It was in this sense that Afro-Jamaicans sought membership in the Afro-Baptist faith, which included the blending and merging of two churches. In the language of Du Bois and Bryan Edwards, the African Church and the Christian Church's approach to life and faith included a "both and approach."

Reverend F. A. Cox in his *History of the Baptist Missionary Society* signals a mixed review of the missionary assessment of Liele's contribution to Baptist faith and traditions combined with his care and compassion for the making of Afro-Baptist faith. On the one hand, Cox commends Liele's thrift and industry as a family man and his response to the call to serve Afro-Jamaicans in his commitment to an Afro-Baptist faith, yet he equivocates concerning any confidence in the instruction provided by Liele and his assistants to the community, which they called Baptist. Cox had this to say:

> Liele having purchased a team of horses, and worked as a carrier, and being an active intelligent man, was employed by the government, and thus procured a comfortable subsistence for his family. He had been pastor of a colored congregation in America; and soon after his arrival in Jamaica, sought every opportunity to communicate religious instruction to the slaves and free people of color. The character of this instruction is somewhat difficult to determine amidst the conflicting evidence that is given; but in all probability, it was very imperfect and intermingled with many false and superstitious notions.[24]

Perhaps, Reverend Cox's ambivalence concerning the character of Liele's teaching of Afro-Baptist faith to both enslaved and freed Jamaicans was Liele's commitment to blend his understanding of the Christian message. We will look at the roving ministry of George Lewis in the parish of Manchester when we give closer attention to the impact of George Liele and his assistants. Lewis was born in Guinea, Africa, was enslaved in Virginia, and after the American War of Independence traveled to Jamaica with the British and there became one of Liele's assistants. According to John Clark in his *Memorials: Baptist Missionaries to Jamaica*, George Lewis was an ardent Baptist in Virginia and came to share the gospel of Christ with Afro-Jamaicans, especially those who were restricted to sugar and slave plantations. Lewis was often arrested for preaching on plantations and was associated with Afro-Jamaicans worshipping at the cotton tree. Clark concludes, "[I]t appears that his religious notions were combined with a great deal of superstition."[25]

The focus on Afro-Jamaican religion, to which Liele would have been exposed during his time in Jamaica, would have been Obeah and Myal. Most scholars regard the practice of Myal as predating Obeah, yet I began with Obeah, taking my lead from Bryan Edwards, the eighteenth-century historian, who mentioned that Obeah was rather universal among Afro-Jamaicans who turned to magic and witchcraft as modes of righting the wrongs committed against them by Europeans in plantation slavery in Jamaica. The turn to Myal, the earliest form of African expression of religion in Jamaica, points to claims Monica Schuler made in her formative essay, "Myalism and the African Religious Tradition in Jamaica." Schuler identifies five marks of Myal religion that were pivotal in the shaping of Jamaican ecclesiology and nation building. Unlike Obeah, which is private and individualistic, Myal is collective with constant rearrangement of its symbols, rituals, and beliefs. Another feature is that the leader is often charismatic and inspired by dreams or visions. There is also a firm confidence that good will prevail and that one task of religion is to prevent misfortune and hasten the breaking-in of a new order of good fortune for the community. Priority is granted to the protection of the community from disease and death. "Myalists believed that all misfortune—not just slavery—stemmed from malicious forces, embodied in the spirits of the dead. The Myal organization provided specialists—doctors—trained to identify the spirit causing the problem, exorcise it, and prevent a recurrence. All problems including bodily illness, were thought to stem from spiritual sources and required the performance of appropriate ritual."[26] The highlight of the Myal ritual was the Myal dance, where "candidates enacted a ritual of death and rebirth by drinking a mixture of cold water and the herb-branched calalu, then dancing until they reached a state of dissociation resembling death. The application of another mixture to the body revived the candidate."[27] The

Myal dance aimed at providing a sense of invulnerability to death caused by European sorcery.

In relating Myalism to Afro-Baptist faith, Schuler indicates that after 1791, Myalism absorbed elements of the faith propagated by Black Baptists. "The geographical limits of Baker's following coincide almost exactly with the core area of an aggressive Myal movement of the 1840s. Because of strict laws against non-Church-of-England preachers, Baker had great difficulty maintaining regular contact with his followers; he could visit them only at night and could not hold Sunday services outside his employer's property."[28] Schuler is insightful in instructing us concerning limits that would have been placed on Liele and his assistants to function in a political context in which only the established Church of England would have had permission to preach in Jamaica with due authorization from the Jamaica Assembly. This was true for all non-conformist churches, which included even the British Baptists. We will note that in 1822, Liele, in desperation, made a trip to the Baptist Missionary Society of London to ask for a letter from the society authorizing him to preach in Jamaica. The Jamaica Assembly forbade all churches except the Church of England to provide documentation granting missionaries permission to teach and preach in Jamaica. Liele, who was not a member of the British Baptists, was refused authorization from the Baptist Missionary Society of London. He returned to Jamaica, and the next we hear of him was from William Knibb, who came to Jamaica as a missionary in February 1825, in which he attended Liele's funeral. The point here is the lack of access Liele and his assistants would have to his congregations after 1808 when the Jamaica Assembly restricted access. This I believe in part explains the equivocations of fellow missionaries concerning the character and nature of the instructions offered by Liele and his assistants to congregants.

Monica Schuler opines that the aggressive posture of Myal filled the void, and the practice of Myal was secretive and not open to the gaze of the master class. Much of Myal teaching and practice of the faith took place under the cover of night. This would also be true of the class meetings that took place in rural areas outside of the gaze of Liele and his assistants, not to mention the gaze of masters and missionaries. Schuler explains:

> The Black or Native Baptist preachers, as men like Baker came to be called, developed an organization. . . . They issued tickets indicating each individual's status—member, candidate, or inquirer—and for instruction they divided their flock into classes, each with its own leader. The leaders became almost totally independent of the preachers and ruled their classes with an iron hand. In time, Baker and his fellow preachers found it impossible to control the content of the leaders' teaching and their ritual, which grew less and less "orthodox" from the Baptist viewpoint.[29]

Schuler points out that there was an explosion of Myalist teaching and ritual in the western parishes of Jamaica where Moses Baker, and other Baptist church leaders, lived. Schuler does not include George Liele in this dilemma as he lived and worked on the eastern side of the island in Kingston and in the capital city of Spanish Town. However, Liele would have faced the same dilemma of not having access to congregations at night. Baker and others of Liele's assistants, Gibb and Lewis, seemed to have found ways to surreptitiously enter plantations at night and share their Afro-Baptist faith. This was not possible for Liele, as he would have had to depend on the emergence of a creole leadership through persons such as Swigle and class leaders who were outside the gaze of masters and missionaries. Schuler suggests that in the blending and merging of Myal and Afro-Baptist faith, it became increasingly difficult to differentiate between them.

The Coming of the Spirit(s)

Of special importance for Myal members and initiates was the inspiration of the Holy Spirit and baptism in the tradition of John the Baptist—by immersion. Schuler suggests that there were several iterations of the Native Baptists, which named their churches after John the Baptist. "The leaders developed a technique for attaining possession by the Holy Spirit and 'dreams' experienced in this state were crucial to a candidate's acceptance for baptism. Without them they could not be born again,

CHAPTER 3

'either by water or by spirit.' Without them they could not be born again."[30] The emphasis of the priority of the Holy Spirit and baptism in a place where there was plenty of water were strong elements of Baptist faith throughout Jamaica and were especially strong in the parish of St. Thomas, where I grew up as a youngster in the 1950s. Strongly associated with the Holy Spirit were gifts of new life and new birth signaled by the biblical mandate to be born again. Much of what Schuler highlights as elements of Myal faith and practice were consonant with Baptist tradition and practice throughout Jamaica.

Noted earlier in this chapter was a reminder that Liele attended a church in Georgia prior to his journey to Jamaica where his pastor, Matthew Moore, belonged to the Separate Baptist tradition—in which gifts of the Holy Spirit and baptism by immersion were required. This would allow Liele to be at home in a context in which leaders, itinerant preachers, and teachers who served in class meetings understood these gifts as essentials to the biblical injunction of being born again. Liele mentioned that his covenant was inspired by the Anabaptist tradition where the baptism of children was viewed as a priority. Could it be that the prominence of children in Liele's covenant was in response to the Myal practice of baptizing young children? The Myal tradition emphasized that baptism would protect the children from evil spirits. This practice of baptizing young people in a river where ancestral spirits lived was an important key to being covered by good spirits. In the understanding of spirits, there was a very thin line between Liele's perspective, shaped by both the Separate Baptist tradition and Myal views encountered in Jamaica. Liele must have heard stories from enslaved Africans about the river being the home of ancestral spirits, as he boated up and down the Savannah River, sharing hymns and verses of the Bible with fellow enslaved persons in Savannah, Georgia. Several of those views underscored the Myal tradition.

Another emphasis among the Myalists that appears in Liele's covenant was their understanding of sin not being primarily against God but against society. Myalists had an explication of sin as sorcery—European sorcery was expressed in the sugar-slave plantation life and culture that demeaned and diminished the humanity of Afro-Jamaicans. "The Myal notion of sin as sorcery, an offence not against God but against society, made it far more this-world-oriented than the Baptist faith. Myal ritual offered a cure for society's ills which, since they were caused by sorcery, could be eradicated by anti-sorcery ritual. For this reason, Myalism was far more relevant to many Afro-Jamaicans than any missionary version of the Christian faith."[31]

Liele had a contextual approach to the needs and existential situation of Afro-Jamaicans as he sought to take their culture and traditions seriously. There was a profound sense in which, unlike the Myalists, he did not seek to give all power to European sorcery, as defined by the Myalists. Afro-Jamaicans' situation of enslavement and loss of power were not primarily sins against God but sins against the people and the society. There were remedies both physical and spiritual that would reverse the sorcery of their oppressor. Liele responded to the needs of society by initiating the tradition of combining education and salvation in local contexts. It became a tradition to use church sanctuaries as schoolhouses during the week for the education of children. Another way in which Liele sought to meet the needs of the populace and blend his practice of ministry with Myal ideology and theology was to rent out his Windward Road Chapel as a hospital and therefore combine healing and salvation.

Liele was also a farmer, and thereby modeled an organic relationship with nature. Myal theology provided the ideological focus for the uprising in 1831 that precipitated the beginning of the end of slavery when class leader "Daddy" Sharpe, a member of the local Burchell Baptist Church, led a revolt against slavery and plantation life in Jamaica. This attack on one of the institutions of European sorcery marked the beginning of the end of slavery in Jamaica. In this attempt of the Myalists to put down slave culture and replace it with freedom, they were able to combine Liele's eschatology of divine judgment at the end of history with their demands of healing of their bodies and a thirst for liberation in the midst of history, believing that even if they sacrificed their bodies in the present circumstance, they would be rewarded in the end with freedom for themselves and their progeny. Liele merged Afro-Baptist faith with Myal worldviews and was able to blend the sacred and the secular, finding the sacred in all things and taking cues from Myal worldviews that saw and understood the spirit in all of life, as they led the charge that sugar-slave plantation life was a sin against society and that God would empower them to change their world.

One way in which we see a coming together of Myal and Afro-Baptist faith that was inspired by Patriarch George Liele was in the combining of their views of spirit. For Liele and Daddy Sharpe, where the spirit was present there was freedom (2 Corinthians 3:17). As Afro-Baptist faith merged with Myal, Afro-Jamaicans were free to be there for one another in their work of liberation. Those whom the spirit set free were free in word and deed. As Myal and Afro-Baptist faith merged, the community began to understand that the present order in which Black lives were being destroyed was incongruous with the new future of freedom the spirit of ancestors and the divine had awakened in them. One of the gifts of the spirit, whether they were spirits of ancestors that could be found at the river or at the cotton tree or at Liele's Windward Road Chapel, was a refusal to accept life dictated by European sorcery as expressed in plantation slavery. Liele and the Myalists were united in the view that the destruction of Black life on sugar and slave plantations was unacceptable. They refused to reconcile themselves to the present order that accepted the crucifixion of Black people trapped on plantations in Jamaica.

In African cosmology there was no loss of the sacred because there was no loss of spirit. It was in the notion of spirit that Liele's Afro-Baptist faith affirmed religion as the source of life and meaning for Afro-Jamaicans because spirit was life-giving and liberating. On most plantations, the only religion allowed was Christianity. For Liele and especially his assistants Baker and Lewis, social context was brutal for enslaved Afro-Jamaicans, as enslavers were constantly reminded that they were in the minority group. In the year when Liele arrived in Jamaica (1783), an enslaved person called Mercury, who lived in the parish of St. Thomas, was found with ten pounds of veal in his possession. "No proof was given that he came dishonestly by it, but he had his right ear cut off; fifty lashes were inflicted at the same time, and he received fifty more twice a month for six months, and during that period was worked in chains." Again, a Black woman called Priscilla ran away from the world her slave owners made for her. She was pursued and, when caught,

"Both ears were cut off. She was placed in chains and sentenced to receive thirty-nine lashes on the first Monday in each month for a whole year."[32]

However, it must be noted that although Liele and the Myalists seemed to have come together in their resistance to what the Myalists termed European sorcery—the organized attempt to destroy Black life—the means by which they experienced spirit that kept body and soul together in the midst of New World slavery's onslaught of Black life were different, at least in the means they traveled to get there. In Myal and Obeah, practitioners' assault on the world of slavery, which sought to dehumanize Afro-Jamaicans, would administer a mixture of gunpowder, grave dirt, and human blood, coupled with the Myal dance, which aimed at conveying the belief to its adherents that Black life was indestructible and would not succumb to the evil practices of the oppressor. An underlying assumption was that the world that was crushing Black people was not permanent—it could be changed through the agency of Black life and powered by manifestation of spirit expressed in Obeah and Myal.

As early as 1774 in Jamaica, one of the few persons who wrote about his observation of the Myal dance, Edward Long, informs us that the introduction of the Myal dance created a society in which those who were members could initiate others into the society. This practice was an early expression of the class-leader-ticket system we looked at earlier in which the members of the class chose their leaders without any reference to Pastor Liele and his assistants. According to Edward Long, this experience in which Afro-Jamaicans were initiated into the Myal society was believed to render them invulnerable to European sorcery and open them to an experience of resurrection.[33] The Myal dance included death and resurrection as the Myal leader illustrated that European sorcery was no match for the gifts of healing that included death and resurrection. The gift of the restoration of life after death was the supreme work of spirit—the spirit that made life worth living. For Liele and the Myalists, there were multiforms of expression of the spirit that resulted in new life after an experience of death. Liele's metaphor that pointed to new life was "being born again," which was occasioned by baptism by water and spirit. We noted earlier that the Myalists highlighted both baptism in the tradition of John the Baptist and the gift of spirit at Baptism, as water was one source of spirit. Liele was clear that new birth engendered by water and spirit provided a baseline that prevented Afro-Jamaicans from falling into the abyss of destruction and loss of hope in the triumph of the human spirit. There was an eschatological horizon for Liele as he would literally hope for a new heaven and a new earth. Liele's background as a Separatist Baptist would indicate that although the earthly sphere was important, because of the loss of power and control of enslaved persons on sugar and slave plantations in Jamaica, they could not foreclose their option to notions of eternal life with God. Yet, this hope for fellowship with God was a basis for the hope in the here and now to enjoy fellowship with each other. For Liele the spiritual and the social merged as there was a vital connection between heaven and earth. A vital and peaceful relationship with God engendered the advocacy for better working conditions and the need to honor the Christian notion that Afro-Jamaicans trapped on plantations, where they were treated as beasts of burden, were nonetheless made in the image of God. Hope in the power and presence of the divine spirit was the basis for a new future both before and after the Parousia.

Both the Myalists and Liele affirmed that the hope engendered by the spirit was not blind, but that the new future promised, whether by the Myal dance or by the return of Jesus, who will return in acts of liberation that include hope for those trapped on plantations in the New World as chains of bondage are broken, children are blessed and protected by divine spirit, and justice and peace become new realities throughout creation. Liele was clear that the final act of the divine spirit was still to come, yet they could witness to the presence of the spirit that attested to the liberating and reconciling activity of the divine whether in Myal or Afro-Baptist faith. At the center of their experience, whether in their memory of acts of new life or liberating possibilities for which they strategized, whether listening to a church covenant written by Liele or participating in a dance of dying and rising, there was hope in divine spirit that sin as European sorcery was no match for the gifts of the spirit in Myal cosmology or Afro-Baptist ecclesiology. Sorcery of all kinds would be defeated, and society would find its equilibrium and the divine plan for creation would be realized.

Liele and His Assistants

Throughout this project, it has been made clear that although George Liele initiated Baptist mission work in Jamaica, he received substantial help from Moses Baker, George Lewis, and George Gibb. Robert Stewart, in *Religion and Society in Post-Emancipation Jamaica*, explains:

> It is important to note that the Baptist acceptance of black leaders who brought their followers with them repeated the original pattern of the Baptist Missionary Society's entry into Jamaica. The first Christian preaching that many of the slaves heard was from black preachers, not from white missionaries. These preachers were forming congregations before the arrival of most of the missionaries, being preceded by the few Moravians who began working in Jamaica in 1754.... The Baptist church in Jamaica was historically a black-initiated church, and white ministers like J. M. Phillippo and William Knibb are preceded in time and importance as pioneers by George Liele, Moses Baker, George Lewis, George Gibb, and Nicholas Swigle, the ex-slave preachers who laid the foundation for the Baptist edifice on the island.[34]

There is widespread agreement that Liele began Afro-Baptist work in Jamaica. Although scholars such as Inez Knibb Sibley in *The Baptists of Jamaica, 1793 to 1965* contend that Liele and Baker began Baptist witness in Jamaica, she tends to forget that it was George Liele who baptized Moses Baker. However, Knibb Sibley correctly acknowledges that Liele began in Kingston, Jamaica, by preaching at the Race Course. "Although often persecuted for doing so, he continued, gathering many to hear him. He then hired a house as a meeting place for his converts. Within seven years George Liele had baptized five hundred on 'their profession of repentance towards God, and faith in our Lord Jesus Christ.' In 1791 he built, and dedicated to the glory of God, the first Baptist church of Jamaica, which was known as the Windward Road Baptist Church at the corner of Victoria and Elletson Roads, Kingston."[35] Knibb Sibley, the great-granddaughter of Missionary William Knibb, makes the bold and provocative claim that Moses Baker made a deeper impact on Baptist work in Jamaica than George Liele. "He [Baker] was instrumental in causing the Baptist Missionary Society of Gt. Britain to begin work in Jamaica. . . . (He) originally hailed from the Bahamas. He, along with his wife, came under the influence of George Liele in Kingston, and both of them were converted."[36] We are reminded by Knibb Sibley that in 1786 Baker and Liele divided Afro-Baptist work between themselves as Baker gave an affirmative response to the invitation of Quaker Lascelles Winn, the owner of the Adelphi estate, for Baker to relocate to the western parish of St. James to provide religious instructions to the enslaved population on Winn's sugar and slave plantation that included enslaved persons bought by Winn who were members of Liele's Windward Road Chapel in Kingston. It was from his new location in St. James that Moses Baker founded the second Baptist church in Jamaica, at Crooked Spring, in 1791. Afro-Baptist witness was decisively shaped by Liele focusing on the eastern parishes in Jamaica and Baker on the western parishes. In his *History of the Baptist Missionary Society*, Rev. F. A. Cox reports:

> A very excellent man, though illiterate, was connected with Mr. Liele's church, of the name of Moses Baker. He came from one of the Windward islands, and went to work in the parish of St. James, where he was very useful to the slaves on an estate belonging to Mr. Winn, which afterwards became the property of Sir. Samuel Vaughan. Mr. Winn had purchased some persons in Kingston, who were members of Mr. Liele's church; and as they were much distressed at losing their religious privileges, he engaged Moses Baker to accompany them as a teacher, promising him support.[37]

John Clark describes the spiritual condition in which Baker found the enslaved people on the Adelphi estate in St. James: "He found them imbued with the superstition known as obeah. Bottles filled with seawater, horns, old rags, and similar things were used for the purpose of witchcraft. Most of the adults were living in concubinage, and some men had two, four and even five wives."[38] We observed in the previous chapter that Du Bois opined that Africans and people of African descent in the New World never converted to Christianity, that they remained Africans in their cosmology, and while their institutions may have become Christian they embraced an African awareness that helped them question oppression and the ways in which European religion was used as a tool of social control. Missionary Clark gestures in this direction in pointing out that the Jamaica in which Liele and Baker sought to make theological sense of the Afro-Jamaican understanding of sin as sorcery refused to embrace European marriage customs, which was above all other factors of immense disappointment to the missionary class, whether white or Black.

Like George Liele his mentor, Baker also had problems with the plantation authorities who did not trust missionaries, whether white or Black. There were slave edicts circumscribing their influence among the enslaved. Missionary Clark reported that Baker at his Crooked Spring Church announced a hymn by Mr. Watts: "We will be slaves no more, since Christ has made us free, has nailed our tyrants to his cross, and bought our liberty." It was reported to the authorities that Baker was teaching sedition and inciting slaves to rebellion. On this charge Baker was arrested and taken to the Montego Bay Police Station. After he received bail, he appeared in court and the charges brought against him were dismissed.[39] Baker, like his mentor George Liele, worked with the Bible in one hand, so to speak, and the hymnal in the other. Worship included a reciprocal relationship between the church hymnal and the Bible—the singing of hymns and the recitation of scriptural passages. It becomes clear that Baker's work in the western parishes of Jamaica flourished, in spite of trial and suspicion from colonial Jamaica as he sought to parlay Christian witness, especially with Liele's Anabaptist covenant, as a basis for his interpretation of Afro-Baptist ways of interpreting the Bible. Baker himself alludes to having a successful ministry as chaplain on the estate of Quaker Lascelles Winn from 1788 when he transferred from Kingston to St. James to work at the Adelphi plantation. Baker in the 1803 issue of *The Evangelical Magazine* states:

> From Christmas-day, I have been prevented preaching, or saying a word to any part of my congregation. From this we can expect nothing but a great falling away of the weaker Christians. The poor destitute flock is left to go astray without a shepherd. Yet, as the Lord has promised he will not forsake us, nor leave us, we have reason to believe, that if God is for us, we will endeavor, by the power of his grace, to hold our

profession unto the end; therefore, we cry and crave to God, night and day, for his great mercy and assistance! We trust God will put it in your power to send us assistance, for the Lord Jesus Christ sake, and for the sake of so many poor souls, that will be totally lost for the want of your assistance! We humbly beseech you all to pray for us, poor distressed creatures as we are. Your kind presents of books I am obliged to lay aside; but I trust in the Lord they will be great help and support, by and by to this small congregation.[40]

Christopher Ballew refers to Baker's letter to the editors of *The Evangelical Magazine (1803)* as a "Macedonia Call" since Baker could not see his congregation at Crooked Spring and his work as chaplain on the Adelphi plantation surviving the new restrictions imposed by the slave laws of 1802. "Baker came to notice when he made an urgent appeal to British Baptists in 1806 because he could not resist the restrictions imposed by the new Slave Laws of 1802. It was this appeal which finally convinced the B.M.S. to commit to a joint work with Jamaican Baptists. . . . He probably had the best local organization. This is why it was to the western group of Baptists that Rowe was sent. Baker had behind him to a limited extent the authority of the Plantocracy."[41]

It is interesting that Liele was equally affected by the new laws of 1802 by the Jamaica Assembly, which was located in the eastern end of the island where Liele practiced ministry, both in Kingston and Spanish Town. Russell mentioned that Baker was influenced to some extent by the plantocracy. It is of interest that at the death of Lascelles Winn, the Quaker owner of the plantation on which Baker worked, his new employer was a Baptist, The Hon. Samuel Vaughn, with connections to the British Baptists. This may explain, in part, why Liele in another area of the island did not join in the contact with the British to request missionaries in 1814, some thirty-one years after Liele and his assistants sought to introduce an Afro-Baptist faith to Afro-Jamaicans. Russell informs us that the first missionary who came to the western section of the island in response to the Macedonia Call by Baker died shortly after his arrival in Jamaica, and Afro-Jamaicans had to await the arrival of Thomas Burchell in 1824. A former deacon and schoolmaster of Liele's church, Jamaican-born Swigle joined Baker and appealed to the British for help with his Gully church, which later became East Queen Street Baptist Church, located in Kingston—a couple of miles from Liele's Windward Road Chapel. Throughout all this time, Liele did not join the chorus asking for help from British missionaries. However, Liele relented and visited the British Baptists in 1822 in England in search of a letter from the Baptist Missionary Society requesting authorization from them to present to the Jamaica Assembly, which requested such a letter after thirty-nine years of Liele's presence on the island as the founder of Baptist work there. The British Baptists declined Liele's request, and he returned to Jamaica, as it is believed, with a broken heart. Liele was not heard from again, and William Knibb, who came to Jamaica in 1825, informed us that he attended Liele's funeral, we believe in 1825.

In the next chapter when the spotlight is turned on the advent and missionary outreach of British Baptists to Jamaica, a full account of the British response to Liele will be given. Horace Russell points out that Baker contrasted significantly with Liele's style of ministry. Baker, who was a convert and former member of Liele's church, was an enthusiast and mystic. On the other hand, Liele excelled at the organization and development of an itinerant ministry, while Baker served as pastor of the second Baptist church formed in Jamaica and excelled as chaplain of the Adelphi estate. Baker also laid the foundations of Baptist work in western parishes of Jamaica.

In the meantime, another contemporary of Baker, Mr. Swigle, who came to prominence as a deacon of Liele's Windward Road Chapel, was the schoolmaster of Liele's church, supervised the school of both freeborn and enslaved persons, and provided leadership in Liele's church. Deacon Swigle was the first creole who came to prominence as a leader in Liele's circle of influence. It was mentioned earlier that when Liele was imprisoned the second time in Jamaica, he appointed his son Paul as interim pastor, which Deacon Swigle interpreted as a sleight of hand, and so in the tradition of the autonomy of the local Baptist church, he withdrew from Liele's church to found his own chapel, named Gully Chapel, which was close to the center of Kingston and attracted many enslaved persons who had to walk to church. Afro-Jamaicans in Kingston found Swigle's

Chapter 3

Gully Chapel a much more convenient location, and by droves they began to leave Liele's church, while also benefiting from the ministry of a much younger pastor.

> In 1797, Liele was imprisoned for debt incurred in the building of his chapel. While in jail his son Paul was appointed preacher and supplied his father's pulpit. The administration of the church was left in the hands of four deacons whose names were not given.... It was during Liele's imprisonment that a damaging schism took place.... The date of the quarrel is uncertain, but it occurred before 1802, since it seemed to have become public knowledge in Britain at that date. In any case Swigle reported in a letter to Rippon dated October 1802 that the relationship between Liele and himself had been repaired.[42]

This was one area in which Baker and Swigle joined forces, with Baker in the west and Swigle in the east, seeking the help of British Baptists to provide missionaries to help their building projects. Swigle informs us that in the interim from 1797 when Liele was imprisoned until 1807 when he was released, Swigle's Gully Chapel exploded in membership as he baptized 111 new members to his Gully Chapel, which became the largest Baptist church in Jamaica in its new iteration—the East Queen Street Baptist Church.

While Liele's work receded, that of his former deacon Swigle became the new future of Baptist work in eastern Jamaica, as he received help from British missionaries replete with financial aid.

> Leile's protégés James Lewis and George Gibb continued to minister in the middle parishes of Manchester and St. Elizabeth while Missionary Thomas Burchell expanded Baptist work in western parishes. But there was a void among Afro-Jamaicans whose interest was centered in the Afro-Jamaican religions of Myal and Obeah. This vacuum was filled by James Lewis and George Gibb. In a lovely turn of phrases, Dianne Stewart's depiction of Liele, Baker, Lewis, and Gibb as North American missionaries provides a lovely segway into a fulsome discussion of their preparatory work for the contributions of the British Baptists.

First, the Native Baptists, who became visible in Jamaica during the last decade of African enslavement (1830s), were described as a distinct sect with connections to the African North American missionaries such as George Liele, Moses Baker, George Gibb, and George Lewis, who first introduced the Baptist faith to Africans in Jamaica. Liele's ministry began in 1784, approximately thirty years before his cohort, Moses Baker, requested assistance from European missionaries in the Baptist Missionary Society of London and fifty years before White missionaries began complaining about Native Baptists in their diaries.[43]

In reference to George Lewis, John Clark informs us that Lewis originally hailed from Guinea, Africa, and worked in Jamaica prior to his traveling to Virginia, where he was influenced by Baptist preachers and became an adherent of the Baptist faith. Armed with Afro-Baptist faith, he returned to Jamaica and became a member of Liele's itinerant circle of preachers, traveling to parishes of Manchester and St. Elizabeth, where he shared his African version of Baptist faith. Clark informs us that Lewis was accountable to one Ms. Valentine, who as his owner gave him permission to travel throughout Jamaica as a peddler and combine this with ministry to enslaved persons on plantations. Missionary Clark informs us that Lewis was repeatedly imprisoned for preaching at sugar-slave plantations especially at night. It was mentioned that Lewis did not formally identify with a particular church in Jamaica and that his practice of preaching included "a great deal of superstition."[44] We are reminded that Liele and the other North American missionaries would have been careful under the scrutinizing gaze and attention of white authorities. It was agreed by those who knew George Lewis very well that he had an effect on the enslaved population who benefited from his ministry—"people left off worshipping the cotton tree, forsook their house idols, lived better lives, and went in search of Christian instruction. 'Whether in pretense or in truth, Christ was preached.'"[45]

George Gibb, the fourth assistant to Liele, seemed to have focused his work as an evangelist in the parishes of St. Mary and St. Thomas in the Vale. He came to Jamaica in 1784, the same year Liele established his church in a house and acquired land to build his Windward Road Chapel. However, of all the North American missionaries who worked and identified with Liele, Gibb stayed outside of the limelight. Winston Lawson informs us: "[Liele] saw the need for added assistance to that of George Gibb, a convert who came with him to Jamaica, and Moses Baker, a barber and enslaved person converted under Liele's preaching. These two colleagues of Liele were to become . . . players in the expansion of the Church's witness in Kingston and its environs and to the Western areas around Montego Bay."[46] George Gibb joined the fraternity, so to speak, of the missionaries from the United States who went to jail. All four—Liele, Baker, Lewis, and Gibb—were imprisoned for their advocacy and preaching the gospel of an Afro-Baptist faith. "[Gibb] was once thrown into Spanish town jail, and confined there four days, for having been caught teaching slaves."[47] In similar fashion to Lewis, it was also Gibb's custom to visit plantations at night and surreptitiously share his Baptist faith with enslaved persons. "He was many times found on estates at night, and cast into the dungeon, and his feet placed in the bilboes, for having dared to enter into a Negro house to teach those by night to whom he did not have access by day."[48] Gibb's personal approach was very successful, as Missionary Clark reported that he attracted hundreds into his church, which practiced triune baptism. There seemed to have been a mystical emphasis to Gibb's approach to baptism, as baptismal services were carried out under the cover of night. This practice of immersing Afro-Jamaicans in holy waters of baptism at night would have Christianized the Myal emphasis of baptism in water as a means of covering the initiate with the presence and power of spirits who could be found in water. Afro-Jamaicans began to associate baptism in rivers or spaces where there was plenty of water as healing streams, and they would seek baptism not only for themselves but for their progeny, as baptism would offer both protection and healing for body and spirit. One can picture baptism at night under a Caribbean moon as enslaved people found healing and protection in their enslaved condition.

Mary Turner, in her *Slaves and Missionaries*, points out that difficult times were ahead for missionaries both Black and white—but especially Black missionaries. Much of the problem revolved around the 1807 law that aimed an attack on preachers to the enslaved population. There was an exception that accommodated the established church to provide instruction to the slave community. "When the Assembly met in October 1807, it passed a new consolidated slave code which made missionary work illegal, but attempted to silence potential criticism on this score by promoting Anglican instruction for the slaves. Clause one stated that slave owners and overseers should give their slaves religious instruction, and clause two specifically limited such instruction to Anglican doctrine."[49] Methodists and Baptists were prohibited from preaching. This was a warning shot in that a Methodist missionary was imprisoned for a month when he defied the order. The practice was that a judge in each parish had to sign off on his satisfaction of the missionary's suitability and qualification to preach. "In this situation a practice developed of allowing the missionaries to work in each parish at the discretion of the magistrates. The precedent for this practice was established by a case arising from the 1802 law. The magistrate in St. Thomas in the East, guided by the custos, Sir Simon Taylor, used the law to charge the Kingston missionary who founded the Morant Bay missionaries, the Rev. Daniel Campbell, with illegal preaching. Campbell was tried at the Kingston assize and, as a missionary licensed by the Kingston magistrates to preach in Kingston, found guilty under the act, of not being 'duly qualified' to preach in the adjacent parish of St. Thomas in the East."[50] Turner points out that from this time until 1828, although missionaries appealed to biblical warrants for their authorization to preach, the magistrates nonetheless decided whether their credentials as ordained qualified them to preach in a particular parish. By refusing to issue a license to preach to a particular missionary, the magistrates could keep the church closed. With the magistrates insisting on being satisfied on the qualifications of missionaries to preach, this, in effect, closed the doors of Liele's church and Black churches in Kingston. Liele's Windward Road Chapel became a hospital as he could not successfully receive authorization to preach. The circumstances were different for Baker since he had the blessing of Hon. Vaughn of the Adelphi estate, where he served as chaplain, and testimonials from his owner that enslaved people under his ministry had become dutiful and obedient. "Moses Baker and George Gibb held congregations together until they died in the 1829s. Once the magistrates had established the right to insist on 'due qualification' before licensing preachers, there was no place in the system for Black Baptists."[51] The problem for Liele and his assistants was that they needed an accrediting organization to vouch for their credentials as preachers. As mentioned earlier, the problem of satisfying a judge that one was qualified to preach occasioned Liele's journey to the Baptist Missionary Society in London to request a letter of accreditation. Liele's request from the British Baptists was declined.

In several cases the congregations established by Liele and his colleagues were taken over by missionaries from the Baptist Missionary Society. While Liele was away in England in 1822 seeking a letter of authorization to preach, his church was taken over by Missionary Coultart. On Liele's return Coultart turned Liele's church over to him, but that congregation never returned to its original vibrancy. With slave preachers being silenced by the magistrates of the planter class and the inflow of missionaries from England on the increase, there were clearly two strands of Baptist witness in Jamaica: the British Baptists, who made their entrée in Jamaica with John Rowe in 1814, and the Baptists led by George Liele. What became increasingly clear was that Afro-Jamaicans established membership in both churches and merged their foundational belief in spirits, dreams, and dance—beliefs in Obeah and Myal—with the Christian church's teaching.

In the next chapter we will focus on the advent of the British missionaries to Jamaica and their contributions to Afro-Baptist ecclesiology and soteriology.[52]

Notes

1. Devon Dick, *The Cross and the Machete: Native Baptists of Jamaica* (Kingston, Jamaica: Ian Randle Publishers, 2009).
2. Philip Sherlock and Hazel Bennett, *The Story of the Jamaican People* (Kingston, Jamaica: Ian Randle Publishers, 1998), 180. Dianne Stewart, in *Three Eyes for the Journey: African Dimensions of the Jamaican Religious Experience* (New York: Oxford University Press, 2005), 128, lists among the Native Baptist leaders who worked closely with Liele, Moses Baker, George Gibb, and George Lewis, "who first introduced the Baptist faith to Africans in Jamaica."
3. Richard D. E. Burton, *Afro-Creole: Power, Opposition, and Play in the Caribbean* (Ithaca, NY: Cornell University Press, 1997), 36.
4. Burton, *Afro-Creole*, 36.

5. Burton, *Afro-Creole*, 37.
6. Stewart, *Three Eyes for the Journey*, 128–29.
7. Stewart, *Three Eyes for the Journey*, 129.
8. Robert J. Stewart, *Religion and Society in Post-Emancipation Jamaica* (Knoxville: University of Tennessee Press, 1992), 124.
9. Stewart, *Religion and Society*, 124–25.
10. Stewart, *Religion and Society*, 125.
11. Stewart, *Religion and Society*, 7–8.
12. Stewart, *Religion and Society*, 8.
13. Mary Turner, *Slaves and Missionaries: The Disintegration of Jamaican Slave Society, 1787–1834* (Urbana: University of Illinois Press, 1982), 52.
14. I recall in 1952, when my grandmother "Mum" died, Grandpa Tata said she wanted the family to sing at her funeral her favorite song, "Sweet Beulah Land." She said "Sweet Beulah Land" was Africa, where she hoped to join the ancestors.
15. F. A Cox, *History of the Baptist Missionary Society: From 1792 to 1842, in Two Volumes* (London: T. Ward, 1842), 183.
16. Dick, *The Cross and the Machete*, 46.
17. Dick, *The Cross and the Machete*, 48.
18. W. M. Duggan, *The First Annual Report of the Jamaica Native Baptist Missionary Society. Spanish Town, 1836*. Angus Library, Regents Park College, Oxford University.
19. John Clark, W. Dendy, and J. M. Phillippo, *The Voice of Jubilee: A Narrative of the Baptist Mission, Jamaica. from its Commencement; With Biographical Notices of Its Fathers and Founders* (London: John Snow, Paternoster Row, 1865).
20. Clark et al., *The Voice of Jubilee*, 3.
21. W. E. B. Du Bois, *The Negro Church* (Atlanta, GA: Atlanta University Press, 1903), 6.
22. Clark et al., *The Voice of Jubilee*, 30.
23. Clark et al., *The Voice of Jubilee*, 31.
24. Cox, *History of the Baptist Missionary Society*, 181.
25. John Clark, *Memorials of Baptist Missionaries in Jamaica, Including A Sketch of Labours of Early Religious Instructors in Jamaica* (London: Yates and Alexander, 1869), 13.
26. Monica Schuler, "Myalism and the African Religious Tradition in Jamaica," in *Caribbean Slave Society and Economy*, Hilary Beckles and Verene Shepherd, eds. (New York: The New Press, 1991), 296.
27. Schuler, "Myalism and the African Religious Tradition in Jamaica," 296.
28. Schuler, "Myalism and the African Religious Tradition in Jamaica," 297.
29. Schuler, "Myalism and the African Religious Tradition in Jamaica," 297.
30. Schuler, "Myalism and the African Religious Tradition in Jamaica," 297.
31. Schuler, "Myalism and the African Religious Tradition in Jamaica," 297.
32. W. J. Gardner, *A History of Jamaica: From its Discovery by Christopher Columbus to the Year 1872*. (London: T. Fisher Unwin, 1909; first published 1873), 178.
33. Howard Stroger, "Coromantine Obeah and Myalism" (unpublished undergraduate honors thesis, Rutgers University, 1966), 101.
34. Stewart, *Religion and Society*, 127.

35. Inez Knibb Sibley, *The Baptists of Jamaica, 1793 to 1965* (Kingston: The Jamaica Baptist Union, 1965), 2. In the description on the cover of the book, Inez Knibb Sibley points out that she was a great-granddaughter of William Knibb, perhaps the most distinguished of the early missionaries to Jamaica.

36. Sibley, *The Baptists of Jamaica*, 2.

37. Cox, *History of the Baptist Missionary Society*, 183. It should be noted that Baker wrote letters to the British Baptist Missionary Society describing his problems with his eyesight and is widely regarded as the author of *The Evangelical Magazine, 1803*. Earlier Knibb Sibley pointed out that Baker was born in the Bahamas. Baker often reported that he was from New York.

38. Clark et al., *The Voice of Jubilee*, 34.

39. Clark et al., *The Voice of Jubilee*, 34.

40. Christopher Brent Ballew, *The Impact of African American Antecedents on the Baptist Foreign Missionary Movement, 1782–1825* (Lewiston, NY: Edwin Mellen Press, 2004), 84. See also *The Evangelical Magazine* (1803), 550–51.

41. Horace O. Russell, *The Missionary Outreach of the West Indian Church: Jamaican Baptist Missions to West Africa in the Nineteenth Century* (New York: Peter Lang, 2000), 14–15.

42. Russell, *The Missionary Outreach of the West Indian Church*, 19.

43. Stewart, *Three Eyes for the Journey*, 128.

44. Clark, *Memorials of Baptist Missionaries in Jamaica*, 13–14.

45. Stewart, *Three Eyes for the Journey*, 102.

46. Winston Lawson, "Pioneer George Liele in Jamaica, the British Colony," in *George Liele's Life and Legacy: An Unsung Hero*, ed. David T. Shannon, Julia Frazier White, and Deborah Bingham Van Broekhoven (Macon, GA: Mercer University Press, 2012), 125.

47. Clark, *Memorials of Baptist Missionaries in Jamaica*, 15.

48. Clark, *Memorials of Baptist Missionaries in Jamaica*, 15.

49. Turner, *Slaves and Missionaries*, 16.

50. Turner, *Slaves and Missionaries*, 16–17.

51. Turner, *Slaves and Missionaries*, 17.

52. It is clear there were different approaches from the Black Missionaries and the British Missionaries to questions of their understanding of church and eschatology.

Chapter 4

The Coming of Missionaries

It is sometimes forgotten that although George Liele and several of his associates were missionaries from North America to Jamaica, they were of African ancestry; they were Black Baptists. What is also unusual is that they came to Jamaica because they were sympathizers with the British cause, and in Liele's case, he had been liberated at the death of his master, a British sympathizer. Members of Henry Sharp's family who were not pleased with the terms of Liele's freedom had him arrested and imprisoned. Liele was able to secure his freedom through his friendship with Moses Kirkland, the commander in charge of the British military in the Savannah area. Colonel Kirkland loaned Liele seven hundred pounds sterling to procure the passage of himself and his family to Jamaica. There was an understanding between Liele and his sponsor to Jamaica that Liele would enter Jamaica as an indentured servant and would work to repay his debt to Kirkland. Liele repaid his debt in two years. John Davis writes:

> Mr. Sharp was an officer in the war and died from wounds received in the King's service. Soon after the death of Mr. Sharp there arose those who were dissatisfied with George's liberation. He was taken and thrown into prison, but by producing his manumission papers was released. To extricate himself from this unpleasant situation Liele became obligated to a Colonel Kirkland. At the evacuation of Savannah by the British he was partly obliged to come to Jamaica, as an indentured servant for money he owed Colonel Kirkland, who promised to

Chapter 4

be his friend in that country.... Thus by force of circumstances George Liele was compelled to leave those among whom he had labored so effectively and thrown into another field where he had opportunity for further service.[1]

Liele, who was born into slavery and had worked as a slave in different states in America, was finally in Jamaica and, although indentured to Col. Moses Kirkland, who had traveled to Jamaica with him, was focused on his calling as the first Black ordained minister of the gospel from Savannah, Georgia, now in Jamaica. Some years later Liele would travel to England on behalf of the Christianity he represented. Liele arrived in Jamaica and saw the precarity of Afro-Jamaicans trapped in the quagmire of slavery that was even more cruel than that to which he was exposed in Georgia and Virginia.

In her important essay "Christianity in the World of George Liele," Deborah Bingham Van Broekhoven asks what it would mean to look at Christianity through the life and times of George Liele, given the impact of the transatlantic world. This approach to Liele transcends the custom among scholars of Black and European varieties of ecclesiology and culture, which has traditionally placed Liele and his ministry in camps of "Black" church and "white" church. An important point here is that Liele's work was not limited to a national context but included international and interregional approaches to ecclesiology.

> The Christianity practiced by Liele was not limited to one nation, colony, or ethnic group but was a faith formed and spread through interaction with colonists and national leaders in the Americas and in England. In turn, this broad vision of Christianity shaped and spread a variety of Christian experience that became widespread and influential in black, white and integrated congregations in Georgia, South Carolina, Jamaica, Nova Scotia, Sierra Leone, and beyond.[2]

According to Van Broekhoven, Liele was prepared to negotiate and interact with both the planter and missionary class in Jamaica because in Virginia and Georgia he interacted with both the plantocracy and preachers. Henry Sharp, Liele's enslaver, was a brother to the wife of

Liele's pastor, Matthew Moore. One gets a sense that Henry Sharp was perhaps the owner and primary benefactor to this plantation church, and since he was a deacon in this church the pastor acceded to his wishes, such as setting Liele apart to witness to enslaved persons on plantations owned by Sharp and later to slaves on plantations along the Savannah River. This was how Liele made his way to Silver Bluff, South Carolina, and became an integral part of the Silver Bluff Baptist Church, where he became reacquainted with his friend David George from their times together as enslaved youths in Virginia.

However, there were significant trends in the wider transatlantic culture that opened up a new world for Liele. The Christianity to which Liele was committed was complex, as it embraced a negative anthropology that shaped the colonial experience and was mostly uncritical of the world that defined enslaved persons living in the context of racial slavery, which taught that Black people were inherently evil. Liele, coming to Jamaica from the North American experience in his turn to Christianity, confessed that he found himself on a path to destruction, and after months of penitence and the embrace of hope beyond this world, gave his life completely to the Christian faith. It was noted in the previous chapter that Liele did not push back against the indigenous religions he experienced in Jamaica in a way that gave comfort to colonial masters both on plantations and the established church and later even from the missionary arm of the British Baptists. Perhaps, because of the new reality that confronted Liele in the Caribbean, that Africans were in a substantial way in the majority and whites in the minority, Liele had to take seriously the practice of indigenous peoples that sin was not constitutive of human life but had its basis in society and that—according to the Myalists and various iterations of indigenous religions in Jamaica—sin was sorcery. Myalists concluded that slavery was a product of European sorcery. This meant that sin was temporal, its basis was anthropocentric, and it could be changed. This may have been one reason for the plethora of rebellions in the Caribbean that ultimately produced the Haitian Revolution. Haitians saw their oppression by the French as a form of European sorcery—and they produced an antidote and overthrew their oppressors and produced the first independent republic in the Caribbean.

Chapter 4

It became increasingly clear that both the British missionaries and members of the Jamaica Assembly did not trust Liele. The phenomenon of a person of African descent providing leadership for the Baptist church in Jamaica from 1783 to 1825 did not cohere with their anti-Black theology and Black people living under a system of racial slavery, who they understood to be inherently evil. It should not surprise us then that about six years after Liele's death, Baptists of Jamaica led by Myalist Daddy Sharpe led a rebellion in Jamaica in 1831 that reminded the plantocracy that they were outnumbered by the indigenous Black population in Jamaica. This rebellion against their colonial masters is referred to as "The Baptist War," and it was clear that the Baptists who participated were from the group shaped by the combination of George Liele and indigenous religious practices. The system of racial slavery and hostile systems of colonial power were not understood by Afro-Baptist faith as sacred—evil expressed in slavery was not permanent. Afro-Baptist faith inspired by Daddy Sharpe and the teachings of Liele and Myal counseled that slavery was an expression of European sorcery and as such could be defeated. According to Van Broekhoven,

> That he lived in a world in which most people of African descent were enslaved complicated and shaped Liele's ministry and theology. During the span of his life, conviction that modern slavery was not Christian and should be abolished grew to become a frequent part of Christian conversation, preaching, and pamphleteering. The twin subjects of slavery and freedom were in the air. Stirred up by the political upheaval of the American, French, and Haitian revolutions and by the religious conviction that began with Quakers and Baptists that slavery was evil and slaveholding was problematic, particularly in a world where Christians were holding other Christians in slavery.[3]

We are reminded that Liele lived in a world in which the majority of enslaved persons were of African descent and this reality would have shaped his approach to theology and ministry. For most of his life in the American colonies, Liele was enslaved and accepted slavery as an integral part of Christian cosmology. While he lived in the American colonies of Virginia and Georgia, even as one who received his license to preach and in 1775 was duly ordained to the Christian ministry, Liele did not critically question the sin of slavery, perhaps because his freedom depended on his silence. The truth was that Christians were leaders in the slave trade and preachers such as Evangelist Whitfield (whose approach to evangelism appealed to Liele) insisted on the enslaved community being allowed to attend evangelical worship services. However, he did not question the social context in which enslaved persons had their humanity diminished and were regarded as beasts of burden. As James Washington writes, "The biblical depiction of a literal 'heaven' and 'hell' has been a cardinal dimension of evangelical cosmic geography since the advent of this movement in the eighteenth century. The classical evangelicals—especially those of a militant bent such as George Whitfield—raised this aspect of the geography of biblical eschatology from a scriptural referent to a serious and indispensable part of Christian soteriology."[4]

In one of his sermons, Whitfield calls on his hearers to imagine themselves in the place of the wretched man [Dives] who was both self-deluding and self-deluded. "Think, I beseech you by the Mercies of God in Christ Jesus, think with yourselves, how racking, how unsupportable the never dying Worm of a self-condemning Conscience will hereafter be to you. Think how impossible it will be for you *to dwell with everlasting burning*."[5]

Matthew Moore, the pastor at Big Buckhead Creek Baptist Church, where Liele was baptized, licensed to preach, and ordained to the Christian ministry, was a disciple of Whitfield and as a "Separate" Baptist would preach in the tradition of Whitfield. This explains in part why Liele, like Whitfield, who had slaves at his Bethesda Orphan House in Savannah, Georgia, would on the one hand encourage attendance of enslaved persons at his churches in Jamaica, and on the other hand would not explicitly critique the system and the world in which enslaved persons lived. "Most churches refrained from antislavery comments as they knew slavery was a sensitive subject among slave-holding Christians. As a slave and then former slave, George Liele was as careful as St. Paul when dealing with the issue of legal bondage, perhaps understanding that his own liberty to preach was conditional upon the approval of slave holders."[6]

Chapter 4

Issues of slavery and freedom were always at the center of attempts to translate the gospel of Christ in Liele's world to the world of those in bondage in the New World. The eschatology articulated by Whitfield undoubtedly informed Liele's approach to the preaching of the gospel of Christ, coupled of course with the precarity of his own freedom to preach in colonial Jamaica. We noted in the previous chapter that Liele had a passion to relate the gospel to Afro-Jamaicans and in this context he understood himself being in the tradition of Psalm 68:31, "Let bronze be brought from Egypt; let Ethiopia hasten to stretch out her hands to God." There were occasions when Liele seemed to make connections between his understanding of salvation—the new life that God makes available through the preaching of the gospel to enslaved persons. One such occasion was perhaps at the celebration of the erection of his church building in Kingston, Jamaica, in preaching from Romans 10:1: "Brethren, my heart's desire and prayer to God for them is that they may be saved." Liele was clearly one of the early church leaders in bringing good news to enslaved Jamaicans.

Liele was probably the first person to do religious work among the slaves of Jamaica, writes John Parmer Gates.

> Up to his time there was not very much effort expended in preaching the Gospel even to whites. . . . Most of the slaves in Jamaica had probably never heard of the Gospel until the Methodists, and the Baptists under Liele, came at the end of the eighteenth century. Some of the Negroes were undoubtedly not far removed from their primitive state, for slave trade with Africa was still in progress. Not infrequently drums were heard that beat out the rhythm for crude sensual dances which, to the whites at times, were dangerously suggestive of earlier African drum beats in preparation for going to war. Belief in witchcraft, the use of charms and other superstitions were common among them. Is it any wonder that Liele attracted attention when, for the first time, he appeared on the Kingston race track preaching the love of God that was in Christ Jesus?[7]

In his important text *Two Jamaicas: The Role of Ideas in a Tropical Colony 1830–1865*, Philip Curtin points out that much of African religions

The Coming of Missionaries

in Jamaica were untouched by European culture. This becomes understandable in Jamaica as Parmer Gates mentioned and Curtin affirms that there was no coming together of Afro-Jamaicans and Europeans for worship on any meaningful scale prior to the coming of missionaries in the 1820s. Although John Rowe, the first British Baptist missionary, came in 1814, he died two years later, and Thomas Burchell came in 1824 followed by William Knibb in 1825. James Phillippo, who later served as a Baptist missionary in Jamaica for some twenty years, calls attention to the two worlds, or as Philip Curtin characterizes it, two Jamaicas, that existed—on the one hand Afro-Jamaica and on the other European-Jamaica. The worlds were separated by color and culture:

> With people of color, indeed, the whites, like the Egyptians in reference to the Israelites, held it an abomination even to eat bread. This senseless prejudice haunted its victims in the "hospital where humanity suffers, in the prison it expiates its offences, and in the grave yards where it sleeps the last sleep." In whomsoever the least trace of African origin could be discovered the curse of slavery pursued him, and no advantage of wealth, talent, virtue, education, or accomplishments, were sufficient to relieve him from the infamous prescription.[8]

It should not surprise us then that enslaved persons not only preferred to worship among themselves but did not trust the interpretation white preachers gave to the scriptures. It was often clear to Black people that the scriptures on the lips of the master class was used to reinforce the subjugation and subordination of the enslaved to the master class. "Many slaves resented having to attend church services conducted by whites. They hated repeatedly being told 'Obey de Massa, obey de overseer, obey dis, obey dat,' while their masters and overseers oppressed and physically abused them. They disliked having to sit in the rear of the church or in the galleries set apart exclusively for them. They cherished meetings of their own where they could relax and enjoy the form of worship that pleased them and uplifted their spirits."[9]

Black people not only loved to worship among themselves, they also craved hearing their own preachers. This made Liele and his associates extremely popular and sought out as preachers by the Black community, especially prior to 1802, at which time preachers were required by law to produce authorization from ecclesial leadership in order to preach. Somehow, the courts and the Jamaica Assembly did not see fit to offer authorization to Liele, who started the Baptist Church in Jamaica and served as its leader. Philip Curtin mentioned quite appropriately, I believe, that Liele was himself a Native Baptist who kept his congregation as orthodox as possible. It seems that much of the distinction among the Baptist churches that owed their origins to George Liele was in the interpretation of "the spirit," the neglect of the written word (the Bible) in part due to the reality that a majority of enslaved Jamaicans were unable to read, and the centrality of dreams especially as it bore testimony to the presence of the spirit as a precondition for baptism in the Baptist tradition. Curtin calls attention to two of Liele's church leaders who departed from Liele's orthodoxy in their embrace of a distinctive emphasis on Native Baptist. He explains:

> The characteristic doctrinal departure from orthodoxy in the early Native Baptist groups was the emphasis on "the spirit" and a corresponding neglect of the written word. Most of the leaders could not read in any case, and the shift accorded with the remnants of African religious attitudes. The followers of both Baker and Gibb were required to be possessed of "the spirit" before baptism was administered. This meant that "the spirit" had to descend on the applicant in a dream, which was then described to the leader. If the dream were satisfactory, the applicant could enter the class. There evolved a regular technique and ceremonial for bringing on the spirit-possession, which included a fast.[10]

Baptism took on a new significance and importance as it was no longer just a symbol and sign of what God through the Holy Spirit had accomplished in the believer but had become a means of grace. A number of Liele's associates, perhaps Gibb and Baker, seemed to have begun the practice of conducting baptisms at night. It was mentioned earlier that Liele's associates had taken Afro-Baptist faith in a new direction and what made it very popular among Afro-Jamaicans was the openness with the Baptist polity and ecclesiology, and as the autonomy of the local church was highlighted it was appropriate for the local church to go in a direction affirmed by local leadership and people.

It became clear that Liele represented the polity and ecclesiology of the Baptist faith, which he embraced in the context of Georgia, from Matthew Moore's church where he was baptized and ordained. Curtin refers to Liele's theological position as orthodox, and Devon Dick as Original. An important distinction between the perspectives of Curtin and Dick is that Curtin proffers different strands of Native Baptists. With Liele's church representing the orthodox in terms of foundational, Curtin presents Liele's associates, Gibb, Lewis, Baker, and Swigle, as representing different iterations of Liele's position. Dick, on the other hand, agrees that there were Native Baptists, yet argues that Liele did not speak of his work in those terms. He offers that Baptist work in Jamaica began with Liele and in that sense his work was original. This distinction between Dick and Curtin is important in our understanding of Liele's contribution to Baptist ecclesiology, practice, and doctrine. A central question in making theological sense of Liele's posture is in relation to indigenous religious practices of Myal and Obeah, understandings of spirit, dreams, worship at cotton trees, or down by the river where Myalists believed spirits resided that had come over with enslaved persons. An important index of answering these questions of Liele's posture in relation to the indigenous religious practices of Afro-Jamaicans is that Liele did not question, censure, or speak out against the practices of these religious positions, especially as they were incorporated in Baptist polity and faith as represented by his associates.

Liele and the Forging of a Transnational Faith

What I find of interest is what Curtin called Native Baptist churches, with an acknowledgment that there were several iterations of Native Baptists, with Liele's church representing the most orthodox among them. Granted, Liele would not have subscribed to notions of spirits gathering at cotton trees inviting Afro-Jamaicans to worship, or that John the Baptist was the head of the Baptist church since he baptized Jesus. There is no evidence that Liele believed claims by Native Baptists who merged Afro-Baptist faith with Myal religion. This is evident from the biblical citations in the Anabaptist covenant produced by Liele and read once per month at Sunday evening service where the ordinance of holy communion was served. Liele was a student of the Bible as was made clear in his letters and the Anabaptist church covenant produced by him. While the covenant regulated the interaction of members with each other, their enslavers, and life within the context of the church, it was not a doctrinal statement that instructed the membership of Liele's church what to believe or how to interpret the faith. With a variety of notions and ideas about "spirits," "the holy spirit," "baptism," "funerals," and even the covenant produced by Liele, he did not provide any theological guidance of how to interpret these elements of the faith. Emphasis was placed on the practice of the faith with room allowed for the interpretation of the faith. There was no guidance on the form that faith takes in the life of believers. The indigenous religious assessment of the spirit informed by the Myal religion stipulates that spirit may guide one or speak to a believer in a dream, or one may worship spirits "down by the river side," or in a forest at night. Liele, who must have known about these understandings of the form the spirit takes, left this door open and placed the emphasis on the authenticity, integrity, and power of the spirit. As a Bible student Liele would have known that the spirit may take the form of a dove, as it was at the baptism of Jesus, or spirit may come as a mighty rushing wind, as in the day of Pentecost, or as a burning bush, as it was in the case of Moses. Spirit may also be feared as in religious expressions of Obeah, or in the form of Jamaican "duppies" at graves of deceased persons.

Liele was cognizant that it would be problematic to say the spirt is here and not there. What was at stake was evidence of the fruit of the spirit—love, patience, joy, and so on. It was this silence of Liele in the critique of Afro-Jamaican religions that allowed some missionaries among the British Baptists to wonder and to charge Liele with being an adherent of Myal and other expressions of Jamaican indigenous religions.

An illustration of Liele's reticence to criticize Afro-Jamaican religion is seen in his relationship to Moses Baker, one of Liele's chief associates who was a leader in Baptist work in the western parishes of Jamaica.

Horace Russell, in his important book *Foundations and Anticipations: The Jamaica Baptist Story, 1783–1892*, calls attention to the leadership Moses Baker provided in the western parishes. According to Russell, in Baker's use of Liele's covenant, Baker excised several sections that he thought were not appropriate, and there was never any comments of disagreement from Liele. Russell points out that it was well known that Baker, who was steeped in Jamaican indigenous religions prior to his conversion and baptism by Liele, would be in a religious trance for several days, which was one of the manifestations of the presence and power of spirit in Myal religion.

> The second challenge, witchcraft continued as a frequent practice on the estate; indeed, its presence appears to have been one of the motivating factors for the appointment of Baker. Most of the slaves were from West Africa and had known the "Mo" houses, in which articles of clothing and the possessions of the deceased were collected as a token of honor to the departed. Here, too, was a center or depository for healing the ailments of body and mind. Thus a house set apart for practices of Obeah, Myal or any other non-Christian celebration or syncretistic worship was not uncommon at this time. . . . It is well known that Baker went into trances for days on end, and indeed at times his overt behavior was similar to that of his opponents.[11]

It was well known that prior to his baptism by Liele, as mentioned by Jamaican historian W. J. Gardner, Baker lived in "utter disregard" of religion.[12] It is quite clear that what Gardner refers to as "utter disregard of religion" would be the practice of Afro-Jamaican religion in the form of Obeah, Myal, and African religious practices. "The negative comments by European missionaries as to Baker's 'strange system' and his associates' 'monstrous superstition' reflect their biased dismissal of African emphases on trances and spirit possession as clearly unorthodox comingling with 'heathen' practices."[13] Curtin points out that prior to 1830, after which there was an appreciable number of missionaries in Jamaica, Europeans in Jamaica did not display much interest in the religious practices of Afro-Jamaicans. This meant that Afro-Jamaicans were free to practice

CHAPTER 4

Myal and Obeah and their preoccupation with spirits was largely unnoticed by the master class.

Before 1830, Curtin writes,

> very few blacks indeed were to be found at the European end of the spectrum. They were not welcome in the Church of England before emancipation, except in rare cases, and, though large numbers of slaves were baptized, it was simply a formality unaccompanied by instruction. The eighteenth-century Established Church was a white man's church, and it was to remain so long after emancipation. The general religious revival in Britain, which was to be a driving force behind emancipation, did not bring a large number of missionaries from the dissenting sects until the 1820s. Long before this, elements of Christianity had come to Jamaica and mixed with African ideas and practices.[14]

Apart from the disinterest that Curtin points to among Europeans as it pertains to Native religious practices, it is instructive that most enslaved persons lived on the premises at the sugar estates. The reality of absentee ownership was a benefit to the enslaved class as their masters resided in Europe and the overseers did not take an interest in religion beyond what affected the production of their work. Added to this reality was the fact that Afro-Jamaicans outnumbered Europeans and lived in remote sections of expansive sugar estates. A point being made here is that Liele did not express any notion of Myal, Obeah, and a variety of indigenous expressions of religion as being a threat to the Christianity that he preached and embodied.

Could there have been another reason for Liele's hands-off approach? Were legal restrictions and the sociological environment in which Liele sought to raise a family, tend his farm, work as a servant of the government, and make room for his contributions as pastor decisive factors? A number of scholars, including Mary Turner in *Slaves and Missionaries* and Maya Jasanoff in *Liberty's Exiles*, suggest that the problem of race on the one hand and limits set by courts of requirements in order to preach to the enslaved class on the other hand literally withdrew Liele's freedom to preach.

Remember the Haitian Revolution

Turner reminds us of the import of the Haitian Revolution in 1791 and its impact on Jamaica in driving French nationals along with their slaves and free people of color and Black persons to settle in Jamaica as refugees.

> The failure of the British invasion attempt launched from Jamaica and the triumph of Toussaint L' Ouverture, leader of the revolution, left Jamaica with a black republic as neighbor just ninety miles away. In St. Lucia the British were defeated by an army of freed slaves, and insurrections followed in the islands of Dominica, St. Vincent, and Grenada, where substantial French minorities had been under British rule for twenty-five years. In Jamaica itself the Trelawny Town Maroons, one of four communities of ex-slaves who had established a territorial base for themselves as a result of a prolonged struggle in the early eighteenth century, rebelled. They were forced to retreat for peace only after a severe campaign in which a hundred man-hunting bloodhounds were imported from Cuba for use against them.[15]

This was a time of immense upheaval for the Caribbean and particularly Jamaica with the Maroons, former African slaves who took to the hills and forests of Jamaica when the British captured Jamaica from the people of Spain in 1655. The Maroons would attack the British from the hills and forests of Jamaica until the British made a peace treaty with them that included ownership of lands and freedom to make their own laws and live by their own traditions. In addition to the dis-ease caused by Haiti and St. Lucia along with insurrections in Dominica, St. Vincent, and Grenada, the Jamaica Assembly and the plantocracy had to deal with missionaries including Liele and fellow Black Baptists proclaiming an eschatology that promised notions of the enslaved and master being equal before God. Further, there were instructions by Baptists, Methodists, Moravians, and Presbyterians that God would judge both the enslaved and the enslaver at the end of history and God's justice would prevail.

Understandably, all preachers in dissenting congregations were suspects and regarded as a threat to the security of the island. Preachers knew they were not trusted by the plantocracy and any suggestion of the abolition of slavery or advocacy of better conditions for the enslaved was dismissed as incendiary. There were riots in Kingston, and church services were banned after dark when an attempt was made in 1791 to destroy a Wesleyan chapel. "The magistrates restored order, but the rioters were acquitted in court. The Wesleyan missionaries lived in the midst of threats and newspaper scandals and their more prominent members were stoned. The Black Baptists suffered worse. Liele and his free colored co-worker, Moses Baker, were charged with preaching sedition and kept in irons while awaiting trial, although they were eventually acquitted."[16]

Mary Turner points out that during the upheaval in Jamaica caused by the Maroons, Liele and his associates fared the worst among the missionaries, and no doubt one reason for their harsh treatment was because they were Black. Moses Baker was of fair complexion in contrast to Liele, whose parents were African slaves. It was unprecedented in Jamaican culture and society to have Black persons preaching the Christian gospel, founding churches, and participating in baptisms and the sacraments of the church. In 1793 when this upheaval in the culture occurred, with the imprisonment of Liele and Baker due to the unrest engendered by the Maroons and a sense of fear that a Black republic was taking roots only ninety miles from Jamaica, Liele was at the pinnacle of his ministerial career in Jamaica. He had recently celebrated the dedication of the Windward Road Chapel in Kingston, along with the procurement of a burial ground (cemetery) in Spanish Town. Baker, on the other hand, was putting down deep roots in St. James, from where he would invite British missionaries to help with Baptist witness in St. James at first and later throughout the island of Jamaica.

Ministry performed among the leaders of Afro-Baptist faith became challenging and difficult. Turner suggests that there was a pattern during the first ten years of Baptist work on the island that shaped the contours of what these churches could expect to unfold in the years ahead.

> The pattern established in the first decade of mission work, uneasy tolerance by the authorities giving way in times of political stress to overt hostility, was repeated in 1802 and in 1807. On each occasion hostility to slave instruction deepened. In 1802, when a large French fleet was

sent to the Caribbean to reconquer St. Domingue, and Jamaica feared invasion, the Assembly, as one of a number of security measures, passed a law to curtail mission work. . . . An act was passed to prevent preaching by persons not duly qualified by law.[17]

A Methodist missionary was imprisoned for a month for refusing to obey the 1807 law. This created extreme hardship for fellow Methodists. The posture of the colonial government in Jamaica was to encourage the Anglican church to provide religious instructions for enslaved persons, in order to enforce the law, that Methodists and other dissenting churches should be prohibited to engage in preaching. The bottom line was that missionary work was now considered illegal. "The missionaries were prepared to dispute the ruling but on seeking legal advice they were told that there was no toleration law operative in the island to which they could appeal. . . . From this time until 1828 missionaries applying for a license continued to take the oath of allegiance and supremacy and subscribe to a scriptural declaration, but the magistrates decided whether their credentials as ordained ministers qualified them to preach in that parish."[18] The new law, which gave the magistrate in each parish the right to rule as to whether the ordination of preachers from dissenting churches were qualified to preach, had the effect of shutting down the Methodist church in Kingston from 1807 to 1814. The magistrate in Kingston withheld certification to preach from Methodists in Kingston. As was always the case, the impact of the ruling of magistrates in Kingston was more severe for the Baptists. Baptist churches in Kingston were all closed. Liele's Windward Road Chapel became a hospital, and this set limits to the growth and operational function of Baptist churches in Kingston. What was especially difficult for Baptists to get around was the insistence of magistrates that clergy persons establish that they were "duly qualified" in order to receive a license to practice ministry. This requirement did not affect Baker, who served as pastor and chaplain in St. James because of his relationship to plantation owner Samuel Vaughn, who provided employment for him on his estate. Samuel Vaughn became a friend of British Baptist missionaries on the north coast of Jamaica and facilitated the procurement of the license to preach. This intervention of planter

Chapter 4

Samuel Vaughn allowed both Baker and Gibb to serve as pastors until they died in the 1820s.

Maya Jasanoff in *Liberty's Exile* agrees with Turner that the political and religious climate in Kingston was quite different for Liele than it was for Baker and his Afro-Baptist ministerial colleagues in the western and northern parishes of Jamaica.

> And George Liele was suspicious not only because he was free and black. His activities as a preacher set a second mark against him. The close connection between abolitionists and evangelism had made certain forms of Christian teaching seem, in the eyes of many Jamaican planters, almost as subversive as republicanism. One Kingston mob even burned the radical Thomas Paine in effigy next to a figure of the evangelical abolitionist William Wilberforce.[19]

Jasanoff opines at the spiritual and emotional journey Liele had to travel between his times in ministry at Silver Bluff Baptist Church in South Carolina and the formation of his own First Baptist Church in Savannah, Georgia, where even in the midst of war between the British and the American colonies he was able to move from his state as an enslaved youth to a life of freedom. His relationship with the British in Georgia through Col. Moses Kirkland, his pastor Matthew Moore, and even his enslaver Henry Sharp, who granted him his freedom prior to his death, must have created sparks of disappointment for Liele as he discovered that the British planters in Jamaica were even more rigid and given to mass enslavement and an ethos of incarceration than the Americans from whom he fled.

> Liele had come to Jamaica as an embodiment of a particular humanitarian promise: by affiliating himself to the British during the war he had secured his freedom and been transported in (nominal) liberty with his family to another British territory.... His work as a Baptist preacher tied him into a larger community committed to a program of individual and collective moral uplift. Liele seemed a perfect illustration of the self-image, championed by abolitionists among others, of a British Empire that would give all its free subjects, regardless of

ethnicity, British liberties, the rule of law, and the chance to partake in cultural enlightenment.... But when the Caribbean blew up in a new revolution, Liele found himself staring into the authoritarian face of the British Empire.[20]

In the language of the Black Atlantic scholars, Liele soon discovered that "there ain't no black in the Union Jack," as reflected in Paul Gilroy's book of the same title.[21] Black people were experienced primarily as slaves whose primary calling and duty was to "make a crop." Churches made it clear that their primary concern was with saving souls of the enslaved and not with disrupting the ethos of plantation life. Even when churches, whether Baptist, Methodist, or Anglican, baptized the bodies of the enslaved persons, it was their way of receiving them into a community that sacralized the system and structure of slavery with the hope that baptism would make enslaved people more obedient and diligent to the demands of the slave master.

Keeping Afro-Baptist Faith Alive

The miracle that occurred in Liele's Jamaica was that in spite of the brutality and inhumanity of slavery, Afro-Jamaicans were able to preserve elements of their indigenous faith as they melded Myal and other forms of indigenous faith with Christianity, especially in terms of their practice of engaging spirit, as they honored their dead and welcomed new life into their world. It has become increasingly obvious that George Liele would have made it clear to his close associates and parishioners that what was at stake was the survival of a faith that oppressed Jamaicans could make their own. Afro-Baptists would have understood that Liele had to satisfy his accusers and produce language to appease them and in all probability feign his compliance and acceptance of their worldviews. Caribbean theologian William Watty speaks to the double consciousness with which Liele had to live:

> Weak and defenseless, kidnapped and alone, the survival of the black man has been due mainly to a combination of outward conformity to white demands and inward skepticism to white systems. In a situation

where those who taught him religion had the same origins and largely the same presuppositions as those who held at his head a loaded pistol, his response was to assent readily and publicly with the necessary "Yes Massa," and to feign acceptance of the readymade imported canons of belief and conduct, but in *camera* he whispered to his fellow captives "but it ain't necessarily so."

Expatriates complain about the practice of Christianity in the Caribbean that there is a marked discrepancy between profession and behavior. From time to time, missionaries have found it necessary to fore-shorten their contract, and negotiate a premature return out of frustration and not a little contempt at this apparent inconsistency. Between creed on Sundays and conduct on Mondays there seems to be a great gulf fixed. . . . A theory is propounded here that when theology is part and parcel of the system of colonial domination, then it is a tribute to people's resilience to be able to survive the impact of colonialism even if it is by dissembling in matters of religion. It is further suggested that, but for that discrepancy, churches, such as they are, could not have been planted in this region.[22]

According to Watty, what was at stake was the survival of a church that could address with integrity and power the need for the restoration of Black life in Jamaica in particular, and the Caribbean in general, a faith that would emerge from the pain and pathos of Afro-Jamaican life buffeted by rabid colonialism and existence in poverty and New World slavery. Watty proffers a framework out of which Liele would seek to engage his people and they would understand the double entendre hidden in the church covenant he presented to them and the Jamaica Assembly and read with relish by plantation owners, who did not understand the "double-speak," which was constitutive of Black-talk in which enslaved persons would read between the lines. Watty insinuates that Liele and the people he served understood that language and Afro-Baptist faith had to be understood in the context of colonial domination and the negative anthropology—that God or the gods made Black people to be servants of white people—and the appropriate place for Black people was to serve the master class as they served God. It is in this context that Liele came to understand that the priority for Afro-Jamaicans was survival with dignity and a profound grasp of the notion that everything African—especially as it pertained to Liele, the leader of Afro-Baptist faith in Jamaica—was regarded with suspicion and often with scorn and contempt. In this context outward conformity did not cancel out critical assessment. Often Afro-Jamaicans would say "Yes Massa" with a full understanding that things were not what they seemed to be.

In the end we learned from Turner and Jasanoff that Liele's active ministry as pastor and leader of Baptist faith came to an end in Kingston, in part, because of his extended time in prison in Kingston due to his inability to pay debts accrued for building material purchased for the erection of his church building, coupled of course with laws of 1802 and 1807 that required him to prove he was duly qualified by law to obtain a license to preach in Jamaica. There were times both in Georgia and Jamaica when benefactor Col. Moses Kirkland intervened on behalf of Liele and through his influence as a British aristocrat saved Liele from extended stays in prison and helped in his contact with folks in Britain to make life livable and manageable. However, this ceased as Kirkland died in 1787, some years after his coming to live in Jamaica. With Kirkland no longer there to protect Liele from the full force of anti-abolitionist wrath, Liele could not serve the church as he was accustomed to in the early years of his ministry in Georgia and Jamaica. According to theologian Watty, one of the problems that would have confronted Liele in his effort to enable the Afro-Baptist church in Jamaica to survive was to become aware of the tension in which Black persons were forced to live in the Caribbean if they desired the Christian church to survive.

Afro-Jamaicans lived in a context in which the evil of colonization and European domination prevailed. Life existed in a context of epistemic violence, shaped by the tension between truth and deceit. A context in which Liele lived was one in which the colonial powers embraced the valorization of caricature and evil in terms of the dehumanization of human beings under the scourge of slavery. Was this why they built an empire on the enslavement of human beings and taught that enslaved persons were to serve the master class as they served God? It must have been most difficult to live in a context of absolute evil and not be affected by it. Was this why Liele in his church covenant accepted human bondage as normative and produced biblical quotations to affirm chattel slavery even for members of his church? It was clear that Liele had no moral scruples with human beings owning other human beings in the context of slavery since he himself owned slaves. We will give full attention to this possible flaw in Liele's owning human beings as slaves when we deal with Liele's travel to the Baptist Missionary Society in London in search of a letter to secure a license for the practice of ministry in Jamaica.

In the meantime, Deacon Swigle broke away from Liele's church and started his own "Gully Chapel" while Liele was in jail for debt incurred in building Liele's Windward Road Chapel. Liele and Swigle became the two leading Afro-Baptist clergy persons in Kingston with the edge granted to Swigle, who was the first Afro-Baptist (Creole) clergy person in Jamaica. It seems that Swigle had an important advantage in that his Gully Chapel was closer to the center of enslaved populations. Jasanoff sums up her understanding of Liele's impact and ministry after the 1790s. "In 1802 the house of Assembly passed a law banning 'the preaching of ill-disposed, illiterate, or ignorant enthusiasts, to meetings of negroes and persons of color, chiefly slaves'—another effort to limit the spread of evangelical language. Partly because of such legislation, Liele himself never returned to regular public preaching after the 1790s."[23] However, this was not the end of Baptist work in Jamaica as seeds planted by Liele bore fruit and there were itinerant preachers throughout the island who combined Liele's orthodoxy with indigenous expressions of the faith. Moses Baker in western parishes started the second Baptist church in Jamaica, the Crooked Spring Baptist Church, and Baker and Gibb continued ministry until the 1820s. In the 1830s, a mere five to six years after Liele's death, the Baptist war kindled fires of liberation throughout the British Commonwealth countries in the Caribbean, and especially in Jamaica, started by Native Baptist Daddy Sharpe. Mary Turner sums up the struggle that confronted Liele and his compatriots, especially in the eastern section of the island—Kingston.

> The B.M.S. proposed originally to send missionaries to assist Liele and Swigle, a scheme to which the Black Baptists had responded with

enthusiasm. When all preachers to the slaves were silenced, however, the B.M.S. shelved the proposal; it was not until 1814 that a man was sent to assist Moses Baker and eventually a missionary took over from him, a pattern followed with other Black Baptist congregations. In other cases the congregation broke up, though some of them, no doubt, became independent sects under their own leaders and merged with the Native Baptist groups.... Which both the Black Baptists and the mission churches engendered.[24]

The action of the Jamaica Assembly in requiring magistrates in each parish to give licenses only to pastors of dissenting churches who could prove that they were duly qualified by law to preach made ecclesial life extremely difficult for pastors and itinerant preachers in Jamaica. It seems that the spotlight was on Liele and fellow preachers especially of the Baptist faith in Kingston. On the one hand, the Jamaica Assembly was located nearby in Spanish Town, so Liele and his compatriots were always under the gaze of the authorities. The second reality to keep in mind was that Liele was accused of sedition, both himself and Moses Baker for articulating language that smacks of an evangelical faith. The root of the problem that confronted Liele, Swigle, and others of Liele's associates in the ministry had to do with suspicion and mistrust from those who represented and administered the colonial government in Jamaica. Would the nature of the proclamation of the Christian faith allow missionaries—Black and white—to make promises of freedom and equality that is offered by the gospel? As mentioned earlier, even prior to the coming of the first British missionary John Rowe in 1814, there was fear among the planter class that the language of freedom and equality before God of all persons, inclusive of enslaved and freed persons, would engender a culture of disloyalty and questioning of an ethos of obedience and trust in the master class. Winston Lawson in his important book *Religion and Race: African and European Roots in Conflict—A Jamaican Testament*, suggests that one of the instruction points to European missionaries that may not have applied to Afro-Baptist missionaries from the American colonies was the importance of reordering the morality and conduct of Afro-Jamaican slaves away from African ways of viewing the world and in its place guiding them toward spiritualized freedom and encouragement to offer fidelity to their masters. This approach was aimed at making enslaved persons more compliant, peaceful, and obedient.

> But it is to relieve them from their servile condition that you visit them—that is out of your power. Nor would it be proper, but extremely wrong to insinuate anything which might render them discontented with a state of servitude or lead them to any measures injurious to their masters. This would be to defeat the object of your mission and excite such opposition as might eventually prevent many other missions. These poor creatures are slaves of ignorance, of sin and of satan; it is to rescue them from this miserable condition by the gospel of Christ that you are now going.[25]

The counsel of the church to its missionaries makes a mockery of the church's understanding of the Christian faith. According to Lawson the church taught and counseled its missionaries to preach the subservience of enslaved persons to the planter class and coached enslaved persons not to run away and avoid enslavement to those who compromised their humanity as sons and daughters of God. Missionaries were instructed that one aim of the teaching of the church as it pertains to enslaved and master class was to make the slave docile and subordinate before the master class in such a way that the master would have no need to punish the enslaved. This no doubt would place the missionary in good graces with the master class. This may have been one good telltale sign why Liele was constantly in poor graces with the master and in the early nineteenth century could not qualify to receive a license to preach in Jamaica, where he began both the practice and tradition of Baptist faith. It is most likely that Liele died in 1825 in Jamaica, so for twenty-three years Liele was out of the public view as a pastor and preacher. There would be an entire generation who would not have been familiar with his name and legacy. And yet the good news in terms of the survival of an Afro-Baptist faith in dialogue and conversation with Afro-Jamaican religions is that Afro-Baptist faith was unhindered by European orthodoxy from 1783, when Liele arrived in Jamaica, to 1824, when Thomas Burchell became the first consequential Baptist missionary to Jamaica. John Rowe, the first

The Coming of Missionaries

British Baptist missionary, arrived in 1814 and survived for two years when he was overcome by tropical diseases. Liele's work had deep roots in spite of his absence from the pulpit, as his work was carried on by Moses Baker, George Lewis, George Gibb, and itinerant preachers, all of whom were baptized by Liele.

In her important book *The Baptists of Jamaica*, the great-granddaughter of Missionary William Knibb, Inez Knibb Sibley, reminds us of the consequential work of George Liele and Moses Baker.

> Although often persecuted for doing so [preaching], he continued, gathering many to hear him.... Within seven years George Liele had baptized five hundred on "their profession of repentance towards God, and faith in our Lord Jesus Christ." In 1791 he built and dedicated to the glory of God, the first Baptist Church of Jamaica, which was known as the Windward Road Baptist Church at the corner of Elletson Roads, Kingston. It was Moses Baker, however, who made an even deeper mark on early Baptist work. He was instrumental in causing the Baptist Missionary Society of Gt. Britain to begin work in Jamaica.... Baker dared to teach and preach the glorious gospel of Jesus Christ despite persecutions and imprisonment and was instrumental in winning hundreds of souls. Thus the second Baptist church in Jamaica was established at Crooked Spring, in the parish of St. James, in the year 1791.[26]

It becomes increasingly clear that toward the end of the eighteenth century Liele became inactive as a pastor and the Jamaican Baptists began to prepare for the coming of British missionaries among them. Because of his connections to plantation owners on the island and the Jamaica Assembly, Samuel Vaughn in St. James and western parishes provided land and financial help for the launching of Baptist churches in the parishes of St. James, Hanover, Westmoreland, and Trelawny. On the other side of the island, there were old connections with the British Baptists due to the advocacy of Liele and Swigle over the years. It also seems that there was a lively contact and relationship between Moses Baker and Dr. John Ryland, president of Bristol Baptist College, pertaining to the possibility of students from the college coming to serve as missionaries in Jamaica. Moses Baker, who received an eye injury in New York where he lived for some time and worked as a barber, mentioned to British Baptists his need for help to sustain and found churches in western Jamaica.

According to Ernest Payne,

> Moses Baker commenced a vigorous attack on superstition and idolatry, and formed a "small society" on the lines laid down by Liele. He met with considerable success, on one occasion baptizing in one day more than a hundred persons. When Winn died, Baker passed into the employ of Samuel Vaughn, for whose slaves he did the same kind of service. There was opposition to be met with, not only from some of the slaves, but also from unfriendly planters. Baker was often charged with sedition and was in personal danger on many occasions. His reputation grew, however, and his influence, until in 1806 the Jamaica Assembly passed a law preventing all teaching and preaching on plantations. It remained in force for eight years, and was a sad blow to men like Liele and Baker, and the latter seemed to have appealed directly to England for help.[27]

Payne, onetime president of the Baptist Union of Great Britain, reminds us that Baker was clear that his work as pastor in western parishes of Jamaica was in tandem with that of George Liele on the other end of the island. Both Baker and Liele were in contact with British Baptists in search of help for Baptist work in Jamaica as the work suffered from the laws of 1802 and 1806 forbidding teaching and preaching to enslaved persons on plantations. The presupposition that informed their request of fellow Baptists in Great Britain was that the British would have a much easier time navigating and negotiating slave culture in which Black missionaries found it extremely difficult to secure license to teach and preach on plantations to the enslaved class. The requests of Baker and Liele bore fruit when John Rowe arrived at Montego Bay in 1814 to meet Moses Baker and fellow Baptist Samuel Vaughn, plantation owner and employer of Moses Baker. Missionary Lee Compere arrived in Kingston in 1816, and he and Rowe offered themselves for missionary service with Jamaican Baptists. Over the years in Jamaica, Liele had sustained contact with British Baptists through correspondence with fellow pastor John Rippon and, as was noted earlier in this chapter, placed on record his desire to partner with British Baptists in advancing Baptist work in Jamaica. However, this request did not at first bear fruit as the Jamaica Assembly in its ruling in 1802 and 1806 forbade the teaching and preaching in public settings or on plantations. However, in 1814, through the pleading of Moses Baker and the instrumentality of Samuel Vaughn, help arrived from Bristol Baptist College in the persons of John Rowe and his wife. "The Rev. John Rowe was met by Moses Baker and the Hon. Sam Vaughn, attorney of the estates on which Moses Baker had taught. Vaughn was said to be 'a Christian layman of liberal views.' He treated the Rev. and Mrs. John Rowe kindly, but warned them of the antagonistic spirit of many of the inhabitants towards the establishment of nonconformist churches in Jamaica. He advised Mr. Rowe 'to first establish his character by opening a school' before attempting to preach."[28]

In all probability Baker had advised Sam Vaughn well to instruct Missionary Rowe of the priority and centrality of teaching and its place in Afro-Baptist understanding of the mission of the church. This was one of the emphases of George Liele as he launched Baptist witness in Jamaica, his insistence that there should not be a division between church and world. As far as Liele was concerned, Baker, who was baptized by Liele and shared in the leadership of Liele's Windward Road Chapel in the formative years, understood that love for the body and the soul should be conjoined. It was a practice in the founding of Baptist churches during the Liele era to begin with the establishment of a school. We recall that Deacon Swigle was appointed headmaster of the school in the Windward Road Chapel, which was for both freed and enslaved persons. This practice had been pivotal in the development of the church in Jamaica, the conjoining of education and salvation. Baptists in Jamaica in the tradition of Liele and Baker enshrined this practice that emphasized the importance of the body—it is the body that is baptized, it is the body that takes holy communion, it is the body that is the temple of the Holy Spirit. To love the soul is at the same time to love the body. In all likelihood, both Liele and Baker drew from the African worldviews extant in Afro-Jamaican culture that so-called secular culture was sacred and there was a special place for music, dancing, and making room for literacy—learning to read in order for Afro-Jamaicans to read the Bible for themselves. In this regard Liele's teaching was filtered through Baker to Vaughn and to the first British Baptist missionary who came to Jamaica in 1814. The ideal was to translate the gospel to serve as a bridge for uniting church and world. The mission of the church was to embrace love for God and neighbor.

It will be noted that even among Baptist missionaries, and here Liele is included, missionaries owned slaves. They bought into the common and popular worldview that slavery was a divine institution that would benefit both slave and master. It was clear that missionaries taught that the Christianizing of the slave would make the enslaved more dutiful and have a positive effect on the master in making him less angry and more kindly disposed toward the enslaved. For whatever reasons we may attribute to Liele, including his predisposition toward the survival of the church in Jamaica and in Georgia, Liele in two articles of his church covenant enjoined slaves to be good servants and to be obedient to their masters. In his "Covenant of the Anabaptist Church, begun in America, December 1777 and in Jamaica, December 1783," Liele enjoins church and plantocracy both in Georgia and Jamaica in articles 15 and 17 that enslaved persons should be compliant and obedient to the planter class.

> Article 15—We permit no slaves to join the church without first having a few lines from their owners of their good behavior. 1 Peter 2:13–16; 1 Thessalonians 3:13
>
> Article 17—If a slave or servant misbehave to their owners they are to be dealt with according to the word of God. 1 Timothy 1:6; Ephesians vi:5; 1 Peter 2:18–22; Titus 2:9–17.

Liele used scripture to advocate the submission of enslaved persons to the master class. What is of interest is that even in cases where the denomination endorses and embraces the posture of the abolitionists, in the case of the British Baptists and the Wesleyan Methodists, there were several ministers of the gospel within those denominations who owned slaves. Earlier we noted the case of George Whitfield, the evangelist who bought eight slaves to work at his orphanage. He cajoled his fellow clergy colleagues to Christianize their enslaved community by allowing them to attend his revivals but failed to enjoin freedom of the body and the human spirit. Masters were told that if they allowed their slaves to attend church and be baptized, then they would discover that a Christian slave was more dutiful and submissive than one who did not attend church. Many Christian preachers, including George Liele, missed the paradox of human beings made in the image of God being slave and Christian at the same time. How could a human being created for fellowship with God and identified as son and daughter of the divine be bought and sold in the marketplace by preachers, and how could custodians of the promises of God buy and sell God's children as beasts of burden? The paradox here was that the church that was built on the promises of God spurned God's command and went after the gods of materiality and capitalism.

> 4. Hear, O Israel: The Lord our God is one Lord; 5. and you shall love the Lord your God with all your heart, and with all your soul, and with all your might. 6. And these words which I command you this day shall be upon your heart; 7 and you shall teach them diligently to your children, and shall talk of them when you sit in your house, and when you walk by the way, and when you lie down, and when you rise. 8. And you shall bind them as a sign upon your hand, and they shall be as frontlets between your eyes. 9. And you shall write them on the door posts of your house and on your gates. (Deut. 6:4–9)

Liele came close to an embrace of the central motif of the Shema in his explication of Romans 10:1, "Brethren, my heart's desire and prayer to God for Israel is that they may be saved," on the occasion of the celebration of the completion of the Windward Road Chapel. Liele was imprisoned and charged with fanning the flames of sedition for awakening the hope for freedom among his congregants. Liele tested the waters of freedom, so to speak, and concluded they were too deep for him and his people to cross over. Jamaica had to await the fervor and rebellion of Daddy Sharpe, a Native Baptist who led a rebellion against the buying and selling of human beings and the plantocracy's depiction of Afro-Jamaicans as chattel. This rebellion was called the "Baptist War" as it was led by Native Baptists. In chapter 5 we will highlight this contribution of the Native Baptists, which recalls the work and legacy of George Liele.

In the meantime, Missionary John Rowe, who had arrived in Montego Bay February 23, 1814, visited Baker's congregation at Crooked Spring in St. James, which had about six hundred members.

> Rowe, being white and having been invited by a member of the Island Assembly was more secure than Baker. . . . After having preached for Baker once or twice he decided to settle permanently in Falmouth where he opened a school in April 1814, and also began a Sabbath School "for children of the poor and slaves whose owners would allow them to attend." He continued his association with Baker, attending worship services and discussing the future of the witness with the elders. Because of the Laws of 1802 and 1807, Baker had suspended the celebrations of the sacraments and one elder confessed that for years he had been deprived of the Lord's Supper. Rowe resisted the temptation to celebrate it however.[29]

Rowe's tenure as a missionary teacher in Jamaica was very short as he died June 27, 1816. Although his tenure among the Afro-Baptist community was cut short, he started a school in Falmouth and was able through his preaching to win to Christ and the church John, the son of Moses Baker.

It increasingly became clear to the leadership of Jamaican Baptists that the presence of white missionaries was indispensable for the future of Baptist work in Jamaica because of the prejudice of the plantocracy and the Jamaica Assembly toward Liele and his associates. It was mentioned earlier the dis-ease of the plantocracy with the missionary class, which was compounded with Black men leading churches and at times performing worship services and baptisms under the cover of night.

ECCLESIAL CENTERS OF AFRO-BAPTIST WORK

Russell informs us that there were three centers of Baptist work in Jamaica prior to the coming of missionaries from Great Britain. The first center was Flamstead–Montego Bay, for which Moses Baker provided leadership. This included Baker's important work at Crooked Spring, which Rowe visited with Baker and which was recognized as the second Baptist church in Jamaica formed by Baker in 1791. The second center was Spanish Town, the capital city of Jamaica and where Liele purchased land for a burial ground (cemetery) that included a house that was used for worship services. "The second was centered at Spanish Town which had grown out of the work of George Liele's able assistant, George Gibb (Gibbs). Gibb had been a member and teacher at the Windward Road Chapel and he was sent to evangelize the north side of the island. His work began as a result of an invitation from a Mr. Laing, the proprietor of the Goshen Estate who had asked George Liele for help."[30] Gibb devoted much time to the North Coast as from there he went to Ocho Rios, where he founded the Ocho Rios Baptist Church and later Guy's Hill and St. Mary. The third center to which Russell draws our attention is Kingston under the leadership of Liele and Swigle. Russell points out that with the coming of the British missionaries, the primary attention was not focused on these centers as Baptist leadership in London emphasized the creation of new work. "However, this proved not to be the case for although Baptists could well look after their own worship needs, the structure of slave society, oppressive and inhibiting as it was, made the white missionary a necessity if Baptists were to continue to have complete freedom to worship due to the newly introduced Consolidated Slave Law."[31] Russell's prognostication bore early fruit as it may be noted that the early Liele made marked progress in colonial Jamaica while his benefactor, Col. Moses Kirkland, was alive. With his demise there were no advocates on the other side of the aisle, so to speak, to stand in the gap for Liele. On the other hand, it was different for Baker and Gibb, who seemed to have the support of Baptist planter, and member of the Jamaica Assembly, Samuel Vaughn. Their witness went on into the 1820s.

The first Baptist missionary from England to Kingston was Lee Compere and his friend Henry Tripp, who was accompanied by his wife. Compere's work in Kingston overlapped with that of John Rowe as they both arrived in 1814, Rowe in the northwest of the island and Compere in the east of Jamaica. It seems most likely that Compere responded to the Macedonia Call, so to speak, from Swigle, Liele's early

CHAPTER 4

deacon and schoolmaster at the Windward Road Chapel. Compere's friend Henry Tripp was a carpenter and builder and was instrumental in moving the erection of the East Queen Street Baptist Church along toward its opening and dedication in 1816. Compere was able to obtain a license to preach from the mayor of Kingston and by 1816 reported a membership of four hundred at the Lord's Supper and indicated that he preached three times on a Sunday. In 1817 Compere became very ill and was succeeded by Missionary James Coultart and his wife, Mary Ann, who arrived in Jamaica May 9, 1817. Coultart had no difficulty receiving license to preach from the mayor of Kingston. Coultart opened a school that was supervised by his wife. Mary Ann supervised both the day and Sunday School. Later her day school reached out to both freed and enslaved persons. Coultart observed that the majority of his members were slaves. Coultart's wife signaled that although the former "Robinson's Chapel," now the East Queen Street Baptist Church, had a membership of about one thousand members "made of Blacks and Browns," there was a problem as Afro-Jamaican culture and religion had surfaced and made worship and church practice awkward. Mary Ann observed that when a member died,

> the relatives and friends meet together in the house of the deceased and feast and sing during the night. They prepare and keep by them their funeral dress which is most gaudy and as costly as their circumstances will permit them to obtain. . . . She reported that there were certain days set aside for fasting and on these days there were testimonies about dreams and visions in which all took part. Indeed, she seemed a little surprised that the 'brown people also, were mainly of the same stamp.' . . . As for her husband, he threw himself into the work and found time to gather some of Liele's Spanish Town members to revive a work there, preaching to them once each fortnight.[32]

Coultart reached out to Liele's people in Spanish Town, where Liele bought land for a burial ground that also had a house where members would gather for worship. To underscore the importance of ceremonies for the deceased, Liele mentioned in his church covenant article XX,

We hold that if a Brother or Sister should transgress, and abideth not in the doctrine of Christ, and he or she, after being justly dealt with agreeable to the 8th article, and be put out of the Church, that they shall have no right or claim whatsoever to be interred into the Burying-ground during the time they are put out, should they depart life; but should they return in peace, and make a concession so as to give satisfaction, according to the Word of God, they shall be received into the Church again and have all the privileges as before granted. (2 John i:9–10; Gal. vi:1–2; Luke xvii:3, 4.)[33]

It was clear that Missionary Coultart understood the importance of funeral ceremonies for the deceased and their families. Therefore, he spent time in Spanish Town reviving Liele's work there and no doubt also in the Windward Road area that was close to Liele's chapel. During this time Liele did not have a license to preach. Most likely he was in bad graces with the colonial government. The British Baptists who were able to relate and communicate with the mayor of Kingston and members of the Jamaica Assembly were able to secure licenses to preach. It was somewhat prescient that Russell gestured in the direction of the necessity for a partnership between Black and white missionaries in Jamaica if the work of growing Baptist churches was to progress. Russell noted the difficulty of Black missionaries receiving licenses to preach and correctly predicted that if the work were to progress there would be need for Black and white missionaries to work together.

During this time Liele was assiduously trying to find the funds to purchase a ticket to visit British colleagues in England who at the beginning of his ministry provided resources to help him complete his Windward Road Chapel and provided a bell for his church and books for his library. But now they were silent and seemingly unresponsive to Liele's needs. John Rippon, to whom he sent his last letter in 1793, was busy at the Carter's Lane Baptist Church, London, where he served as pastor from 1771 to 1834. Later this church was led by Charles Hadden Spurgeon. There was no sign or indication that there was any correspondence between Liele and John Rippon after 1793. Liele adopted the posture of patriarch of the Native Baptists whose emergence he inspired and whose polity and reliance on the spirit he shared. Liele planned and no doubt saved for his visit to Baptist colleagues in colonial England. He would learn that there "ain't no Black in the Union Jack."

In the meantime, the trek of missionaries continued to Jamaica. Jamaica Baptists became increasingly aware that as the white keys of the piano need the black keys to make harmonic melody so was the need for Black and white missionaries to advance the work of the Christian church in Jamaica. Missionary Compere became very ill and on leaving for the United States introduced British missionary James Coultart to the island. Coultart arrived in Jamaica May 9, 1817, and after a short stay in Old Harbor he moved to Kingston, where he served as pastor of "Robinson's Chapel," which he mentioned had a membership of about seven hundred communicants. According to Coultart most of his membership were enslaved persons. His leadership was consequential as he presided over the opening and dedication of the East Queen Street Baptist Church in January 1822. Commenting on the tenure of Missionaries Mary Ann and James Coultart, Russell states, "The hectic pace took its toll on the couple. Mary Ann became ill and died Wednesday, October 8, 1817. . . . She was buried in the Kingston Parish churchyard. . . . Her husband himself ill, retired to Port Royal to recuperate but continued to visit Spanish Town to keep the work going."[34]

THE BUYING AND SELLING OF HUMAN BEINGS

Coultart left for England in 1819 and was succeeded by Christopher Kitching. While in England he raised funds for the completion of Robinson's Chapel, the New East Queen Street Baptist Church, which was dedicated in January 1822, with a seating capacity of two thousand members. For many years this was the largest Baptist church in Jamaica. Writing to the General Committee of the Baptist Missionary Society of London in 1823, James Coultart acknowledged that he had departed from the policy and instructions of the church family from which he had come to Jamaica as he was the owner of two enslaved persons and sought direction from the General Committee of how to proceed. Minutes from General Committee Meeting of December 18, 1823, state:

A letter was received from Mr. Coultart, dated London, December 16, acquainting the Committee with the circumstances under which he became possessed of two domestic slaves and requesting their advice how to act on the matter, on which it was, Resolved, that in the opinion of the Committee, if any circumstances would justify the purchase of Negroes, Mr. Coultart was justified in the cases he had specified, but that as the purchase or sale of slaves is decidedly opposed to the fundamental principles of the mission it is the unanimous decision of the Committee that missionaries ought not under any circumstances whatever, to have anything to do with this odious traffic.

Resolved, that the foregoing resolution be communicated to Mr. Coultart, impressing upon him the necessity to procure the manumission of the persons referred to, and requesting him to meet the Committee to discuss the subject at our next monthly meeting; Resolved further that the said Resolution be forwarded to each of our brethren in the island, accompanied with a distinct and positive intimation that, should any missionary be found hereafter to purchase a slave or slaves, it would be considered as immediately dissolving the connection between him and the society.[35]

The British Baptist were very clear that "the purchase or sale of slaves" by missionaries who were sponsored by their organization was against the fundamental principles of the Baptist Church of Great Britain. However, it is of interest that the minutes make an allowance for Mr. Coultart buying and selling of slaves because of his extraordinary circumstances. It is appropriate to expect the Baptist Missionary Society to offer understanding and forgiveness for the purchase of slaves, granted that Missionary Coultart's wife died and he was very ill; and then be emphatic in insisting "that, should any missionary be found hereafter to purchase a slave or slaves, it would be considered as immediately dissolving the connection between him and the society." It was very difficult to monitor the social and moral activities of missionaries in Jamaica from the vantage point of the Missionary Society in England. A few years after they responded to Missionary Coultart's admission that he bought slaves, the Missionary Society at their quarterly committee meeting July

30, 1828, wrote to James Phillippo, one of the more popular missionaries, who gave twenty years in service to Jamaica, that they received information that he also had purchased slaves. "Resolved, that immediate inquiry be made respecting certain slaves said to have been purchased by Mr. Phillippo; that he also be informed that the Society cannot charge itself with the expense of the school at Spanish Town."[36]

In a subsequent meeting the society stated that they received a letter from Mr. Phillippo of Spanish Town "containing very satisfactory explanation respecting the slaves alleged to have been recently purchased by him."[37] It becomes increasingly clear that several missionaries both Black and white had no moral difficulties with the buying and selling of slaves.

On the other hand, Liele was able to find the financial resources to travel to England to implore his British colleagues to provide him with a letter to present to the Jamaica Assembly in order for him to secure a license to preach in Jamaica. It was somewhat strange and yet a reality in a white-Black world in which the people in the colonial government with power to make decisions, such as who could teach and preach with the freedom to interact with the enslaved populace, were all white. But more than that, white folks determined the contours and shape of one's freedom. Liele was not able to secure a license to preach in Jamaica and so traveled to England to meet with the Committee of the Baptist Missionary Society. Missionary John Clark makes it clear:

> About 1822, Mr. Liele paid a visit to England, but soon returned, and a few years afterward died. Mr. William Knibb attended his funeral, and believed him to be a God-fearing man. One of his daughters became a member of the Hanover Street Church, and two of his grandsons attended East Queen Street School in 1830. One of these afterwards became a member of the House of Assembly, and frequently showed good ability and love to his country.[38]

While Liele was away in England, British Baptist missionary Joshua Tinson served as pastor of Liele's church in 1822. Tinson arrived in Morant Bay, Jamaica, May 31, 1822, and had hoped to serve churches in St. Thomas in the East but was unable to obtain a license to preach from the magistrate there. Because of this inability to secure a license to preach in St. Thomas, he went to Kingston and there in Liele's absence in 1822 he was invited to serve as interim pastor. He succeeded in obtaining a license to preach in the town in which Liele was denied one, with the proviso that Liele was not qualified under the law. There does not seem to be any white missionary who was constantly denied license to preach, as was the case with George Liele. As Rev. F. A. Cox, missionary to Jamaica, writes,

> The church under the pastoral care of Mr. Tinson, which assembled in an old building a mile from Kingston, had been blessed with a gratifying portion of prosperity,—upwards of three hundred having been added by baptism, and many were inquiring the way of salvation. But the dilapidated state of the building in which the people met, its inconvenient distance from the city, and a desire to provide additional means of religious instruction for a numerous and ill-supplied population, induced many of the members, encouraged by the missionaries, to seek an eligible situation in Kingston, with a view of removing the church. Suitable premises accordingly have been obtained, the greater part of the members withdrew, to form a new church; the place was opened on the 24th December 1826; and on January 7th 1827, the church was formed, consisting of two hundred and eighty-two town members, and about two hundred living on estates on different parts of the country.[39]

Cox informs us of some of the difficulties that confronted Liele in 1822 on his visit to London to consult with members of the Baptist Missionary Society to give him a letter to take to the magistrate in Kingston to certify that he is qualified before the law to teach and preach at his church in Kingston. However, it became clear that there were other problems that confronted the venerable Rev. George Liele in his ministry in Jamaica. His Windward Road Chapel, built in the 1790s, was in 1822 in need of repairs and was mentioned in Cox's missive as dilapidated and in need of major repairs. Added to these realities that confronted Liele was the pressing need to preach and his constant refusal of a license to teach and preach; additionally, there were two newer Baptist churches served by missionaries and these churches, Hanover Street Baptist Church and East Queen Street Baptist Church, were in closer reach of the enslaved community. In a profound sense the white missionaries had replaced Liele and they seemed not to have had any interest in helping him secure a license to preach. Cox commenting on the opening and dedication of Hanover Street Baptist Church stated,

> Many of the people [Liele's people] and deacons had long desired to have a chapel in the city, both from the inconvenience of the old place and to meet the wants of those who were willing to attend but could not travel so great a distance. Premises were soon engaged in Hanover Street, and after some necessary alterations and repairs, a commodious place of worship in a good locality was opened on the 24th of December 1826, when Messrs. Phillippo, Flood and Knibb took prominent parts in the interesting services.[40]

It was mentioned earlier by Missionary John Clark of Brown's Town Baptist Church that William Knibb, who arrived in Jamaica in February 1825, attended the funeral of George Liele. This is the only witness we have to anyone who attended the funeral. It is widely assumed that Liele was buried at the small burial plot at the Windward Road Chapel. The sense one gathers is that in 1825 worship services may not have been held there anymore, and Liele may have rented it out once more as a hospital and the premises used as a burial ground for a select number of persons. In the following chapter on Liele and nation building, we will give attention to the contributions of Missionaries Thomas Burchell and William Knibb in western parishes of St. James and Falmouth, in Trelawny, along with James Phillippo in the capital city of Jamaica, Spanish Town. Before we look at Liele's meeting in England with the secretary of the Baptist Missionary Society of London, and Secretary Dyer's stating Liele's reason for being in London in 1822, we will look at Inez Knibb Sibley, who was the great-granddaughter of William Knibb, and her description of the arrival of British missionaries to Jamaica between 1816 when John Rowe and Lee Compere arrived in Jamaica, Rowe in western parishes and Compere in Kingston. While her list is not inclusive of all the missionaries, it does list those who provided leadership among the missionaries.

> Among those who established the Baptist churches in this pioneering stage were Lee Compere, who began work at East Queen Street Baptist Church; James Coultart, who, besides consolidating work at East Queen Street, bought land for a church at Mount Charles, in St. Andrew; Thomas Godden, who began work at Spanish Town; J. M. Phillippo, after whom the Phillippo Baptist Church in Spanish Town is named; and Thomas Burchell, who established churches in five parishes in the West. Thomas Knibb, and English school master at the "Gully School," also began work at Port Royal. His life's span was cut short within a few months, and he died saying: "If I had a thousand lives I would give them all to Jamaica." Following on came William Knibb, who took his brother's place at the school in Kingston, and afterwards went to Sav-la-mar and Falmouth, serving Jamaica from 1825–1845. We think with gratitude to God of others, amongst them, Benjamin Dexter . . . who established work at the Alps in the hinterland of Trelawny in 1835; James Mann who worked with Thomas Burchell. . . . And Walter Dendy who founded Bethtephil church in 1839. . . . John Clarke whose name is bound up with Brown's Town. . . . Who laid the foundation of Baptist work in Jamaica.[41]

Liele observed that the missionaries from England for the most part were able to receive license to preach in Jamaica while he and the Afro-Baptists were denied. In what seems to be a final effort to resolve the difficulty of not being able to obtain a license to teach and preach in his church or any place in Jamaica, George Liele traveled to England to meet with members of the General Committee of the Missionary Society. His request of the society was twofold. His primary request was for a letter to take back to Jamaica to present to the mayor of Kingston to certify that he was qualified before the laws of Jamaica to teach and preach. The second request was for a missionary to accompany him back to Jamaica to vouch for his credentials. This must have been a very humiliating meeting for Liele, to go to British Baptists as Marcus Garvey would say, "with hat in hand" to beg for a letter vouching for his credibility and authority to teach and preach in Baptist churches that he founded in Jamaica, and if the Missionary Society was unable to grant his request of providing this letter of recommendation, then he would ask for a missionary to accompany him, who would speak on his behalf to the authorities in Kingston. In the minutes of the Baptist Missionary Society, May 21, 1822, it is stated:

> Mr. Burls reported that he and the secretary [John Dyer] had seen and conversed with George Liele, a black minister from Jamaica, who has come to this country with a view to procure a license for preaching himself, or a minister to accompany him back to Jamaica under the sanction of the Committee, on which it was "Resolved., That the Committee cannot sanction the application of Mr. Liele unless it be concurred in by those brethren in connection with us, who are already in the island."[42]

Missionary John Clark sums up for us a reading of Liele's contribution to Afro-Baptist witness in Jamaica:

> Mr. Liele appears to have been a good man, and devoted to the work of his Divine Master. He baptized Moses Baker, was a light in those days, shining in a dark place, and among dark people. He has been charged, by men who came to Jamaica long after his decease, with teaching false doctrine, and following superstitious practices.[43]

In preparation for his visit to England, Liele made a will, dated February 12, 1822. Liele stated that he owned slaves:

> I give, devise, and bequeath unto my dear and beloved wife, Hannah Hunt Liele, all my lands and tenements with all and singular the buildings thereon standing, erected and built, to hold the same to her, her heirs and assigns forever. I give, devise, and bequeath unto the said Hannah Hunt Liele my Negro slaves named Neptune, Anney, and her son James, Betsy and her children Indjoe and Nancy, Peggy and Margaret, for—and during the run of her natural life and no longer and from immediately after the decease of the said Hannah Hunt Liele, then I

do this by my will absolutely manumize, enfranchise and set free from all manner of bondage and slavery whatsoever all and singular the said slaves with their then and future issue, offspring, and increase in as full and ample as if they had been born of free parents and never had been slaves.[44]

There is a paradox that comes to the fore in Liele's admission, prior to his voyage to England, that he owned eight slaves. Liele in his teaching and preaching and his care for others gestures in the direction of one who leads though values—values of freedom and equality.

The paradox is this: How could Liele, who knew firsthand the scourge of being a slave and the personal power of being free, become the owner of eight slaves? We recall that he had a rather large farm and that he worked for the colonial government and owned horses to help him remove spent cartridges from the city streets. Perhaps these enslaved persons helped with those tasks. Perhaps Liele's eschatology may have allowed him to sacrifice the present for a future hope. Toward the end of the will in a note to his executrix and executor he stipulates that eight slaves are to be set free in the end, at the death of his wife, Hannah, and then they should be treated as if they were born of free parents. The vision of the end of slavery for these eight slaves and their children did not transform their slavery. Both Liele and Baker were known through their songs to call attention to the power of the eschaton transforming the inhumanity of slavery: "We will be slaves no more, since Christ has set us free."[45]

It could be that for Liele the future resided in the community called church and specifically the Anabaptist church. His will was clear that those who would benefit from his estate in the end would be those who adhere to the Anabaptist faith. Slaves who stayed in the arc of the covenant, so to speak, would be saved.

In the following chapter particular attention will be given to Liele's contribution to nation building in Jamaica through the agitation and transformation effected in community through a realized eschatology.

CHAPTER 4

NOTES

1. John W. Davis, "George Liele and Andrew Bryan, Pioneer Negro Baptist Preachers," *Journal of Negro History* 3, no. 2 (1918): 120–21.

2. Deborah Bingham Van Broekhoven, "Christianity in the World of George Liele," in *George Liele's Life and Legacy: An Unsung Hero*, ed. David T. Shannon, Julia Frazier White, and Deborah Van Broekhoven (Macon, GA: Mercer University Press, 2012), 23.

3. Van Broekhoven, "Christianity in the World of George Liele," 24.

4. James M. Washington, "The Origins of Black Evangelicalism and the Ethical Function of Evangelical Cosmology," *Union Seminary Quarterly Review* 32, no. 2 (1977): 107.

5. Washington, "The Origins of Black Evangelicalism," 107.

6. Van Broekhoven, "Christianity in the World of George Liele," 25.

7. John Parmer Gates, "George Liele: A Pioneer Negro Preacher," *The Chronicle: A Baptist Historical Quarterly* 6, no. 3 (July 1943): 119–29, 123.

8. James M. Phillippo, *Jamaica: Its Past and Present State* (London: John Snow, 1843; reprinted, Westport, CT: Negro University Press, 1970), 148.

9. William E. Montgomery, *Under Their Own Vine and Fig Tree: The African American Church in the South, 1865–1900* (Baton Rouge: Louisiana State University Press, 1993), 33.

10. Philip D. Curtin, *Two Jamaicas: The Role of Ideas in a Tropical Colony, 1830–1865* (New York: Atheneum, 1970, originally published at Cambridge: Harvard University Press, 1955), 33–34.

11. Horace O. Russell, *Foundations and Anticipations: The Jamaica Baptist Story, 1783–1892* (Columbus, GA: Brentwood Christian Press, 1993), 13–14.

12. W. J. Gardner, *A History of Jamaica: From Its Discovery by Christopher Columbus to the Year 1872* (London: T. Fisher Unwin, 1909; first published 1873), 344.

13. Winston Lawson, "Pioneer George Liele in Jamaica, the British Colony," in *George Liele's Life and Legacy: An Unsung Hero*, 125–26.

14. Curtin, *Two Jamaicas*, 31–32.

15. Mary Turner, *Slaves and Missionaries: The Disintegration of Jamaican Slave Society, 1787–1834* (Urbana: University of Illinois Press, 1982), 13.

16. Turner, *Slaves and Missionaries*, 13.

17. Turner, *Slaves and Missionaries*, 14–15.

18. Turner, *Slaves and Missionaries*, 17.

19. Maya Jasanoff, *Liberty's Exiles: American Loyalists in the Revolutionary World* (New York: Alfred A. Knoff, 2011), 270.

20. Jasanoff, *Liberty's Exiles*, 271.

21. Paul Gilroy, *There Ain't No Black in the Union Jack: The Cultural Politics of Race and Nation* (Chicago: University of Chicago Press, 1987).

22. William W. Watty, "The De-Colonization of Theology," in *Troubling of the Waters*, ed. Idris Hamid (Trinidad, WI: Rahaman Printery, 1973), 49–50.

23. Jasanoff, *Liberty's Exiles*, 271.

24. Turner, *Slaves and Missionaries*, 17–18.

25. Winston Lawson, *Religion and Race: African and European Roots in Conflict—A Jamaican Testament* (New York: Peter Lang, 1996), 96.

26. Inez Knibb Sibley, *The Baptists of Jamaica* (Kingston: Jamaica Baptist Union, 1965), 2. Sibley dates the completion and dedication of Liele's Windward Road Chapel as 1791. Ernest A. Payne dates it as 1793. See Ernest Payne, "Baptist Work in Jamaica Before the Arrival of the Missionaries," *The Baptist Quarterly Incorporating the Transactions of the Baptist Historical Society*, New Series, Volume VII (1934–1935): 19–26, 21.

27. Payne, "Baptist Work in Jamaica Before the Arrival of the Missionaries," 22. For a full description of Liele's covenant, see Payne, "Baptist Work in Jamaica Before the Arrival of the Missionaries," 20–26, 24–26. For discussion of the covenant, see Noel Leo Erskine's *Plantation Church: How African American Religion Was Born in Caribbean Slavery* (New York: Oxford University Press, 2014), 174–76.

28. Inez Knibb Sibley, *The Baptists of Jamaica*, 3.

29. Russell, *Foundations and Anticipations*, 23.

30. Russell, *Foundations and Anticipations*, 24.

31. Russell, *Foundations and Anticipations*, 24.

32. Russell, *Foundations and Anticipations*, 27.

33. Payne, "Baptist Work in Jamaica Before the Arrival of the Missionaries," 20–26, 26.

34. Russell, *Foundations and Anticipations*, 27.

35. Baptist Missionary Society General Committee Minutes, 1819–1823. Committee Meeting December 18, 1823, 36–37. Angus Archives, Regents Park College, Oxford University.

36. Baptist Missionary Society General Committee Minutes, 1827–1830. Quarterly Committee Meeting July 30, 1828, 96. Angus Archives, Regents Park College, Oxford University.

37. Committee Meeting October 13, 1828, 13

38. John Clark, *Memorials of Baptist Missionaries in Jamaica, Including a Sketch of the Labours of Early Religious Instructors in Jamaica* (London: Yates and Alexander, 1869), 11.

39. F. A. Cox, *History of the Baptist Missionary Society, From 1792–1842* (London: T. Ward, 1842), 55–56. See also Christopher Brent Ballew, *The Impact of African American Antecedents on the Baptist Foreign Missionary Movement, 1782–1825* (Lewiston, NY: Edwin Mellen Press, 2004), 53–54.

40. F. A. Cox, *History of the Baptist Missionary Society, From 1792–1842*, 174. See also Ballew, *The Impact of African American Antecedents on the Baptist Foreign Missionary Movement*, 56.

41. Inez Knibb Sibley, *The Baptists of Jamaica*, 4.

42. Baptist Missionary Society of England Committee Minutes, October 1819–July 1823. Minutes for May 21, 1822, 203–204.

43. John Clark, *Memorials of Baptist Missionaries in Jamaica*, 11.

44. Shannon, White, and Van Broekhoven, eds., *George Liele's Life and Legacy*, 166.

45. Phillip Sherlock and Hazel Bennett, *The Story of the Jamaican People* (Kingston, Jamaica: Ian Randle Publishers, 1998), 201.

Chapter 5

The Man and His Legacy

The Baptist Church provided the first Black missionaries to the enslaved population in colonial Jamaica through the work of their leader, George Liele, and his assistants, Moses Baker, George Lewis, and George Gibb. Liele and his assistants understood their church as a Black church, were explicit in the connection of their work to Ethiopia, and understood one of their aims as the salvation of the people of Ethiopia (Africans) in Jamaica. Mary Turner writes:

> Before the Black Baptist preachers and missionaries started work, no attempts had been made by the planters to influence directly the slaves' ideas about life and the universe. The slaves, however, stripped of country and family, had to exercise some form of control over their environment. They adapted the techniques developed in their homelands to serve their new needs. Deprived of priests and organization, theological distinctions became blurred and a common pattern of religious practice emerged. . . . The idea of the supreme being is thought by some authorities to be indigenous and to pre-date missionary activity. In any case, the role assigned to the supreme being in these religions is quite different from that assigned to the Christian God. God in West Africa is the great creator but not the great law giver; among the Yoruba and the Ibo he is not worshiped and is given less attention than the nature gods and ancestors.[1]

It becomes increasingly clear that enslaved people in Jamaica and in the Americas did not sit around to wait on the missionary whether

Chapter 5

white or Black to introduce them to religion or religious practices that would ameliorate the cruel conditions of chattel slavery, but rather they plumbed the depths of their indigenous faith in search of tools to overthrow the conditions of slavery and welcome the emergence of emancipation that would accord freedom and equality to the children of God who were consigned by many missionaries and planters who viewed them as inferior and preached that God had made Africans and their descendants to make a crop.

In this chapter I will revisit Afro-Jamaicans' press for liberation and emancipation through the exercise of their theology and ministry of spirit expressed in different iterations. Their passion for liberation did not begin with missionaries. However, in their critique of missionary theology, enslaved Jamaicans took from it what was useful in their management of life in plantation culture, and through running away or burning sugar estates that provided a context of their bondage, Black people were willing to make the ultimate sacrifice of offering up their own bodies and that of their children in the march toward their liberation as a people. Their religion of spirit, enabled by the presence of ancestors, priests, diviners, mediums, and doctors, enabled the journey toward liberation. The main point being observed here is that the foundation for Liele's work in Jamaica was laid by Afro-Jamaicans in the practice of Obeah and Myal. It is of first importance that Liele on no occasion ever criticized the work of Afro-Jamaicans in their practice of Obeah and Myal. This is in stark contrast to the posture and practice of Liele's associates—the British missionaries. Could it be that Liele understood the work of Afro-Jamaicans as a necessary foundation for his own explication of the Baptist covenant that conjoined his work in Georgia and Jamaica?

In the previous chapter I noted that Afro-Jamaicans understood sin as sorcery—the plotting and planning of the enemy to affect and turn their world upside down. Evil machinations did not emerge out of nowhere but were viewed as a direct consequence of the evil intent and planning of the enemy, and through careful observation and planning the enemies' plans could be thwarted. One of the consequences of this way of viewing the world was that sin was not the last word and had no power of its own. Sin, sorcery—in its form as slavery could be destroyed. With the help of ancestors, healers, diviners, and through their religions the enslaved community could dream of a better day.

> Every event, every illness, is assumed to have a cause, a spiritual root, a religious significance, and the specialists are there to rationalize, ritualize, or cure it. Mediums communicate directly between god and man; they are possessed and speak in tongues.... Death itself is always regarded as caused by bad magic or a revengeful spirit, and burial ceremonies incorporate rituals intended to reveal who had wished death on the corpse. But death itself is not seen as a great divide.... Life after death is envisaged as a form of family reunion where life continues like life on earth.[2]

One of the interpretations of the religious practices with which Liele and his associates would have become acquainted in Jamaica was connected to Obeah and Myalism, and one approach to understand the relationship between them was that of sorcery and the response to it through renewed life and liberation. Forms of evil and sin are understood as Obeah, and the overcoming of these manifestations of evil whether in sickness, or the loss of property or life, is understood as Myal. Missionaries and planters were often unable to differentiate between Obeah and Myal and so they believed that one way to neutralize the power of Obeah and Myal was to baptize Afro-Jamaicans.

> The superstitions which prevail in Western and Central Africa have been brought to the West Indies and may be comprehended under the two systems of obeahism and myalism; the first of which is entirely mischievous, and the other professes to counteract it. The principal actor(s) in the former are old men, generally Africans. These pretend to have powers over others, even at a distance.... One of the plans which the overseers adopted during slavery, for breaking the spell of obeahism ... was to procure baptism for the Negroes.... Latterly, however, baptism or as they call it, christening, has become so common, that it seems to have lost its charm. And the doctor or Myal-man, is resorted to, that he may neutralize the power of the Obeah-man.[3]

Perhaps, having been a slave himself, Liele understood that enslaved people caught in the tragedy of chattel slavery would try any means necessary to keep intact their own dignity and freedom as sons and daughters of God.

M. G. Lewis, in his *Journal of a West Indian Proprietor*, in 1816 referred to Christianity as white Obeah. The set of circumstances that led Lewis to make a connection between Christianity and Black Obeah had to do with the sense of powerlessness Lewis as a plantation owner experienced in the presence of Afro-Jamaican religion. Lewis writes of an Obeah-man called Adam who attempted to poison an attorney and discovered that his plan failed because Bessie, a house slave, had betrayed him. Obeah-man Adam cursed Bessie, her health declined, and her four children died, one after another. Lewis tried white Obeah to counteract Adam on two levels. He appealed to a false eschatology offering Bessie hope in a heaven beyond the skies for herself and her children. It is worth noting at this point a distinction between Liele's (who was in Jamaica at this time) eschatology and that of M. G. Lewis. In earlier chapters it was observed that Liele in his articulation of an Afro-Baptist faith appealed to African Americans and Afro-Jamaicans to enact a linkage between earth and heaven. In "The Covenant of the Anabaptist Church, begun in America, December 1777 and in Jamaica, December 1783," Liele spells out in articles VIII and XX ways in which eschatology—the hope for peace with God and neighbor—becomes transformative in the present situation. Article VIII specifies that it is of first importance for members of the community called church to be there for each other. If one falters the person who was wronged should reach out to the wrongdoer and if that gesture is refused, then the community should in love and generosity be there with the one who broke covenant. Liele cites Matthew 18:15–18. The threat of judgment is real because if the person who broke the covenant fails to return to the community, then the fracture and possible breaking of covenant becomes real. Liele seems to imply that Christ is among the membership both faithful and unfaithful as community. He cites Matthew 18:18: "Truly I say to you, whatever you shall bind on earth shall be bound in heaven: and whatever you loose on earth shall have been loosed in heaven." However, in article XX, "We hold if a Brother or

Sister should transgress, and abideth not in the doctrine of Christ, and he or she, after being justly dealt with agreeable to the 8th article . . ." It is quite clear that for Liele there is some notion of what he terms "the doctrine of Christ" in article XX that serves as a hermeneutical key in the maintaining of ecclesial community. Liele cites Luke 17:3–4: "Be on your guard! If your brother sins, rebuke him; and if he repents forgive him. And if he sins against you seven times a day, saying, 'I repent,' forgive him." It becomes increasingly clear that Liele anchored his teaching about sin in his understanding of church and community. What is bound on earth is also bound in heaven, and the doctrine of Christ, according to Liele, includes the doctrine of God as father and spirit.

The emphasis of slave owner M. G. Lewis was not about keeping together the enslaved community or the positing of an eschatology that would join heaven and earth, as Liele suggests. On the contrary, he sought to keep intact his power over the enslaved community as masters were expected to do in relation to enslaved workers on his plantation. He embraced the Christian ways of embracing the world and understood Christianity, white Obeah, as a means of controlling the practice of African religion that sought to interrupt the logic and ethos of plantation life. Plantation owner Lewis was perturbed concerning the power of African religion as practiced in Jamaica and its power to interrupt plantation life. Lewis confesses:

> In short, I know not what I can do with him, except indeed make a Christian out of him! This might induce the negro to believe, that he has lost his infernal power by the superior virtue of the holy water, but, perhaps he may refuse to be Christened. However, I will at least ask him the question and if he consents, I will send him—and a couple dollars—to the clergyman—for he shall not have so great a distinction as baptism from massa's own hand—and see what effect "white obeah" will have on removing the terrors of this professor of the Black.[4]

George Eaton Simpson shares with us a sense of the ethos informing both the established and dissenting churches in Jamaica in 1816, within a year or two in which Lewis spoke of Christianity as white Obeah and sought in response to the power of Black Obeah, as practiced by Adam the Obeah-man, to request of the Anglican parson, to baptize Obeah-man Adam with a wish that baptism would neutralize Black Obeah. It seemed to have been the practice for plantation owners to offer payment to the parson to perform the baptism. Simpson explains:

> The temper of the early nineteenth-century Jamaica was reflected in a resolution of the Assembly in 1815 to consider at its next meeting the state of religion among the slaves, and especially to investigate the "dark and dangerous fanaticism of the Methodists, Moravians and Baptists." Rather than abandon 350,000 slaves in the island to the dissenters, the Jamaican legislature enacted a law in 1816 providing for the appointment of Anglican curates to instruct Africans.... The minister received a fee for each slave who was baptized and registered as a member of the church. One rector baptized and registered 5,000 of the 24,000 blacks in his parish in six months. Slaves regarded baptism as a charm against sorcery, and many were baptized several times.[5]

Simpson indicates that this practice of baptizing Afro-Jamaicans by the established church was short-lived. Plantation owner Lewis informed us that what the clergy of the Anglican church offered was baptism "as Christening," and this ritual was short-lived. A majority of Afro-Jamaicans who hailed from Africa attributed special significance to the presence of spirit mediated by water. Liele underscores this in the inclusion of baptism as one of the ordinances of his church. In article iii of "The Covenant of the Anabaptist Church," Liele states, "We hold to be baptized in a river, or in a place where there is much water, in the name of the Father, and the Son, and the Holy Ghost" (Matt. 3:13, 16, 17; Mark 16:22–24; Matt. 28:19). When the established church agreed to practice baptism through sprinkling, they went against a tradition that was about thirty-two years old and implemented by Liele and his associates. Liele on occasion would mention that he practiced baptism at the sea in Kingston and at the river in Spanish Town. Simpson explains:

> In the British possessions the Church of England was the religion of white settlers and officials in the seventeenth and eighteenth centuries;

it was not a missionary church for the slaves.... In Jamaica, the Native Baptists were without serious competition for forty years (1780–1820) as George Gibb, Moses Baker, and other subordinates in George Liele's "leader system" founded their own groups and as these split into still more cult groups. During this period a reinterpretation of Christianity spread throughout the island, and by 1830 the Native Baptists had become "another religion competing with Christianity of the European missionaries."[6]

White Obeah was no match for Black Obeah. Lewis had to agree for Bessie to see a Black Obeah-man who lived in the mountains to alleviate her suffering.

As we probe the religious foundations on which Liele built his work in Jamaica, it is instructive to note Dr. Du Bois's depiction of indigenous Black religion that Africans brought to the New World, which Du Bois terms "the Black Church," refers to Obeah and other iterations of Black religion. Black religion first brought to the New World by native Africans was not at first a Christian church—it was an African church immersed in the "heathen rites" of Obeah and voodoo worship. According to Du Bois, it took about two centuries for these African religious practices to become Christian, "with a simple Calvinistic creed, but with many of the old customs still clinging to these services. It is this historic fact that the Negro Church of today bases itself upon the sole surviving social institution of the African fatherland, that accounts for its extraordinary vitality ... the Church became the center of amusements, of what little spontaneous economic activity remained, of education, and of all social intercourse."[7]

The main point Du Bois seeks to make is that native Africans provided a religious basis for the creation of the Black church, with a measure of diversity and plurality, as religions as diverse as Islam, Christianity, and African traditional faith were all present among Africans who were brought to the New World in chains. The interpretive key for Du Bois was the presence of African priests who saw the need for equilibrium in the culture and found the freedom to practice their art of religion, Obeah. Du Bois helps us understand that there were few tools available to African peoples with which they could seek to dismantle the house of bondage built by the oppressor class. The main tool available to the oppressed class was religion. Liele seems to have been conversant with African ways of thinking and perhaps this was why he often spoke of his mission and ministry to Ethiopians and created in Georgia and Jamaica worship and educational experiences that honored the world of spirits, ancestors, and an Anabaptist approach to life. Liele shared with the indigenous approaches to religion that confronted him in Jamaica a sense that the doctrine of Christ was their way of witnessing to the divine in their midst as this was expressed in ministries of humility both in the washing of each other's feet and in admitting children into the membership of the church.

Afro-Baptist Faith as Praxis

There are a number of explicit ways in which Liele through his church covenant did theology from the bottom up and represents a worldview that is praxis oriented. Early in the exposition of his covenant, he critiques orthodox Baptist polity by legislating, in a covenant that guides both theology and polity in his church, mandates that were to become not merely an ethical ideal but a gospel mandate. This was revolutionary with a church comprised of more than 90 percent of the membership being enslaved persons. This was not the policy or practice of British Baptists but emerged from Liele's own experience of being an enslaved person in Georgia. Liele as a member of the Separate Baptist Church in Savannah undoubtedly shaped a number of the polity and doctrinal statements in his covenant from ecclesial positions in Georgia and later in Jamaica.

It may be helpful at this point to note the possible influence of George Whitfield on Liele's teaching in his church covenant and a possible theological relationship with Whitfield. Charles O. Walker in "Georgia's Religion in the Colonial Era, 1733–1790" informs us that the Rev. George Whitfield may be called the Father of the Particular Baptists in Georgia.

> The Reverend George Whitfield can indirectly be called the "Father of the Particular Baptists" in Georgia.... The Regular or Particular Baptists were Calvinistic and very conservative in their worship, doctrine, evangelism, and church extension. Formal confession of faith, such as the London, Philadelphia, and Charleston were very important to them. Separate Baptists tended to follow zeal more than confessions. Dependence upon the Holy Spirit for guidance and the absolute authority of the Bible were most important to them.... Perhaps the Sandy Creek Association can be taken as the most radical group, for it at one time held nine Christian rites: Baptism, the Lord's Supper, love feasts, the laying on of hands (upon each member), feet-washing, anointing the sick, the right hand of fellowship, the kiss of charity, and the devoting of children.[8]

Understandably it would have been easier for the kiss of peace and the washing of feet to take place in Jamaica under Liele's leadership rather than in Big Buckhead Baptist Church in Georgia where Liele as an enslaved person worshipped with at least eight other enslaved persons who were owned by Liele's master, Deacon Henry Sharp, whose sister was married to Pastor Matthew Moore. Charles O. Walker concluded a description of the ordinances by acknowledging that gradually these ordinances were dropped. Deacon Henry Sharp had eight slaves and one presumes Liele's parents were included, although he never mentioned them in the Jamaican context. How would the washing of feet work in a church in which the majority of the membership is white and several of the Black persons are slaves to Deacon Sharp? Perhaps even the pastor, who seemed to have come to Georgia in 1764 with Henry Sharp, worked at the behest of Deacon Sharp. The ethos was different in Jamaica, where the majority of Liele's membership were enslaved persons steeped in their native religion who were beginning under the tutelage of Liele to discover that membership in Liele's church did not cancel out Afro-Jamaican ways of worship. Although the majority of Liele's membership were enslaved, there were persons such as Deacon Swigle and certainly in the earlier years Moses Baker and others of Liele's associates who were freed. Did the issue of class play a role in Liele's church in Jamaica? If the issue of race were a problem in Matthew Moore's

CHAPTER 5

Big Buckhead Baptist Church in Georgia, it is clear that class would have been an issue in Liele's church in Jamaica. Liele does not offer any insights to the practice of feet washing and the kiss of peace as rites of his church. Walker points out that several Baptist churches in Georgia did not adhere to these rites and gradually the practice was dropped. "They insisted on an 'Experience of Grace' which was to be publicly confessed before a person was received into the church and baptized"[9] In the Afro-Baptist context in Jamaica, an "Experience of Grace" as testimony took precedence over feet washing and the kiss of peace. Testimony, dancing, and praying in the spirit replaced these rites as observed by Separate Baptists in Georgia.

The "experience of grace" was always at the core of Liele's contribution, and according to David Shannon this experience of grace allowed Liele's faith in Christ to direct his life and ministry in spite of the perils of slavery. David Shannon argues that Liele's theology of grace provides a touchstone for his "black theology of liberation," stating, "The background for understanding George Liele as well as his message to the people is found in the New Testament, John 13:13: Ye call me Master and Lord; and ye say well: for so I am" (Translation by Shannon). This phrase is the foundation of George Liele's theology and, therefore, the beginning of a "black theology of liberation"[10]

Shannon informs us that a black theology of liberation is grounded both in the African-American experience of slavery and other forms of oppression such as humiliation and loss of dignity. Shannon reminds the reader that Liele often called attention to the suffering engendered by the children of Israel in Egypt and that Liele as a slave in Georgia epitomized the suffering of Israel in Egypt and hence embodies a starting point for a black theology of liberation. It is worth noting that Liele's suffering did not cease when he and his family landed in Jamaica in 1783 as an indentured servant of Col. Moses Kirkland. He was twice imprisoned in Jamaica, on one occasion for preaching from Romans 10:1 where he compared the suffering of Afro-Jamaicans to that of the children of Israel. He was charged with sedition and his feet and upper body placed in stocks. Shannon suggests that suffering is the midwife of Black liberation and in Liele's case it was chattel slavery. Liele's parents were known only by their first names, Nancy and Liele. For some time Liele was known only by his first name, George, until he assumed his father's first name, Liele. Shannon reminds the reader that Liele was converted by a white preacher, Matthew Moore, but was always clear that his ministry was to fellow enslaved persons in Georgia and later to Afro-Jamaicans who were caught in the web of slavery. Shannon cites Liele: "Desiring to prove the sense I had of my obligation to God, I endeavored to instruct . . . my own color in the Word of God: the white brethren seeing my endeavors . . . gave me a call at the quarterly meeting to preach before the congregation."[11] On the basis of his sermon to the Big Buckhead Baptist Church in 1773, Liele received a license to preach in Georgia. While in Jamaica Liele was denied a license to preach, and perhaps about 1806 joined with Moses Baker in requesting the British Baptists to send missionaries to fill the void occasioned by several Black Baptists being denied the opportunity to preach. Moses Baker through the aegis of his employer, Samuel Vaughn, who was a member of the Jamaica Assembly, made it possible for Baker to preach until the 1820s. This courtesy was not extended to Liele and there is good evidence to suggest, that in all likelihood, Liele did not do much preaching after 1808. The situation was much different in Georgia as Liele was the first African American who was licensed to preach and consequently ordained by the same church and pastor in 1775.

"Liele's conversion to Christianity is one of the key experiences toward a liberation theology. Before his conversion, Liele's sense of right and wrong, instilled in him first by his father and second by Matthew Moore, a white Baptist minister, drove him to seek salvation. Although he joined Moore's church, engaged in Bible study, prayed and did good work, it was his conversion that stimulated his deep love for Christ. He describes this important epiphany: 'I felt such love and joy as my tongue was not able to express.'"[12] Liele's passion to minister to fellow enslaved persons happened in Georgia as an enslaved person who belonged to Deacon Henry Sharp, who after Liele's conversion made it possible for Liele to visit with fellow slaves and engage in the practice of reading among them, sharing verses of hymns, and explaining verses of the hymns to members of the enslaved community. It was this boating along the Savannah River in his visit to plantations along the river that allowed Liele to venture as far as Silver Bluff, South Carolina, where he was instrumental in the founding of the Silver Bluff Baptist Church and was the first Black preacher to minister in that context. This was pivotal in the conversion of David George and his acceptance of the role as elder in the church during the absence of Elder Palmer, who corralled the group together for worship. On one of these occasions at Silver Bluff, Liele preached in the cornfield, and David George in an expression of conviction sought Liele's counsel on how he should overcome his fear of leading the flock at Silver Bluff. Liele's answer was prayer. Liele seems to explain that prayer is the atmosphere in which grace thrives. He encouraged David George to spend time in prayer and this David George found helpful.

LIELE OPENED DOORS—TO SCHOOL AND TO CHURCH

One of the hidden passions of Liele was the teaching of literacy, using his time among fellow enslaved persons on plantations along the Savannah River to read among the people. He may not have had the confidence or the opportunity to teach the enslaved to read and write, but he read among them and sang among them and would explain the meaning of verses of the hymns to fellow enslaved persons. Liele was able to build on this passion to share words and interpret words with the enslaved and it seems that all the time Liele had in mind whetting the appetite for literacy with the goal of placing the Bible in the hands of the enslaved. In the Jamaican context one goal was to help Afro-Jamaicans understand that the Great Ancestor of Myal and other indigenous expressions of religion was also the God of the Bible. It was observed in the previous chapter that Liele's approach to literacy was to have a teaching master, Nicholas Swigle, in his church provide school for both enslaved and free persons. Further, wherever meetinghouses were formed in the hill country—often called classes, which later became churches—the experience in ministry began with a school. This became a permanent addition in churches in Jamaica as the space for church was the same space used for schools during the week. In fact churches became sponsors for school, and with Liele's model in mind there was a link between salvation and education. This practice was most helpful as Liele taught in the Jamaica church that it was poor stewardship to have the space for worship on Sundays locked and chained the other days of the week. This space was used for education, and in the tradition of Liele two books that were central at church were also useful in school, the hymnal and the Bible. In school students were taught to sing many of the Psalms.

David Shannon made the bold claim that one way of highlighting the hermeneutical key to Liele's approach to ministry and his Black liberation theology is tied in the phrase, "Jesus is my Lord and Master." Shannon cites Liele in his letter to John Rippon in the Baptist Annual Register, for 1790, 1791, 1792, and part of 1793. "I always had a natural fear of God from my youth, and was often checked in conscience with thoughts of death, which barred me from many sins and bad company. I knew no other way at that time to hope for salvation but only in the performance of my good works. I requested of my Lord and Master to give me work, I did not care how mean it was, only to try and see how good I would do it."[13] According to Shannon here we see a flowering of Liele's theology of "The Experience of Grace." "It seems clear that at first, Liele was unaware of the facts of salvation before his conversion. However, as he learned more about Christianity, he changed his way of thinking from a works-based salvation to that of a grace-based salvation."[14] There is clearly a Christocentric point of departure to Liele's understanding of work. When Liele made this theological discovery, of the sufficiency of God's grace, he was still an enslaved person in Georgia accountable to Henry Sharp as a master. But in his explication of John 13:13 he finds the language to superimpose on notions of an earthly lord and master to whom even his master becomes accountable to his Christ, the heavenly Lord and Master. This is one way in which Liele transposes an eschatology at the end of history when he will meet his savior face to face in a proleptic understanding of the hope for a future with his Christ being available and operative even in plantation culture. According to Shannon one may imagine Liele saying "I may call Henry Sharp lord and master but there is one above him, one who transcends him who is present with me in the here and now, it is this lord I seek to serve, who gives me work to do, and it does not matter how menial or humble this work may be."

Liele's goal was to see how well he could perform this work, seeing he was empowered by the experience of grace. It is in this sense that Shannon may be correct in identifying Liele as the father of Black liberation theology.

Shannon, a New Testament scholar, juxtaposes a relationship between Liele and St. Paul. He argues that for both, the experience of their conversion was pivotal in the development of a theology of grace. There is a sense in which one could speak of a pre-conversion period in the lives of both men. Paul was devoted to notions of the rule and the role of the law in his life as a Pharisee prior to his meeting Christ on the road to Damascus. While Paul did not disavow the presence and need of the law in one's life as a Christian, it became increasingly clear that the law was not pivotal or central after the Damascus Road encounter. What became central was his theology of the cross of Christ. "God forbid that I should glory save in the Cross of Christ my Lord" (Galatians 6:14). There was a new methodology—it was no longer the way of the law—it was now the way of grace. Even talk about faith was now faith formed through grace and talk about sin was itself an act of grace.

> Like the Apostle Paul, George Liele was a man of great faith who accepted Jesus as his Lord and Master and committed himself to spreading the gospel. Like Paul also, Liele's conversion was key to his understanding and faith. Some scholars suggest that the radical impact of Paul's conversion (call) is redefined by his relationship between God and the Jews and the Gentiles. Paul's experience with God led him to a new focus. . . . George Liele's faith was grounded in an intimate relationship with God. He used the study of the Bible as a source to overcome the negative and hostile experiences of enslavement . . . Bible study was a source of inspiration for their songs, sermons, prayers, testimonials, funerals and rites of passage.[15]

LIELE AND PAUL?

Shannon does not make a connection between salvation and liberation in his discussion of Liele's engagement with the context of slavery in which he lived. He reminded us that Liele engaged in Bible study and that his conversion, like that of the Apostle Paul, served as a hermeneutical key as he lived out his call. But what may we ask of the loss of freedom in which Afro-Americans and Afro-Jamaicans were forced to live? What are we to make of Liele's and Shannon's lack of rebuke to the master class concerning the cruelty of masters and white ministers in their commitment to make enslaved people submissive? What about the autonomy of enslaved persons and their rights to live as sons and daughters of God? What was their rebuke to masters who abused enslaved persons? What of the responsibilities of churches to the enslaved when white preachers and in some cases Liele, as we note in his church covenant, use scripture to keep Black people in a place of subservience? What is the point of reading the Bible when the Bible was used against the poor and enslaved, admonishing slaves to be obedient to their masters, and Liele including in the church covenant that in accepting Afro-Jamaicans in his church he needed a note from the master attesting to the good behavior of the enslaved persons. Enslaved persons were told by the church to be devoted to their masters, to accept their status in life as chattel, and to be faithful in their service to their masters as unto God. Where is the word of rebuke to masters? A dilemma being pointed out is the danger of the church taking the side of the oppressor who buys and sells human beings against "the least of God's children." A former enslaved person, Frederick Douglass, helps to frame this issue:

> But the church of this country is not only indifferent to the wrongs of the slave, it actually takes sides with the oppressor. . . . Many of its eloquent Divines, who stand as the very lights of the church, have shamelessly given the sanction of religion and the Bible to the whole slave system. They have taught that man [woman] may, properly be a slave; that the relation of master and slave is ordained of God; that to send back an escaped bondman to his master is clearly a duty of all the followers of the Lord Jesus Christ; . . . They strip the love of God of its beauty and leave the throne of religion a huge, horrible, horrible repulsive form. It is a religion for oppressors, tyrants, manstealers, and thugs.[16]

It is quite likely that when Douglass mentions eloquent Divines who send back slaves to their masters, he included St. Paul, who in a letter

CHAPTER 5

addressed to Philemon but intended for the entire church, calls on Philemon to receive back Onesimus who apparently went to Paul who was in prison without the knowledge of his slave master Philemon. Carolyn Osiek in her commentary on Onesimus's return to Philemon writes:

> A new relationship has come about between Paul and Onesimus during the visit (v. 10), probably the baptism of Onesimus, . . . such as Onesimus's determination to become an apostle like Paul. . . . If baptism is intended in verse 10, which is most likely, this is a good example of the autonomy of household slaves to make their own decisions about conversion even where the *paterfamilias* is Christian. . . . Paul wants to keep Onesimus for ministry work with him but sends him back for reconciliation with Philemon and his approval for this new work. Paul asks Philemon to accept a new level of relationship with Onesimus, probably including the manumission of the slave.[17]

This esteemed New Testament scholar, on the one hand, posits something of a correlation between George Liele and St. Paul particularly around the issue of conversion. Their conversion was a new point of departure for them as they saw the world differently. In the case of George Liele, he discovered a new love for the enslaved community with whom he shared verses from *Watts Hymnal* and verses from the Bible both in Georgia and in Jamaica. With Bible in one hand, and the Hymnal in the other, one could argue that Liele like Paul in his letter to Philemon condemned the practice of slaves running away from their masters. There were no instances of Liele running away from his master unlike his mentee David George, who it seemed was constantly on the run from cruel masters. In Ephesians 6:5, servants are enjoined to be obedient to their masters and if they confess to be Christians, are expected by both missionary and master to set a wholesome example for those who are not Christians by not running away. In his church covenant, "The Covenant of the Anabaptist Church, begun in America, December 1977 and in Jamaica, December 1783," Liele writes:

> Article XV. We permit no slaves to join the Church without first having a few lines from their owner for good behavior. (1 Peter ii:13–16;

1 Thess. iii:13.) Article XVII. If a slave or servant misbehave to their owners they are to be dealt with according to the Word of God. (I Tim. 1:6; Eph. vi:5; I Peter ii:18–22; Titus ii:9–11.)

I am especially interested in Liele's appropriation of what he understood to be the word of God as expressed by St. Paul. In Ephesians vi:5, Paul writes: "Slaves, be obedient to those who are your earthly masters, with fear and trembling, in singleness of heart, as to Christ."

It is quite clear in this context that Liele would not have encouraged enslaved persons who would run away or disobey their masters. On the contrary, they were expected to serve their masters as they served Christ. Missionaries and masters who were invested in the promotion of slavery would quote and preach from Ephesians, Timothy, Romans, and Philemon. The argument from Philemon was most persuasive as Onesimus was enjoined by Paul to return to the setting and scene of his oppression in a context in which as a slave he was expected to apologize to the master for running away. Carolyn Osiek's interpretation of the letter to Philemon—that Onesimus was asked by Paul to return to the house of bondage and no doubt offer words of regret for running away, as a way to embrace the possibility of reconciliation, does not take into account the imbalance of power between master and slave. It is not inconceivable that Onesimus returned to the house of bondage with love in his heart for the master, but we may ask what value is love without the power to self-actualize? Reconciliation between master and slave is impractical when it is done within the existing structure of master-slave relationships. The master-slave order needs to be abolished and both are seen and understand themselves as equal before God. What is required here is a new order in which slave and master are abolished and it is replaced by a new creation. Paul stumbled on this insight when he stated, "If anyone is in Christ—she is new. The Old is past and lo all things are become new" (2 Cor. 5:17). The inbreaking of the new transforms the house of bondage to a site of renewal and transformation. It was difficult to practice the love of Christ in the house of bondage. The old forms of oppression had to give way to the inbreaking of God's reign of peace and love.

CHAPTER 5

Horace Russell, the celebrated Caribbean theologian, points out that the circumstances in Liele's world may have forced him to buy and sell persons in Jamaica and thereby compromise his quest toward the complete and total liberation of Afro-Jamaicans. Russell reminds us that Liele in arriving with his family in Jamaica, January 1783, had with him a letter from Col. Moses Kirkland, the commanding officer of the British forces for the evacuation of Savannah, to Archibald Campbell (1739–1791), the acting governor of Jamaica since 1781. Liele, who was indentured to Kirkland, worked to repay his debt to Kirkland.

> Liele's job was to carry shot from the naval base in Port Royal into Kingston and to collect abandoned pieces about the town. It appears to have been a large enterprise, and according to his account in the *Jamaican Gazette* (an official government publication) and from his will and that of his wife Hannah, it appears Liele bought enslaved persons to carry out his business. It was not an unusual practice in Caribbean urban centers for former enslaved persons to own slaves. . . . There was even a woman in Kingston who allowed her enslaved person, a Baptist, to be an evangelist for the Moravians. Liele was a creature of his social times, and his action was a compromise.[18]

Additionally, Liele owned a large farm and buildings in the city of Kingston and may have rationalized his need for owning eight enslaved persons. Liele's wife, Hannah Hunt Liele, indicated in her will that her husband, George Liele, overstated his ownership of eight slaves when three of the enslaved persons named, Betsy and her two children Nancy and Cudjoe, were her property and she desired to pass them on to her daughter Lucy [Liele] Price. The will procured by Hannah Hunt Liele states:

> A Negro woman named Betsy, and her children are from (mistake or inadvertence) directed to be manumitted at my decease but as the said Negro woman slave named Betsy and her children, Nancy and Cudjoe, are my sole and separate property, my said and late husband George Liele had no power to make such bequest. It is therefore my will and desire that the said Negro Woman slave named Betsy, and her children

Nancy and Cudjoe, and their future issue, offspring and increase shall form part of my estate and pass under this my will and go to my said daughter Lucy [Liele] Price to hold to her the said Lucy Price and to her heirs and assigns forever.[19]

George Liele wanted at his death to free all eight slaves that he claimed he owned. His wife begged to differ as she claimed Betsy and her two children belonged to her and she would will them to her daughter Lucy.

It is extremely difficult to live in a culture in which human life is denigrated and dehumanized and not be touched and affected by this practice. Liele and his family became owners of slaves, participating in the buying and selling of human beings. George Liele at his death willed that all eight enslaved persons be set free—granted they remain adherents of the Anabaptist faith. His wife wanted Betsy and her two children to be passed on to her daughter Lucy.

With Liele's impending death in 1825, about three years after his return from London in search of authorization from the British Baptists to secure a license to preach in Jamaica, Liele could have been at rest in the knowledge that, his flaw of enslaving human beings aside, he had prepared the next generation that would succeed him, to strike a blow for freedom.

Native Baptists Press for Freedom

It was merely six years after Liele's death that Native Baptist deacon Daddy Sharpe struck a blow for the freedom of enslaved persons in Jamaica and throughout the British Commonwealth. The Baptist War, as this uprising was called, had its roots in a prior rebellion against British colonialism when the Maroons of Jamaica sought to overturn plantation slavery in Jamaica. The Maroon rebellion of 1760, led by Ashanti warrior and Obeah-man Tacky, was one of the bloodiest revolts staged by Afro-Jamaicans. Led by Tacky, the warriors prepared for war by mixing rum with gunpowder and grave dirt. Blood drawn from the arm of each participant was added, and then the mixture was drank in turn by each warrior. The drinking of this mixture signaled the covenant to fight until death.[20] This was certainly a part of the backdrop for the Baptist War led by Daddy Sharpe aimed at taking on the colonial government in a quest to overthrow the institution of slavery in the British Commonwealth. An additional reason for the Baptist War, according to Winston Lawson, was sparked by news from England that the Anti-slavery Society was committed to immediate emancipation and that the House of Commons in April 1831 had taken steps to abolish slavery. A rumor ensued among the enslaved population in Jamaica that freedom should not be denied and delayed any longer because it had already been granted by the king and his ministers in England but was being withheld from enslaved persons by white people in Jamaica.

> They were therefore ready and anxious to take hold of the news from England in 1831 that abolition was imminent. Anyone, therefore, who stood in the way of their realizing their dream of freedom from an unworkable and demoralizing circumstance, be they planter, politician or preacher would be denounced as Knibb and his colleagues were at Salter's Hill on that fateful December 27 when the accumulated pressures of alienation and the frustrated resentment of pacification and acquiescence to the status quo, made them declare with bitter disappointment, that "the man must be mad to tell us such things."[21]

Although the Native Baptists deviated from Liele in interesting ways—for example, Liele in his church covenant states that he baptized in the names of the Father, the Son, and the Holy Ghost (article iii)—the Native Baptists emphasized the presence and power of the spirit and this emphasis on the spirit provided a connection point with Myal and Obeah religions. In a system of slavery that denied the leaders of the Native Baptists political power—operating under the aegis of the spirit—they were free to make theological connections as they saw fit and not be tied to Baptist orthodoxy, as Liele was expected to do in relation to his colleagues from the Baptist Missionary Society in London. Native Baptists carved out their own theological space; in this church John the Baptist was seen as the leader since he baptized Jesus and, so to speak, accepted Jesus into his church. As the Native Baptists merged African perspectives with Liele's teaching, they formulated a reinterpretation of Christianity that would endure even under the onslaught of European theological beliefs. "By 1830 the doctrine and organization of the Native Baptists had become a thoroughly integrated part of Negro culture—another religion competing with the Christianity of the European missionaries."[22]

The Baptist War of 1831, led by Daddy Sharpe, signaled the beginning of the end of slavery in Jamaica. Afro-Baptists fighting for emancipation in and around Montego Bay brought to a climax the long struggle of Afro-Jamaicans for freedom and liberation from British colonization. The struggle over the years took the form of enslaved people running away, many, as in the case of the Maroons of Jamaica, fleeing to the hills and organizing periodic attacks, or the Maroons under the leadership of Tacky pledging to fight until death. The focus of this war, however, was Black Baptists organizing to withdraw their labor and attack the institutions that kept them enslaved. Because of this the brunt of their attack was on the institutions of the plantation. A total of 120 buildings on the estate were torched as Afro-Jamaicans insisted that they were human beings who had a right to emancipation; they had a right to withdraw their labor and attack the institutions that kept them in slavery. Enslaved Jamaicans were clear that they were not asking for kindness from the master class, they were demanding the freedom to which they were entitled. More than twenty thousand Afro-Jamaicans were involved in the uprising. The focus was not a call to arms but for enslaved persons to withdraw their labor and thereby crush the monster of slavery. Mary Turner puts the uprising in the Baptist War in perspective:

> The Baptist War, however, was essentially the Native Baptist War; its leaders shaped mission teaching to their own ends and used mission organization for their own purposes. . . . The Baptist historic connection with the Black Baptist churches founded by Liele and Baker in the eighteenth century had meant that, throughout the slavery period, there was a stronger tendency for the Baptist mission members to enjoy, like Sharpe, dual status as mission members and as Native Baptists. . . . General Ruler Sam Sharpe, "director of the whole and preacher to the rebels" claimed in the account he gave to Wesleyan missionary, Henry Bleby, who had several conversations with him in jail, that he planned not armed rebellion but what would today be called mass passive resistance. After the Christmas holidays, when the cane harvest

was due to begin, the slaves were to sit down and refuse to work until their masters acknowledged that they were free men and agreed to pay them wages.... The main body of arguments, however, related to religion.... Sharpe and his aides proclaimed the natural equality of men and denied, on the authority of the Bible, the right of white men to hold the black in bondage. The text, "No man can serve two masters," persistently quoted by Sharpe, became a slogan among the slaves. To protest against slavery was a matter of "assisting their brethren in the work of the Lord . . . this was not the work of man alone, but they had assistance from God."[23]

Edward Hylton, one of Daddy Sharpe's followers, tells of being in the hills and receiving a message from Daddy Sharpe to attend a meeting at Johnson's house at Retrieve estate in St. James. The gathering took the form of a prayer meeting. After the meeting, Daddy Sharpe, William Johnson—who became one of the leaders of the Baptist War—Hylton, and a few others remained behind. "After a while Sharp spoke to them in a low, soft tone so that his voice would not be heard outside. According to Hylton, he kept them spell bound while he spoke of the evils and injustices of slavery, asserted the right of all human beings to freedom and declared on the authority of the Bible, that the White man had no more right to hold Blacks in bondage than the Blacks had to enslave the Whites."[24] The meeting went on late into the night as they agreed on a strategy to overturn slavery. They covenanted not to work after the Christmas holidays but to seize the right to freedom in faithfulness to each other. "If backra would pay them, they would work as before. If any attempt was made to force them to work as slaves, they would fight for their freedom. They took the oath and kissed the Bible."[25] It became clear that Daddy Sharpe did not intend a violent confrontation with plantation owners. What he had in mind was a peaceful protest against the planters proposing and insisting on the enslaved community working without wages during the Christmas holidays. The nonviolent protest would take the form of a labor strike. The plan was that on the day after the Christmas holiday an overseer or a driver would go to the "busha" on each estate and inform him that the slaves would not work until they agreed to pay wages. The bushas were to be kept on the estate until they agreed to pay for work.

The leadership of the Native Baptists had organized themselves into a trade union arm of their church, advocating and negotiating wages for the slaves. Philip Curtin suggests that what in fact occurred was the Native Baptists skillfully had detached the Baptist missionary organization from white missionaries and found a way to use church structure and offices as a trade union leader would negotiate on behalf of his constituency—fellow enslaved Afro-Jamaicans. Winston Lawson highlights the theological, socioeconomic, and Afro-religious environment into which Daddy Sharpe, a leader of the Native Baptists, raised his dark hand in striking a blow for freedom, which signaled the beginning of the end of slavery not only in Jamaica but also in the British Commonwealth. According to Lawson, Sam Sharpe and his followers who carried on the work of George Liele and Moses Baker were clear about the theological presuppositions that informed their planned assault against the scourge of slavery in the British Empire. Perhaps in a tradition among Afro-Jamaican Baptists that has its roots in the teaching of Liele and Baker, who planted theological seeds in Jamaica concerning the equality of all persons before God, Sam Sharpe in the tradition of Liele insisted that white people did not have any right to enslave Black people just as Black people did not have such a right to enslave whites. All human beings are on level ground as they stand in the presence of God. This was the reason why in Baptist churches in Jamaica the communion table from which the ordinance of the Lord's supper was served was never placed in the area of the pulpit from which the leader teaches and sermonizes, but always on the ground floor, where all who enter the sanctuary are equal before God. Lawson speaks of this equality of all persons in the presence of God as "natural equality." Another way in which Liele addresses the question of the equality of all persons before God was in article V in his church covenant, which was widely circulated among Afro-Baptists in Jamaica: "We hold to the ordinance of washing one another's feet" (John xiii:2–7). Lawson reminds us that Daddy Sharpe, patriarch of the Native Baptists, affirmed the natural equality of all persons before God, as he would recite his favorite biblical text, often joined by his associates: "no one can serve two masters."

Lawson further highlights the socioeconomic context in which Sharpe and his associates planned their assault on the culture and house of bondage so artfully created by their oppressors.

> It must be borne in mind that as has been indicated above, the social context in which Sharpe and his colleagues planned their strike against slavery, was one of extremely dire economic circumstances. There had been a long six-month period of drought that extended into May 1831 when heavy rains finally came, thus affecting farming enormously. Along with this natural disaster there occurred an epidemic of small pox, cholera and dysentery.... The religious context was one in which the North coast of Jamaica had been a major center of Baptist and to a lesser extent Methodist mission since 1824, with Burchell in Montego Bay and Knibb going to Falmouth. The parishes of St. James, Trelawny, Hanover and Westmoreland, struck with natural disasters and economic crises, were prime territories for the blossoming of this world-affirming and hopeful Afro-Christian religion, that would counter the pie in the sky escapism of Missionary theology. Not surprisingly in these very parishes there had been at this time, a noticeable "outpouring of the Spirit," with revivals yielding far great attendance at the Chapels, than was the case previously.[26]

According to Lawson a revival of indigenous religion erupted in Jamaica as Afro-Jamaicans gave expression of their disappointment with missionary theology and its promise of an escapist theology that pointed to a better life by and by and a gradual approach to freedom. Freedom was an eschatological promise that would descend like a cloud from the heavens.

On December 27, 1831, Missionary William Knibb, visiting Moses Baker's chapel at Crooked Spring, now Salter's Hill, tried to persuade enslaved persons that rumors about freedom having been granted by the king of England were untrue. The congregation was immensely disappointed with Missionary Knibb, and many persons left the chapel very offended at his remarks. Afro-Baptists began to complain, "The man . . . must be mad to tell us such things."²⁷ William Knibb had won the confidence of the Jamaican people since he began missionary work in the island in 1825, and no doubt he had a special place in the hearts of Afro-Baptists since he was the only missionary who could talk about being at the funeral of George Liele, I believe in 1825. Knibb was accustomed to swaying Afro-Baptists with his charismatic preaching, but with his compatriot Thomas Burchell, pastor of the Baptist church in Montego Bay, on leave in England because of ill health, and the rumor extant that Burchell would soon return with the free papers from the king of England, Knibb had to stand alone. He addressed Afro-Baptists:

> I am pained—pained to the soul, at being told that many of you have agreed not to work anymore for your owners, and I fear this is too true. I learned that some wicked person has persuaded you that the King of England has made you free. Hear me! I love your souls and I would not tell you a lie for the whole world; I assure you that it is false, false as hell can make it. I entreat you not to believe it but go to your work as formerly. If you have any love for Jesus Christ, to religion, to your ministers, to those kind friends in England who helped you to build this chapel, and who are sending a minister for you, do not be led away. God commands you to be obedient.²⁸

William Knibb, one of the most revered missionaries to Jamaica, whose effigy is placed on the premises of the Falmouth Baptist Church, in Falmouth, Jamaica, pled with Afro-Jamaicans to work on plantations over the Christmas holidays against the counsel of a pivotal leader of the Native Baptist church. His mini-sermon models discourse of colonial theology in the tropical islands of the Caribbean. He begins the sermon with a plea for enslaved Jamaicans to consider his pain; he is pained that Afro-Jamaicans, under the leadership of Daddy Sharpe, have decided not to work over the Christmas holidays in 1831. He fails to mention anything about the conditions under which these enslaved persons work and that generations of Afro-Jamaicans have worked without pay for close to three hundred years. The missionary is pained because he is the representative of the plantation masters and wants to see their will and wishes being enacted. Jamaicans responded, "The man . . . must be mad to tell us such things." It is interesting that Knibb's sermon was given in Baker's chapel at Crooked Spring, the second-oldest Baptist chapel in Jamaica. This chapel was the home of many of the original members of the Native Baptist community.

When Missionary Burchell joined Baker in 1824, one of the first places he preached was Baker's church at Crooked Spring. Daddy Sharpe was a member of this church, and Baker agreed for a slice of the membership of his church to become members of Burchell chapel in Montego Bay. Daddy Sharpe and others of the Native Baptist persuasion became members of this missionary Baptist church. Afro-Baptists were always members of two churches, their indigenous spirit-centered church and the missionary church. Now as they became restless and began to envision a life free from plantation restrictions and the cruelty of the master, they began to plan Emancipation Day. They began to dream of freedom coming like a thief in the night, coming in spite of the advocacy of Knibb on behalf of the plantation owners. Missionary Knibb informed the congregation gathered in Baker's former church that he loved their souls. He did not define souls for the congregation, but it would have been helpful if he considered their bodies as sites for liberation. It is clear Missionary Knibb was on a quest to persuade Afro-Jamaicans to return to the plantation over the Christmas holiday to work—without pay—for the master class. One of the demands that Daddy Sharpe had on behalf of the community he represented was that they would no longer work without wages, and it was understood by the community that when freedom and emancipation came, they would remove as far as they could from the site of the plantation. Missionary Knibb was clearly not on the side of freedom and liberation for the enslaved population. Missionary Knibb in his zeal to please the enslaver broke the third commandment: "You shall not take the name of the Lord your God in vain: for the Lord will not hold him guiltless who takes his name in vain" (Exodus 20, 7. RSV). Knibb in using the sacred scriptures as a tool of social control petitioned a congregation comprised of enslaved persons, "If you have any love for Jesus Christ, to religion, to your ministers, or to those kind friends in England who have helped you to build this chapel, and who are sending a minister for you, do not be led away. God commands you to be obedient."

The Man and His Legacy

One understands that in the wake of an uprising by Afro-Jamaicans, Knibb and other missionaries of dissenting churches were expected by plantation owners to deliver for the owner class by getting disgruntled slaves to be obedient to the orders of plantation owners. Missionaries were expected to persuade enslaved persons to return to work and keep the economy rolling and the export of sugar on track. The problem was word was out that the anti-slavery group in England was on the side of freedom and emancipation was imminent and that Thomas Burchell was in England and would return with the free papers. Knibb was in no position to deliver to the plantation owners their hope that slaves would return to work. Representing the voice of the people, Daddy Sharpe exclaimed, "We have worked enough already, and we will work no more; the life we live is too bad, it is the life of a dog, we won't be slaves no more, we won't lift hoe no more, we won't take flogging anymore."[29]

Daddy Sharpe and his compatriots Dove, Linton, Dehaney, and other freedom fighters seized the right to fight for justice and interpret the message of liberation through the hermeneutic of freedom. With Daddy Sharpe's announcement, enslaved persons began to see themselves through the lens of freedom. It is reported that when Daddy Sharpe was apprehended, he said that he "had rather die than be a slave." The price paid for freedom by Sharpe and his community was very high.

> In many instances criminals were condemned during the morning and executed between two and four o'clock. Of 106 slaves tried in St. James 99 were convicted, six executed, one pardoned and two dismissed. Of the 99 convicted, 84 were sentenced to death; in Westmoreland, 33 of the 64 convicted were sentenced to death. Other punishments in St. James included one sentence of 500 lashes, one of 300 lashes and life with imprisonment, one of two hundred lashes with six months imprisonment, and so the dreadful story of barbarity went. . . . Sam Sharpe learnt of the executions while in prison. He himself was tried in Montego Bay on 19 April. He was publicly hanged there on 23 May 1832. At no time did his courage, his nobility of spirit shine more brightly than on the day of his execution. . . . He addressed the assembled crowd in a clear, unfaltering voice, admitted that he had broken the laws of the country and declared that he depended for salvation

upon the Redeemer who shed his blood for sinners upon Calvary . . . Sharpe declared that the missionaries had nothing whatever to do with the uprising.[30]

In the aftermath of the Baptist War, some six hundred Afro-Jamaicans were killed by British forces. In their defense they killed fourteen whites. But the seeds were sown for the destruction of slavery in Jamaica. On August 1, 1834, Lord Stanley introduced the following act to the British Parliament:

> Be it enacted, that all and every person who on the first day of August, one thousand eight hundred and thirty four, shall be holden in slavery within any such British colony as aforesaid, shall, upon and from any after the said first day of August, one thousand eight hundred and thirty four, become and be to all intents and purposes free, and discharged of and from all manner of slavery, and shall absolutely and forever manumitted.[31]

It is worth noting that in the freedom granted to enslaved persons in the British Commonwealth there was the proviso that freedom was granted within the context of an apprenticeship. Persons six years and older were to register as apprentices and continue to work for their former owners—as field hand for twelve years and domestic help for seven years. Children younger than six years old and those born after the act's passage were free. This interpretation of the new freedom Afro-Jamaicans thought they had won was interpreted by the heirs of Daddy Sharpe, and as a part of the legacy of George Liele and Moses Baker it met with stiff resistance from freedom-loving Jamaicans. The system of apprenticeship was resisted throughout Jamaica by the working class. "Slave owners in Jamaica received compensation from the British Government amounting to $6,616,927 (transpose to pounds sterling) for the loss they were expected to suffer when they no longer controlled the forced labor which had been the mainstay of their opulent life style. . . . Emancipation struck at the heart of [the] system of slavery by introducing the payment of wages to laborers."[32] The apprenticeship system of slavery did not work out the way it was planned. Emancipation came like a thief in the night, in 1834 as a limited version of emancipation and in 1838 with the end of the apprenticeship system and full emancipation.

With emancipation Afro-Jamaicans had to relinquish their cottages and their family plots and seek new space to live. Several of the ex-slaveowners wanted to sell their lands, but they chose to sell large acreages, which was beyond the financial reach of the peasantry—those who had stepped into the new freedom made possible by the host country England. Afro-Jamaicans wanted just enough to grow their crops and find living space to raise a family and bury their dead.

The church was appropriately suited to offer this service to Afro-Jamaicans. During the first years after emancipation, churches were crowded with the new Black people. The world Black people occupied during slavery had to be demolished. It was a world in which they were not free to be human. The task confronting the church in Jamaica and the Caribbean was not to arbitrate between master and slave but between free people. Both Baptist and Methodist missionaries were proactive in procuring large tracts of lands that they subdivided into smaller plots and used to create free villages for Afro-Jamaicans who were displaced because of their new-won freedom from the sugar plantations. Baptists saw their membership triple while the membership of the Methodists doubled as Afro-Jamaicans were moved with gratitude for the leadership provided by churches in their journey to emancipation. With the success in membership and the large attendance of Afro-Jamaicans at worship, missionary churches assumed that Black religion, Myal and Obeah, were on their way out. Philip Curtin explains:

> In 1846, the Native Baptist congregations in the sugar parish of Vere, were stronger than all the European churches together. Even in Kingston, Native Baptists in 1860 made up half the churchgoing population.... To make matters worse, the semi-Christian cults were not the only rivals of the missionaries. At the far end of the religious spectrum, the more African Myal religion revived after the disappearance of the strict control of the slave system, and the practice of obeah increased. Obeah was still essentially private and secret, but Myalism took the form of open outbreaks of local hysteria that were bound to attract attention. One disruption, "the great Myal procession," moved

through northwestern parishes from December 1841 through most of 1842. Another major outbreak came to the southeast in 1846, and there were still other occurrences in the country side during 1848, 1852, and 1860.[33]

THE GREAT REVIVAL

Curtin concludes that with the advent of emancipation, the native form of religion mingled with Liele's emphasis on the power and presence of spirt had a firmer grip on the country than European orthodoxy. No doubt Afro-Jamaicans would remember the melding of Liele's and Baker's emphasis on the spirit that synchronized with Myal notions of spirits of ancestors and as a living presence among them coupled with the need for healing and praying, especially over the sick. Philip Curtin points out that in 1860 mission churches launched a united assault in an attempt to dislodge the last vestiges of African religion in Jamaica. The revival aimed at weaning Afro-Jamaicans from their African ways. Worship focused on praying, fasting, and dancing in the spirit. The high point came when the Native Baptists set aside the last Sunday of April 1860 for God's arrival in Jamaica. Gradually, missionaries began to discover that the revival had turned African. Indigenous religion resurfaced and the revival embraced the practices of Myal coupled with Liele's emphasis on the spirit, prayer, singing, and room for dancing in the spirit, prophesying, and spirit seizure. The revival was a rejection of European orthodoxy.

Leonard Barrett comments on the Great Revival that swept Jamaica in 1860–1861:

> How can this Great Revival be interpreted? Was it really a revival of Christianity? The answer is no. There was no Christianity to revive among the slaves. What actually happened was a result of the confused state in which the Blacks found themselves after the Emancipation of 1838. Their expectation that Emancipation would result in freedom and self-betterment was disappointed and instead they found themselves disenfranchised, landless, homeless and without the means to support themselves. The missionaries, who played a great role in the liberation movement, had built up their expectations of a better life in a free Jamaica, but this proved to be nothing more than empty talk. The Great

Revival is thus better understood as a rejection of Christianity and a revival of the African force-vitale. . . . What really took place was a forcible amalgamation of Christianity with the African ethos.[34]

Barrett was quite clear that something new happened in the Great Revival. According to him there was no Christianity there to be revived. It was clear that what was revived was the teachings of Black missionaries from America: George Liele, Moses Baker, George Gibb, and George Lewis. According to Barrett what occurred at the Great Revival was an amalgamation of Black Baptists' viewpoints with Afro-Jamaican indigenous teachings on spirit, the power of dreams, prayer and healing of the weary, and learning from Myalist teachers that sin was sorcery and there was a remedy for white sorcery. Afro-Jamaican Baptists highlighted spirit possession, and many spoke in tongues. Liele once had members leave his Windward Road Chapel because they practiced speaking in tongues, and Liele was not so persuaded. According to Richard Burton, when white Baptist missionaries arrived from Britain and tried to take over Black Baptist churches, a rupture ensued between those of the Native Baptist persuasion and British missionaries. "The Black Baptist preachers and their congregations split off to follow their own style of worship, which, giving a Christian form to long-established Myalist practices, emphasized music and dancing, 'spirit possession' and speaking in tongues."[35] Burton in agreement with Barrett points out that it was difficult and somewhat impossible to expect Liele and his associates from the United States, who had twenty-eight years of autonomous leadership in Jamaica prior to the coming of British Baptists, to surrender their "Afro-Christianity" for a "Euro-Christianity" that was out of touch with the indigenous culture. This was what was special about the theological and cultural contributions that Liele and his associates made in their approach to healing, that of respect for the dead, spirit possession, prophesying, dreams, dancing, and sin as sorcery, which were all deeply connected to the indigenous beliefs of Afro-Jamaicans. With the coming of emancipation in 1838, indigenous expressions of religion flourished in Jamaica. Afro-Jamaicans became suspicious that orthodox Christianity offered by the missionaries was an attempt to keep Afro-Jamaicans in their place and preserve the old order of structural injustice. Missionaries had an investment in keeping the social conditions the way they were as in many cases they were invited to the island by the plantation owners, as was the case of Missionary Thomas Burchell. It is of interest that Burchell preached his first sermon at Crooked Spring, the second Afro-Baptist church built in Jamaica by Moses Baker. Baker encouraged about half of his congregation to form the congregation in Montego, which was named after Missionary Burchell. This church should have been named after Daddy Sharpe, its most consequential member.

> [I]t was their happiness to drop anchor in Montego Bay, on the 15th of January 1824. . . . On landing, Mr. Burchell's first object, agreeably to the instructions of the Committee, was to seek an interview with the Hon. Samuel Vaughn, one of the proprietors, and the acting attorney of the estates on which Mr. Tripp had been located. . . . Mr. Vaughn informed him, therefore, that his family had determined on giving up service on one of their estates altogether; and would require his services on the other, viz. Flamstead only once on every alternate Sunday; and further, that as the house intended for the missionary had been converted into a hospital for the Negroes, he must seek residency elsewhere. On the following Lord's day, January 25th he commenced his labors at Crooked Spring, by preaching from Luke 2:10: "And the angel said to them, 'Be not afraid; for behold I bring you good news of a great joy which will come to all the people.'"[36]

Although freedom had come, the lives of Black people had changed for the worse. After emancipation there was a general deterioration in living standards. During slavery, the master class provided the basic amenities for the enslaved. With slavery being abolished the enslaved had to leave slave quarters quite often with nothing to help her/him carve out new space to live. There were issues with health care and land reform. For the first time, enslaved persons had to provide their own housing and sanitation, land to cultivate and on which to raise a family, and space to bury their dead. Afro-Jamaicans began to complain that the issue of racial prejudice exploded as the masses of Afro-Jamaicans were denied their full humanity. In this context the Native Baptists saw their churches as spaces of resistance and hope against attempts to set the new peasantry aside in their quest to affirm their new-won freedom.

DEACON PAUL BOGLE AND REVIVALIST ALEXANDER BEDWARD

It may not surprise us then that with the reality of racial turmoil and a sense that Afro-Jamaicans were being excluded from opportunities for advancement on the island, another Afro-Baptist leader, Deacon Paul Bogle, of the Baptist church in Stony Gut in the Parish of St. Thomas in the East, led a revolution in an attempt to create space for hope to flourish for Afro-Jamaicans. The central issue that brought the leadership skills of Deacon Bogle to the fore focused on October 7, 1865, when a court session in Morant Bay was disrupted by protests organized by peasant farmers. The court ordered the leader of the protest, Charles Middleton, arrested, but when the police sought to enforce the order, Paul Bogle, pastor of a Native Baptist church, and others rescued him from the officers. The following Monday, October 9, Lewis Dick, another peasant farmer, was found guilty by the court for trespassing on the Middleton plantation. When fined by the court, he was instructed by the Native Baptist pastor Bogle to appeal the fine because the lands were owned not by the Jamaican government but by the British government. As may be expected, the court issued an order for the arrest of Bogle and twenty others for disrupting the will of the court. In an attempt to arrest Bogle, the police proceeded to his house only to discover that Bogle had anticipated their visit and had had the house surrounded by about three hundred members from his church. The members seized the police as Bogle made them swear "to forsake the White and Brown" and cast their lot with him.

> The seizing of the police created alarm but the oath created even more, prompting the Custos, the chief magistrate of the parish, to call out the volunteers and immediately request reinforcements from the governor in Kingston. The governor communicated the information to the general who readied the troops to sail to Morant Bay by Thursday, 12 October. On that Wednesday, 11 October, a meeting of the vestry was called to enact regular business, but word had already come that

troops had been seen coming by land to Morant Bay over the mountains. Alarmed at the turn of events, the rioters struck, killing the custos, Baron Von Ketelholdt; the Rector Rev. Victor Herschell; and other members of the vestry, Charles Price, Capt. Edward Hutchins, Lieutenants Halt and Reid; together with several other members of the volunteer force. Since the court was also in session, several justices were injured along with some police who came to their aid. Meanwhile, Bogle and his followers returned to Stoney Gut . . . and in the local chapel . . . he thanked God for the victory that had been given to them by the Divine hand.[37]

Native Baptist pastor Paul Bogle, his wife, and other members of the family were hanged. The soldiers launched a full-scale attack against the citizenry, killing many of them. In retaliation for the 29 white persons killed and 34 others seriously injured, the homes of all would-be protestors were burned and their crops destroyed. The official records state 1,000 homes burned, 354 people executed by court-martial, 50 shot without trial, 25 shot by the maroons, ten "killed otherwise," and 600 flogged.[38] The Bogle rebellion, another religious response to oppression in the parish of St. Thomas, hardly went beyond the Native Baptist church led by Bogle. Bogle used his congregation as a way of launching a full-scale attack against white rule in Jamaica. He appealed to his congregation to forsake the white and brown persons who wielded political power in Jamaica and for them to cast their lot with him. Pastor Bogle talked about seeing white and Black walls in Jamaica and that the Black wall was gaining supremacy. Bogle's successor, Alexander Bedward, who like George Liele represented the nonviolent pole of Baptist witness and leadership, would often quote Bogle's formulation of the white and Black wall in Jamaica. Bogle and his followers chose death rather than peacemaking with the inequalities and injustices sponsored by the government of Jamaica. Perhaps Bogle and his people did not die in vain. "The blood of Christians is seed" of the church.[39] We may call the roll and acknowledge Liele, Baker, George Lewis, George Gibb, Sam Sharpe, and now Paul Bogle as foundation stones in the building of an independent Jamaica.

The Man and His Legacy

One of the foundation stones in this beautiful building being erected in Jamaica that came to a climax in the celebration of Emancipation Day on August 1, 1838, and Independence Day (1962) is the best-known revivalist in Jamaica, Alexander Bedward, who stands in the tradition of George Liele and Moses Baker. The main key in Alexander Bedward's commitment to the revival of Jamaica and perhaps why he is looked to as the foremost evangelist in Jamaican tradition and history was his practice of healing–salvation as healing through baptisms. He also saw himself in the tradition of Paul Bogle and taught that Afro-Jamaicans should overthrow white rule in Jamaica. On one occasion he called on Jamaicans to remember the "Morant War," which was led by Native Baptist pastor Paul Bogle. Born in 1859, Bedward grew up in Jamaica with a deepened sense of the revivalist spirit and embodied a vision of a renewed Jamaica. In a visit to Colon, Panama, he received a vision to return to Jamaica and save the souls of Afro-Jamaicans. In the tradition of the Myalists, the spirit instructed him to fast three times per week, during which the gift of healing would be bestowed on him. This coupling of the gift of the spirit with healing is of first importance as healing emerged as one of the antidotes to sin as sorcery. Unlike white iterations of religion, the healing administered by Bedward focused on the body as the point of departure for addressing the need for liberation. Healing was for weary bodies, as the body became the site of healing. There were yards scattered throughout Jamaica that were called "Balm Yards" in response to Jeremiah's query, "Is there no balm in Gilead? Is there no physician there?" (Jeremiah 8:22). These were usually run by revivalist preachers, who would answer, "There is a balm in Gilead, to heal the sin sick soul." Jamaicans who needed healing for weary souls and bodies made their way to balm yards.

With the gift of the revivalist spirit, Bedward began his ministry in Jamaica in 1895, in Kingston, Jamaica. Albert Raboteau captures the essential theology and practices of the revivalist:

> In two of these groups, Revival and Pocomania, services culminate in African-style possession. However, it is the Old Testament prophets, the four evangelists of the New Testament, the apostles and the archangels, and the Holy Ghost who take possession of the members, not

the gods of Africa. Revivalists believe that God the Father created the world and dwells in the "highest heavens." He never descends to visit the services or to possess believers. Jesus, according to the members of Revival, does visit their services and a "love feast" is held in his memory, but he like the father, does not possess.

Deceased members, however, may return to possess their relations among the faithful.[40]

Raboteau is very helpful in allowing us to view a distinction between religion in Jamaica pre-Liele and post-Liele. Pre-Liele both the form and the content were African. Post-Liele the form remains African but the content is shaped by the Bible, especially Old Testament prophets and the gospels of the New Testament. Notions of the triune nature of God also seem to come through. It is still the custom in Jamaican religious traditions that the spirit, not the Father nor the Son, visits worship.

One of the marks of the ministry of Bedward was his emphasis on the use of water from the Mona River in Kingston as a balm for healing weary souls and bodies. George Liele was often called the baptizer, and his baptism was more in the tradition of John the Baptist, for repentance. In the case of Bedward, while he would not exclude repentance, the focus was on healing. Even the river where he would perform baptisms was referred to as a healing stream. Salvation was offered as healing. To be saved was to be healed, and he called on his nation, Jamaica, to come to the river for healing. Bedward attracted the most oppressed among the poor, the group at the bottom of the social ladder from which Rastafari would emerge in the 1930s. In a context in which the government did not provide health care for its citizens, the Revivalists, through baths, and in Bedward's case baptisms, provided healing for weary, forlorn, and sick bodies.

Ennis Barrington Edmonds in his important text *Rastafari* ties together for us the link that holds together the bond among Daddy Sharpe, Paul Bogle, Alexander Bedward, and George Liele. According to Edmonds, Daddy Sharpe, Paul Bogle, and Alexander Bedward forged a connection between religion and resistance. Edmonds states:

The Man and His Legacy

The 1831 rebellion, aimed at destroying the plantation owners and securing freedom for the slaves, was inspired and orchestrated by Sam Sharpe, who was a "daddy," or priest, in the slave religion and at the same time a deacon in the Baptist Church. In addition, Paul Bogle, another deacon in the Baptist Church, incited and led the Morant Bay Rebellion in 1865. The nexus between religion and resistance continued with Alexander Bedward. Explicit Ethiopianism in Jamaica had its beginnings in the eighteenth century with George Liele.... Liele's sermons, which highlighted the African and Ethiopian elements in the Bible, usually began with the call, "Arise ye sons of Ethiopia." ... The significance of George Liele and the native Baptist movement is they blended Afrocentricity, biblical messianism, and apocalypticism with Ethiopianism to create a liberative vision among Jamaicans of African descent.[41]

Edmonds has not provided any sources to substantiate his claim that Daddy Sharpe aimed at destroying plantation owners in his attempt to secure freedom for Afro-Jamaicans. Philip Curtin and others point out that what was at stake was Daddy Sharpe's attempt to use Afro-Jamaicans as a passive nonviolent group to make demands for wages and days off over the Christmas holiday in 1831. It so happened that even with the best plans for a nonviolent revolt, the master class responded violently, and Sharpe and his people were caught up in a violent response.

LEILE AND RASTAFARI

On the other hand, Edmonds is correct in his claim that Liele would often begin with the salutation, "Arise you Sons of Ethiopia." There was definitely an Ethiopian hermeneutic that informed the expectations of Liele and his community, as Liele would cite Psalm 68:31, "Let bronze be brought from Egypt; let Ethiopia hasten to stretch out her hands to God." Liele and his community would often refer to each other as Ethiopians. My sense is that the expression, "Arise you Sons of Ethiopia" was an expression of greeting rather than a phrase imbued with theological and sermonic content.

Edmonds reminds us that Rastafari, which is indigenous to Jamaica, tapped into Liele's emphasis on Ethiopia and developed a faith on

Jamaican soil that remembered George Liele and Marcus Garvey. Rastafari was born out of the pain of oppression and suffering. This pain and suffering fired the hope for liberation. One leader of the faith was Sam Brown, who makes a connection between the Rastafari faith and Marcus Garvey. Brown points out that Garvey left the political scene in Jamaica in the 1930s. Afro-Jamaicans were purposeless and Rastafari emerged to provide focus and direction for the masses of Jamaicans. The coronation of Haile Selassie in 1930 caused a great stir among the populace, and many began to study their Bibles more closely. They recalled how Garvey the prophet said, "Look to Africa where a Black King shall arise—this will be the day of your deliverance."[42] The relationship with Garvey allowed many of Garvey's ideas to be included in the development of the movement. By 1933 Rastafari began to teach that Ras Tafari (the baptismal name of Haile Selassie) was God, the "King of Kings," and the "Root of David," using the biblical texts Revelation 5:1–5; 19:16 to support their claim.

The twin concepts of the divinity of Haile Selassie and the redemption of Black people have distinguished the Rastafari faith from other movements that seek to create Black awareness and Black consciousness. Rastas began to teach that Africa is in Jamaica. This became a call for the Africanization of Jamaica. Jamaicans did not have to migrate to Africa; there was an inward migration in similar fashion to Christians announcing that the Kingdom of God is within. It is in this sense that Rastafari went beyond Garvey as Garvey taught the physical return to Africa. Their leader Haile Selassie, though absent (Rastas are not comfortable in talking about the absence of their leader Haile Selassie), is present among them as community. It is in the community of I's, as each member affirms his or her identity as an I, that the new life-giving community is forged.[43]

As Afro-Jamaicans sought to make connections between their faith and resistance, they employed various means. For Liele and his associates they called upon their faith, a confidence that Jesus was Lord and Master, and this meant in the existential situation whether in Georgia or in Jamaica, it was Christ as Lord and Master who had the decisive word and gave him confidence that salvation was through faith and not through works. Confession of sin was a step on the way to conversion, and it was these two strands of faith that were central and pivotal. In Georgia, through his pastor Matthew Moore he learned and absorbed the teaching of George Whitfield and embraced the priority of a life powered by the spirit of God. In Jamaica he was able to blend his understanding of spirit, baptism, and healing with indigenous expressions of faith and thereby gave Afro-Jamaicans confidence in their own reading of the Bible and an opportunity to learn and understand that the God of the Bible was the God of their ancestors.

An examination of the leaders in the Jamaican culture who agitated and fought for emancipation and liberation betray the hand of George Liele. This is the case with Daddy Sharpe, whose uprising was a precursor to emancipation in the British colonies throughout the Caribbean, and then Baptist deacon Paul Bogle, who protested and led an uprising against the injustice in post-emancipation Jamaica as emancipation had left Jamaicans homeless, landless, and in persistent poverty. Alexander Bedward, along with Revival and Rastafari spiritualities, highlighted the priority of the healing of body and soul as a way to keep the "balm in Gilead." In all these expressions of faith and life, we can see the hidden hand of George Liele and his associates Moses Baker, George Gibb, and George Lewis.

NOTES

1. Mary Turner, *Slaves and Missionaries: The Disintegration of Jamaican Slave Society, 1787–1834* (Urbana: University of Illinois Press, 1982), 52.

2. Turner, *Slaves and Missionaries*, 53.

3. Dianne Marie Burrows Stewart, "The Evolution of African-Derived Religions in Jamaica: Toward a Caribbean Theology of Collective Memory" (PhD diss. Union Theological Seminary, 1997), 40.

4. M. G. Lewis, *Journal of a West India Proprietor* (Boston: Houghton-Mifflin Company, 1834), 126.

5. George Eaton Simpson, *Black Religion in the New World* (New York: Columbia University Press, 1978), 29.

6. Simpson, *Black Religion in the New World*, 21–22.

7. W. E. B. Du Bois, *The Negro Church* (Atlanta, GA: Atlanta University Press, 1903), 5.

8. Charles O. Walker, "Georgia's Religion in the Colonial Era, 1733–1790," *Viewpoints: Georgia Baptist Historical Society* 5 (1976): 17–44, 29, 31, 32.

9. Walker, "Georgia's Religion in the Colonial Era, 1733–1790," 32.

10. David T. Shannon, Julia Frazier White, and Deborah Van Broekhoven, eds., *George Liele's Life and Legacy* (Macon, GA: Mercer University Press, 2012), 71.

11. Shannon et al., *George Liele's Life and Legacy*, 72.
12. Shannon et al., *George Liele's Life and Legacy*, 73.
13. Shannon et al., *George Liele's Life and Legacy*, 75–76.
14. Shannon et al., *George Liele's Life and Legacy*, 76.
15. Shannon et al., *George Liele's Life and Legacy*, 78.
16. Philip S. Foner, ed., *The Life and Writings of Frederick Douglass: The Pre–Civil War Decade, 1850 to 1860* (New York: International Publishers, 1975), 197.
17. Carolyn Osiek, *Abingdon New Testament Commentaries: Philippians & Philemon* (Nashville: Abingdon Press, 2000), 127.
18. Horace O. Russell, "Prologue," in *George Liele's Life and Legacy*, 8.
19. Vernitia Shannon, "The Last Will and Testament of George Liele," in *George Liele's Life and Legacy*, 148.
20. Philip Sherlock and Hazel Bennett, *The Story of the Jamaican People* (Kingston, Jamaica: Ian Randle Publishers Limited, 1998), 143.
21. Winston Arthur Lawson, *Religion and Race: African and European Roots in Conflict—A Jamaican Testament* (New York: Peter Lang, 1996), 153.
22. Philip D. Curtin, *Two Jamaicas: The Role of Ideas in a Tropical Colony, 1830–1865* (New York: Atheneum Press, 1970), 34.
23. Turner, *Slaves and Missionaries*, 154–55.
24. Sherlock and Bennett, *The Story of the Jamaican People*, 214.
25. Sherlock and Bennett, *The Story of the Jamaican People*, 214.
26. Lawson, *Religion and Race*, 167–68.
27. Sherlock and Bennett, *The Story of the Jamaican People*, 216.
28. John Howard Hinton, *Memoir of William Knibb* (London: Houlston and Stoneman, 1847), 118.
29. Trevor Munroe and Don Robotham, *Struggles of the Jamaican People* (Kingston, Jamaica: E. P. Printery, 1977), 16.
30. Sherlock and Bennett, *The Story of the Jamaica People*, 226–27.
31. James M. Phillippo, *Jamaica: Its Past and Present State* (London: John Snow, 1843; reprinted, Westport, CT: Negro University Press, 1970), 169.
32. Sherlock and Bennett, *The Story of the Jamaican People*, 230–31.
33. Curtin, *Two Jamaicas*, 169–70.
34. Leonard E. Barrett, *Soul-Force* (Garden City, NY: Anchor Press/Doubleday, 1974), 115.
35. Richard D. E. Burton, *Afro-Creole: Power, Opposition and Play in the Caribbean* (Ithaca, NY: Cornell University Press, 1997), 37.
36. William Fitzer Burchell, *Memoir of Thomas Burchell: Twenty-Two Years a Missionary in Jamaica* (London: Benjamin L. Green, Paternoster Row, 1849), 51–52.
37. Sherlock and Bennett, *The Story of the Jamaican People*, 213.
38. Sherlock and Bennett, *The Story of the Jamaican People*, 260.
39. Hans von Campenhausen, *The Fathers of the Latin Church* (Stanford, CA: Stanford University Press, 1964), 13.
40. Albert J. Raboteau, *Slave Religion: The "Invisible Institution" in the Antebellum South* (New York: Oxford University Press, 1978), 28.

41. Ennis Barrington Edmonds, *Rastafari: From Outcasts to Culture Bearers* (New York: Oxford University Press, 2003), 33, 35.
42. Barrett, *Soul-Force*, 158.
43. For a complete guide to the history, theology, and culture of Rastafari, see Noel Leo Erskine, *From Garvey to Marley: Rastafari Theology* (Gainesville: University Press of Florida, 2007).

Bibliography

Ballew, Christopher Brent. *The Impact of African-American Antecedents on the Baptist Foreign Missionary Movement, 1782–1825*. Lewiston, NY: Edwin Mellen Press, 2004.
"Baptist Missionary Society General Committee Minutes, 1819–1823. Committee Meeting." Oxford University: Regents Park College, December 18, 1823. Pp. 36–37. Angus Archives.
"Baptist Missionary Society General Committee Minutes, 1827–1830. Quarterly Committee Meeting." Oxford University: Regents Park College, July 30, 1828. P. 96. Angus Archives.
"Baptist Missionary Society General Committee Minutes, 1827–1830. Committee Meeting." Oxford University: Regents Park College, October 13, 1828. P. 13. Angus Archives.
"Baptist Missionary Society of England Committee Minutes, October 1819–July 1823. Minutes for May 21, 1822," May 21, 1822. 203–204.
Barrett, Leonard E. *Soul-Force*. Garden City, NY: Anchor Press/Doubleday, 1974.
Beckles, Hilary. *Caribbean Slave Society and Economy: A Student Reader*. Edited by Hilary Beckles and Verene Shepherd. New York: The New Press, 1991.
Brooks, Walter H. "The Priority of the Silver Bluff Church and Its Promoters." *Journal of Negro History* 7, no. 2 (April 1922): 172–96. https://doi.org/10.2307/2713524.
———. *The Silver Bluff Church: A History of Negro Baptist Churches in America*. Washington, DC: Press of R. L. Pendleton, 1910.
Burchell, William Fitzer. *Memoir of Thomas Burchell: Twenty-Two Years a Missionary in Jamaica*. London: B. L. Green, Paternoster Row, 1849.
Burton, Richard D. E. *Afro-Creole: Power, Opposition, and Play in the Caribbean*. First edition. Ithaca, NY: Cornell University Press, 1997.
Canzoneri, Antonia. "The History of Bethel Baptist Church, Nassau." Department of Archives, 1994. Bethel Baptist Church.
Chevannes, Barry, ed. *Rastafari and Other African-Caribbean Worldviews*. London: MacMillan Press Ltd., 1995.
Clark, John, W. Dendy, and J. M. Phillippo. *The Voice of Jubilee: A Narrative of the Baptist Mission, Jamaica, from Its Commencement; With Biographical Notices of Its Fathers and Founders*. London: Paternoster Row, 1865.
Clark, John. *Memorials of Baptist Missionaries in Jamaica, Including a Sketch of the Labours of Early Religious Instructors in Jamaica*. London: Yates and Alexander, 1869.

Bibliography

"Colonial Office Papers on Microfilm." Public Archives, 1826. Co 23/81 Folio 316 ff. 1826.

Conference, Association of Caribbean Historians. *A Selection of Papers Presented at the Twelfth Conference of the Association of Caribbean Historians (1980)*, 1989.

Cox, Francis A. *History of the Baptist Missionary Society from 1792–1842, Volume 2*. London: T. Ward, 1842.

Curtin, Philip D. *Two Jamaicas: The Role of Ideas in a Tropical Colony, 1830–1865*. New York: Atheneum, 1970.

Davis, John W. "George Liele and Andrew Bryan, Pioneer Negro Baptist Preachers." *Journal of Negro History* 3, no. 2 (April 1918): 119–27. https://doi.org/10.2307/2713485.

Dick, Devon. *The Cross and the Machete: Native Baptists of Jamaica—Identity, Ministry and Legacy*. Kingston, Jamaica; Miami: Ian Randle Publishers, Jamaica, 2009.

Douglass, Frederick. *The Life and Writings of Frederick Douglass, Vol. 2: The Pre–Civil War Decade*. Edited by Philip S. Foner. New York: International Publishers, 1975.

Drake, St. Clair. *Redemption of Africa and Black Religion*. Chicago: Third World Press, 1970.

Du Bois, W. E. B. *The Negro Church*. Edited by Alton B. Pollard III. Atlanta, GA: Atlanta University Press, 1903.

Duggan, W. M. *The First Annual Report of the Jamaica Native Baptist Missionary Society*. Oxford University, 1836.

Edmonds, Ennis Barrington. *Rastafari: From Outcasts to Culture Bearers*. Oxford; New York: Oxford University Press, 2003.

Erskine, Noel Leo. *Plantation Church: How African American Religion Was Born in Caribbean Slavery*. New York: Oxford University Press, 2014.

———. *From Garvey to Marley: Rastafari Theology*. Paperback edition. Gainesville: University Press of Florida, 2007.

Gardner, Robert G. "Primary Sources in the Study of Eighteenth-Century Georgia Baptist History." *Viewpoints: Georgia Historical Society*, no. 7 (1980): 59–119, 103.

Gardner, William James. *The History of Jamaica: From Its Discovery by Christopher Columbus to the Year 1872*. London: T. Fisher Unwin, 1909. First published 1873.

Gates, John Parmer. "George Liele: A Pioneer Negro Preacher." *The Chronicle: A Baptist Historical Quarterly* 6, no. 3 (July 1943): 118–29.

Gilroy, Paul. *There Ain't No Black in the Union Jack: The Cultural Politics of Race and Nation*. Chicago: University of Chicago Press, 1987.

Hamid, Idris, ed. *Troubling of the Waters. A Collection of Papers and Responses Presented at Two Conferences on Creative Theological Reflection Held in Jamaica*. Trinidad, WI: Rahaman Printery, 1973.

Hinton, John Howard. *Memoir of William Knibb, Missionary in Jamaica*. London: Houlston and Stoneman, 1847.

Holifield, E. Brooks. *Theology in America: Christian Thought from the Age of the Puritans to the Civil War*. New Haven, CT: Yale University Press, 2003.

Hopkins, Dwight N., and Edward P. Antonio. *The Cambridge Companion to Black Theology*. New York: Cambridge University Press, 2012.

Jasanoff, Maya. *Liberty's Exiles: American Loyalists in the Revolutionary World*. New York: Alfred A. Knopf, 2011.
Klein, Herbert S. *Slavery in the Americas: A Comparative Study of Virigina and Cuba*. Chicago: Quadrangle Books, 1971.
Lawlor, Jim. "Shadrach Kerr: Priest and Missionary." *American Baptist Quarterly* 26, no. 4 (2007): 388–402.
Lawson, Winston Arthur. *Religion and Race: African and European Roots in Conflict—A Jamaican Testament*. New York: Peter Lang, 1996.
Lewis, Matthew. *Journal of a West India Proprietor: Kept during a Residence in the Island of Jamaica*. Edited by Judith Terry. Boston and New York: Houghton Mifflin Company, 1834.
Montgomery, William E. *Under Their Own Vine and Fig Tree: The African-American Church in the South, 1865–1900*. Baton Rouge: Louisiana State University Press, 1993.
Munroe, Trevor, and Don Robotham. *Struggles of the Jamaican People*. Kingston, Jamaica: E. P. Printery, 1977.
Osiek, Carolyn. *Abingdon New Testament Commentaries: Philippians & Philemon*. Nashville, TN: Abingdon Press, 2000.
Payne, Ernest A. "Baptist Work in Jamaica before the Arrival of the Missionaries." *Baptist Quarterly* 7, no. 1 (January 1, 1934): 20–26. https://doi.org/10.1080/0005 576X.1934.11750306.
Phillippo, James Mursell. *Jamaica: Its Past and Present State*. London: John Snow, 1843; reprinted, Westport, CT: Negro University Press, 1970.
Pugh, Alfred Lane. "The Great Awakening and Baptist Beginnings in Colonial Georgia, the Bahama Islands, and Jamaica (1739–1833)." *American Baptist Quarterly* 26, no. 4 (2007): 357–73.
Raboteau, Albert J. *Slave Religion: The "Invisible Institution" in the Antebellum South*. First edition. Oxford; New York: Oxford University Press, 1978.
Rippon, John D. *Baptist Annual Register, for 1790, 1791, 1792, and Part of 1793, Including Sketches of the State of Religion among Different Denominations of Good Men at Home and Abroad*. Volume 1. London, 1790.
Russell, Horace O. *The Missionary Outreach of the West Indian Church: Jamaican Baptist Missions to West Africa in the Nineteenth Century*. New York: Peter Lang Inc., International Academic Publishers, 2000.
———. *Foundations and Anticipations: The Jamaica Baptist Story, 1783–1892*. Columbus, GA: Brentwood Christian Press, 1993.
Sernett, Milton C., ed. *Afro-American Religious History: A Documentary Witness*. Durham: Duke University Press, 1985.
Shannon, David T., Julia Frazier White, and Deborah Van Broekhoven, eds. *George Liele's Life and Legacy: An Unsung Hero (The James N. Griffith Endowed Series in Baptist Studies)*. First edition. Macon, GA: Mercer University Press, 2012.
Sherlock, Philip Manderson Sir, and Hazel Bennett. *The Story of the Jamaican People*. First Paperback edition. Kingston, Jamaica: Ian Randle Publishers, 1998.

Sibley, Inez Knibb. *The Baptists of Jamaica*. Kingston, Jamaica: Jamaica Baptist Union, 1965.
Simpson, George Eaton. *Black Religion in the New World*. New York: Columbia University Press, 1978.
Stewart, Dianne M. "The Evolution of African-Derived Religions in Jamaica: Toward a Caribbean Theology of Collective Memory (PhD Dissertation)." Union Theological Seminary, 1997.
———. *Three Eyes for the Journey: African Dimensions of the Jamaican Religious Experience*. Oxford; New York: Oxford University Press, 2005.
Stewart, Robert J. *Religion and Society in Post-Emancipation Jamaica*. First edition. Knoxville: University of Tennessee Press, 1992.
Stroger, Howard. "Coromantine Obeah and Myalism, 1700–1833: African Survivals in Jamaica and Barbados (Unpublished Undergraduate Honors Thesis)." Rutgers University, 1966.
Stuckey, Sterling. *Slave Culture: Nationalist Theory and the Foundations of Black America*. Second edition. Oxford; New York: Oxford University Press, 1987.
Thomas, Edgar Garfield. *The First African Baptist Church of North America*. Savannah, GA: E. G. Thomas, 1925.
Turner, Mary. *Slaves and Missionaries: The Disintegration of Jamaican Slave Society, 1787–1834*. Urbana: University of Illinois Press, 1982.
Von Campenhausen, Hans. *The Fathers of the Latin Church*. Stanford, CA: Stanford University Press, 1964.
Walker, Charles O. "Georgia's Religion in the Colonial Era, 1733–1790." *Viewpoints: Georgia Baptist Historical Society* 5 (1976): 17–44.
Washington, James Melvin. *Frustrated Fellowship: The Black Baptist Quest for Social Power*. Macon, GA: Mercer University Press, 1990.
———. "The Origins of Black Evangelicalism and the Ethical Function of Evangelical Cosmology." *Union Seminary Quarterly Review* 32, no. 2 (1977): 104–16.
Webber, Thomas L. *Deep Like the Rivers: Education in the Slave Quarter Community, 1831–1865*. New York: W. W. Norton and Company, 1981.
Whelchel, L. H. Jr. *The History and Heritage of African American Churches: A Way Out of No Way*. St. Paul, MN: Paragon House, 2011.
Wilmore, Gayraud S. *Black Religion and Black Radicalism*. First edition. Garden City, NY: Doubleday, 1972.
Woodson, Carter G. *The History of the Negro Church*. Washington, DC: Associated Publishers, 1921. https://www.biblio.com/book/history-negro-church-carter-g-woodson/d/1432634343.

INDEX

abolition, 116, 118, 121, 128, 164
Adam (Obeah-man), 148, 150
Africa: beliefs, 17, 151, 174–77; Christianity with traditional practices of, 21, 22, 42, 49, 51, 56, 66, 74, 114, 145, 149; cosmology, 88, 92; Jesus-Africa question, 23
African Americans: Ethiopians, 75; migrating to Jamaica, 21, 31; with traditional practices of Africa, 49, 56. *See also* slavery
African Church, 17, 51, 79–82, 151
African Methodist Church, 50–51
African Methodist Episcopal Church, 52
Afro-Baptist faith, 53, 55, 76, 94, 97, 116, 148; with African Church and Christian Church, 82; in Bahamas, 13; indigenization, native Baptist movement and, 70–72; John 3:5–7 and, 67; Myal religion and, 84–88, 90, 112; persecution and, 98; popularity of, 110–11; as praxis, 152–56; slavery and, 106; slaves and, 68, 74, 82, 85; sustaining, 119–30
Afro-Baptist sacred cosmos, 52
Afro-Baptist work, 91, 92, 130–34
Afrocentricity, 181
Afro-Creole (Burton), 66–67
Allen, Richard, 45
Amos. *See* Williams, Amos
Anabaptist Church, 26, 86, 141, 152, 163. *See also* "The Covenant of the Anabaptist Church, begun in America, December 1777 and in Jamaica, December 1783"
Anney (slave), 140
Anti-slavery Society, 164
apocalypticism, 181
apprenticeship system of slavery, 172–73
arrests: of Baker, 30–31, 93; of Lewis, George, 83; of Liele, George, 103
Asbury, Francis, 60
Augusta Institute, 12, 48. *See also* Morehouse College

Index

Bahama Islands, 2, 9, 33, 48, 65, 68; Baker and, 92, 102n37; Williams and, 12–14

Baker, Moses, 57–59, 66, 69, 76, 78–79, 85, 153; Afro-Baptists Faith and, 125–27, 130; arrest of, 30–31, 93; Bahama Islands and, 92, 102n37; Baptist Missionary Society of Gt. Britain and, 91–92, 125; with "The Covenant of the Anabaptist Church," 65; Crooked Spring Church and, 92–94, 122, 125, 130–31, 168–70, 176; *The Evangelical Magazine* and, 93–94, 102n37; Flamstead–Montego Bay and, 130–31; Great Revival and, 175; legacy, 125, 178, 183; with license for preachers, 118, 155; as Native Baptist, 21–22; native Baptist movement and, 91–100; Obeah worship and, 81; in prison, 98, 116; as protégé of Liele, George, 33, 34, 55, 56, 65, 73, 91–100, 100n2, 125, 140, 145, 151; sedition accusations against, 93, 116, 123, 126; on slavery, 141; spirit and, 110, 174; in trances, 113; transnational faith and, 112–13

Ballew, Christopher Brent, 24, 94

"Balm Yards," 179

baptisms: Anabaptist Church and, 26, 86; born again with, 86, 89–90; as charm against sorcery, 150; of children, 86; with dreams and Holy Spirit, 85–86, 110; for healing, 179, 180, 183; of Jesus Christ, 22, 69, 111, 164; by Liele, George, 62, 91, 125, 140, 150, 164, 180; of Liele, George, 40, 42, 44; Myal religion and, 86, 89–90, 98, 147; to neutralize Black Obeah, 147, 150; of Onesimus, 160; slaves and, 119, 150; with spirit seizure, 22

Baptist Annual Register, 35n8

Baptist Church: with African traditional practices, 21; as chosen people, 39; orthodoxy of, 70

Baptist Missionary Society of Gt. Britain, 91–92, 125

Baptist Missionary Society of London, 30, 78, 84, 97, 134–35, 138

The Baptists of Jamaica (Knibb Sibley), 91, 125, 143n26

Baptist War (1831), 34–35, 87, 106, 122, 129–30, 163–72, 181

Barrett, Leonard, 174–75

Bedon, Selina. *See* Williams, Selina Bedon

Bedward, Alexander, 177–81, 183

Bennett, Hazel, 54–57

Bessie (house slave), 148, 151

Bethel Baptist Church, Bahama Islands, 48

Betsy (slave), 140, 162–63

the Bible: Afro-Jamaicans with, 183; authority of, 16, 49, 153, 166; 1 Corinthians 15, 54; with coronation of Haile Selassie, 182; "The Covenant of the Anabaptist Church" and, 112; Deuteronomy 6:4–9, 129; Ephesians, 128, 160, 161; Galatians, 35, 158; John, 67, 154, 157; Joshua 6:21, 51; literacy and, 12, 13, 34, 128; Luke 17:3–4, 149; Matthew, 9, 148; New Testament, 154, 158, 160, 179–80; Old Testament, 179–80; 1 Peter, 39, 128; Psalm 68:31, 48, 108, 181; Revelation 5:1–5; 19:16, 182; Romans 10:1, 23, 61, 76, 108, 129, 154; with singing of hymns, 25, 43, 54, 58, 93, 156; slaves and, 3–4, 9, 34, 50–51, 54–58, 110, 159; as storybook, 74; 1 Thessalonians 3:13, 128; Timothy, 26, 128, 161; Titus, 27, 128, 161
biblical messianism, 181
Big Buckhead Baptist Church, 16, 40, 43–44, 47, 107, 153–55
Bishop, Josiah, 47
Black churches, 8, 13, 31, 99, 104, 145; Du Bois on, 17, 151; independent, 6–7, 28, 40–49
Black consciousness, 182
Black liberation, 154
Black liberation theology, 157–58

Black life, 88–89, 120, 121
Black Obeah, 147, 150, 151
Black-talk, 120
Bleby, Henry, 165
Blight, Gilbert, 33
blood, 26, 28, 89, 163, 171, 178
bodies, healing of, 179, 180, 183
Bogle, Paul, 177–81, 183
born again, 9, 53, 67, 85–86, 89–90
Botsford, Edmund, 40
British Baptist Missionary Society, 2, 18, 32–33, 58, 76–77, 102n37
Brooks, Walter H., 6–7, 8, 10–11, 13
Brother Amos. *See* Williams, Amos
Brown, Sam, 182
Bryan, Andrew, 1, 8; conversion of, 36n15; as protégé of Liele, George, 12, 14, 33, 48, 53, 67; as slave, 9, 10, 47
Bryan, Hagar (wife), 9, 53, 67
Bryan, Jonathan, 48
Bryan, Sampson (brother), 10
Buckhead Creek Church. *See* Big Buckhead Baptist Church
Bull, Stephen, 8
Burchell, Thomas, 76, 79, 94, 96, 109, 124, 138–39; Crooked Spring Church and, 170, 176; slavery and, 168–69, 171
Burchell Baptist Church, 87
Burls (Mr.), 32, 140
Burma, 1

Index

Burton, Richard, 66–67, 175

Calabar College, Jamaica, 12, 34
Calvinism, 16, 51–52, 61, 151, 153
Campbell, Archibald, 18, 24, 162
Campbell, Daniel (Rev.), 99
Canada, 1–2, 9, 14, 31, 33, 65, 104
Canzoneri, Antonina, 13
Carey, William, 1
Carter's Lane Baptist Church, London, 33, 37n51, 133
certificate of freedom, 18
Charleston, South Carolina, 8–9, 49, 51–52, 153
Charleston Association, 40
children: in Anabaptist Church, 26, 86, 152; in apprenticeship system of slavery, 172; baptism of, 86; of missionaries, 77; in schools, 11, 87, 130; as slaves, 61, 62, 130, 140–41, 148, 162–63, 172; slaves as God's, 9, 18, 19, 51, 53, 57, 129, 146, 159; of Williams, Amos, 13
Christianity: with African traditions, 21, 22, 42, 49, 51, 56, 66, 74, 114, 145, 149; cosmology, 106–7; Creo-Christianity, 67; Great Revival as rejection of, 174–77; planters and, 59–60; slavery and, 106–7, 109, 120, 123–24, 128–29, 141; slaves and, 19–22, 25–27, 30–31, 41, 59–60, 91, 128–29; spread of, 104; as white Obeah, 148, 149

"Christianity in the World of George Liele" (Van Broekhoven), 106
churches: African Church, 17, 51, 79–82, 151; African Methodist Church, 50–51; African Methodist Episcopal Church, 52; Baptist Church, 21, 39, 70; Black, 6–7, 8, 13, 17, 28, 31, 40–49, 99, 104, 145, 151; Methodist Church, 25, 29, 30, 50–51, 117; Moravian, 33; "Mothers," 58, 73; Native Baptist Church, 21–22, 34–35, 65, 73, 77–78, 111–12, 163–74, 177–78; Negro Baptist, 6–8; schools and, 11–12, 28–29, 34, 54, 56, 87, 94–95, 127, 132, 139, 156–58. *See also* Anabaptist Church; *specific churches*
Church of England, 59, 67, 84, 114, 150–51
Clark, John (Rev.), 15–16, 31–32, 62, 71–72, 139; on African cosmology, 92; on funeral of Liele, George, 138; on Lewis, George, 82–83, 97; on licenses for preachers, 136; on sin as sorcery, 93; on slavery in Jamaica, 81
class leader, 85, 87; as spiritual guides, 21, 73; ticket system and, 71, 72–75, 76, 89, 151
class meeting, 71, 78, 84–86

Coke, Thomas, 30, 60
Compere, Lee, 126, 131, 134, 138–39
concubinage, 74, 92
confession: of faith, 153; of sin, 16, 75, 182
Consolidated Slave Law, 131
Cook, Joseph, 8
Cooke, Stephen, 25
1 Corinthians 15, 54
cosmology: African, 88, 92; Christian, 106–7; Myal, 90
cotton trees, 69–70, 83, 88, 97, 111
Coultart, James, 78–79, 100, 132–35, 139
Coultart, Mary Ann (wife), 132, 134, 135
"The Covenant of the Anabaptist Church, begun in America, December 1777 and in Jamaica, December 1783" (Liele, G.): articles of, 2, 25–27, 74, 128, 148–49, 160–61; on baptism, 86, 150; the Bible and, 112; role of, 28, 65; on slaves and obedience, 128–29, 160–61
Cox, F. A. (Rev.), 23–24, 74–75, 82, 102n37, 137, 176
Creo-Christianity, 67
creoles, 66, 68, 73, 80, 85, 95
Cromwell, Oliver, 24
Crooked Spring Church, 92–94, 122, 125, 130–31, 168–70, 176

The Cross and the Machete (Dick, D.), 65–66, 75–76
Cuba, 68, 115
Cudjoe (slave), 162–63
Curtin, Phillip, 21–22, 108–11, 113–14, 167, 173–74, 181

"Daddys," 57, 58, 71, 73, 75. See also Sharpe, Sam "Daddy"
Daddy Sharpe. See Sharpe, Sam "Daddy"
dancing: Afro-Jamaican culture and, 127, 154, 174; Myal, 67, 83–84, 89–90, 100, 174–75; spirit possession and, 21, 57, 66
Davis, John (Rev.), 77
Davis, John W., 9, 103–4
Dead River Church, South Carolina, 13
death row, 28, 61
death sentence, 171
Dehaney (Mr.), 171
Dendy, Walter, 139
Deuteronomy 6:4–9, 129
Dexter, Benjamin, 139
Dick, Devon (Rev.), 65–66, 75–78, 111
Dick, Lewis, 177
double consciousness, 119–20
"double-speak," 120
Douglass, Frederick, 43, 159
Dove (Mr.), 171
dreams, 69, 83, 85–86, 110–11
drumming, 21, 70, 108

Du Bois, W. E. B., 17, 79–82, 92, 151–52
Duff, John (Rev.), 77
Duggan, William (Rev.), 77–78
Dunmore (Earl), 7
Dyer, John, 32, 138, 140

East Queen Street Baptist Church, 95–96, 132, 134, 138–39
East Queen Street School, 31, 136
Edmonds, Ennis Barrington, 180–81
education: literacy, 12–14, 18, 34, 51, 54, 128, 156; salvation and, 156–57. *See also* schools
Edwards, Bryan, 24, 80, 82–83
Edwards, Jonathan, 44, 65
Egypt, 20, 48, 51, 57, 108–9, 154, 181
emancipation: Great Revival and, 174–77; in Jamaica, 30, 35, 70–71, 91, 165–66, 172–77; Revolutionary War and, 7, 8
Emancipation Day (1838), 179
England, 29, 30, 135–36, 164; Carter's Lane Baptist Church, 33, 37n51, 133; Church of England, 59, 67, 84, 114, 150–51; Liele, George, in, 31–35
enslaved people. *See* slaves
Ephesians, 128, 160, 161
Erskine, Leo, 12
Eternity of Hell Torments (Whitfield), 45

Ethiopian Baptist Church, 17–19, 23, 33, 48–49, 61, 75
Ethiopians, 75, 152, 181, 182
Europe, 22, 109, 174
European sorcery, 84, 86–90, 105–6, 175
evangelical movement, 57, 65, 66
The Evangelical Magazine, 93–94, 102n37
Evans, Thomas, 33
evil spirits, 74, 86

faith, 78–85, 111–14, 153. *See also* Afro-Baptist faith
farmers, protests, 177–78
feet washing, 26, 152–54, 167
financial incentives, for baptizing slaves, 150
First African Baptist Church, Savannah, 9, 10, 17, 48
First African Baptist Church of Augusta (Silver Bluff Church), Georgia, 11–12, 48. *See also* Springfield Baptist Church, Georgia
"The First Annual Report of Jamaica Native Baptist Missionary Society" (Duggan), 77, 78
Flamstead–Montego Bay, 130–31, 176
folk beliefs, 57, 66
fornication, 27, 74
Foundations and Anticipations (Russell), 113

Index

Francis, Henry, 10
freedom: Black liberation, 154; Black liberation theology, 157–58; for indentured servants, 18; Native Baptist Church with slavery and, 163–74; search for, 49–54; for slaves, 7, 8, 13, 15, 32, 35, 49–54, 75, 87, 103, 108, 135, 148, 160, 162, 165–66. *See also* Maroon population, Jamaica
Freetown, Sierra Leone, 1, 4, 14, 31, 48
Frustrated Fellowship (Washington), 39, 61–62
funerals, 101n14, 112, 132, 158, 176; ceremonies, 133; of Liele, George, 31–32, 84, 95, 136, 138, 169

Galatians: 5:1, 35; 6:14, 158
Galphin, George, 5, 7
Galphin, Jesse (Jesse Peter), 7, 10–12, 14, 33, 48
Gardner, Robert G., 2
Gardner, W. J., 21, 55, 113
Garrettson, Freeborn, 39, 41, 60
Garvey, Marcus, 139, 182
Gates, John Parmer, 20, 24–25, 46, 108–9
Gaulsing, Jesse (Rev.), 9
Gayle, Samuel, 33
General Baptists, 39

General Committee, of Baptist Missionary Society of London, 134–35
George, David (Rev.): conversion of, 4–7, 35n8, 67, 156; as protégé of Liele, George, 1, 4–6, 12, 14, 16, 33, 48, 53; in Sierra Leone, 9, 31; Silver Bluff Church and, 10, 11, 12, 35n8; as slave, 4, 5, 7, 11, 105, 160
Georgia Education Association, 11
"Georgia's Religion in the Colonial Era, 1733–1790" (Walker), 16–17, 152–53
Gibb, George, 21–22, 55, 110, 131, 178, 183; Great Revival and, 175; in Jamaica, 69, 78–79, 85, 91, 96–99, 122; as protégé of Liele, George, 91, 96–99, 100n2, 125, 145, 151
Gilroy, Paul, 119
Godden, Thomas, 139
Gordon, Ernie (Revd. Canon), 59
grace, experience of, 16, 17, 154, 157–58
Great Awakening, 40–41, 57, 60
Great Britain, 24, 69, 91–92, 115, 125–26, 130
Great Revival, 174–77
Gully Chapel, 95–96, 122, 139

Haile Selassie "Ras Tafari" (Emperor of Ethiopia), 182
Haiti, 56, 68

Haitian Revolution (1791), 29–30, 50, 54, 105–6, 115–19
Halt (Lieutenant), 178
hangings, 5, 24, 25, 171, 178
Hanover Street Baptist Church, 138
Haynes, Lemuel, 47
healing, of bodies, 179, 180, 183
health care, 176, 180
hell, 3, 42, 44–45, 53, 61–62, 107, 169
Herschell, Victor, 178
History of the Baptist Missionary Society (Cox), 74–75, 82, 102n37, 176
Holifield, E. Brooks, 51–52
Holy Spirit, 16, 85–86, 110, 112, 127, 153, 179–80
Hosier, Harry, 47
hospitals, 87, 99, 109, 117, 138, 176
House of Assembly, Jamaica, 18, 25, 29–33, 53, 122, 136
Hutchins, Edward (Capt.), 178
Hylton, Edward, 166
hymns, singing of, 25, 43, 54, 58, 93, 156

Ibo people, 145
indentured servant, 15, 18, 60–61, 68, 103–4, 154, 162
Independence Day (1962), 179
Independent Baptists, 30, 75–76
indigenization, Afro-Baptist faith and, 70–72

Indjoe (slave), 140
Islam, 151

Jack, Gullah, 51, 52
Jamaica: African Americans migrating to, 21, 31; *The Baptists of Jamaica*, 91, 125, 143n26; Calabar College, 12, 34; emancipation in, 30, 35, 70–71, 91, 165–66, 172–77; House of Assembly, 18, 25, 29–33, 53, 122, 136; Liele, George, in, 1, 14–31, 54–62, 65–66, 103–4, 118–19; Maroon population, 28, 34, 69, 115–16, 163, 165, 178; "Myalism and the African Religious Tradition in Jamaica," 83; Native Indians hanged in, 5, 24; Race Course, 14, 16–18, 62, 81, 91; *Religion and Society in Post-Emancipation Jamaica*, 30, 70–71, 91; Rowe in, 76; slavery in, 14–15, 18–22, 24–28, 33–35, 50, 54–56, 61–62, 66, 70, 76, 81, 87, 118; Spanish Town, 94, 98, 116, 123, 131–34, 136, 138–39. *See also* Windward Road Chapel, Jamaica
Jamaica Assembly, 25, 61, 94–95, 115, 120, 130, 155; with "The Covenant of the Anabaptist Church," 28, 65; with licenses for preachers, 123, 133, 136, 139–40; Liele, George, and,

106, 110, 125; permission to preach from, 84; with teaching and preaching outlawed on plantations, 126–27; Vaughn and, 131

Jamaica Native Baptist Missionary Society, 77, 78

Jamaican Gazette, 162

James (slave), 140

Jasanoff, Maya, 14–15, 30, 31, 114, 118–19, 121–22

Jesus-Africa question, 23

Jesus Christ, 25, 27, 53–54, 90; Afro-Jamaicans with, 70, 74, 81–82; John the Baptist and, 22, 69, 111, 164; Liele, George, and, 44, 46; with slavery, 22

Jim Crow, 11

John: 13:13, 154, 157; 3:5–7, 67

Johnson, William, 166

John the Baptist, 22, 69, 85, 89, 111, 164, 180

Joshua 6:21, 51

Journal of a West Indian Proprietor (Lewis, M. G.), 148

Judson, Adoniram, 1

Judson, Ann, 1

Killick, William (Rev.), 77

King, Martin Luther, Jr., 12

Kiokee Baptist Church, 40, 42

Kirkland, Moses (Col.), 7–8, 24, 118; as benefactor to Liele, George, 18, 103, 121, 131; Liele, George, as indentured servant to, 15, 18, 60–61, 68, 103–4, 154, 162

Kitching, Christopher, 134

Knibb, William, 31–32, 84, 91, 95, 102n35, 109, 136, 139; at funeral of Liele, George, 138, 169; with slavery, 164, 168–71

Knibb Sibley, Inez (great-granddaughter), 91, 102n35, 102n37, 125, 138–39, 143n26

Laurens, Henry (Col.), 8

Lawlor, Jim, 13

Lawson, Winston, 98, 123–24, 164, 167–68

leader system. *See* class leader

Leland, John, 41

Lewis, George, 21, 69, 78–79, 83, 85; Great Revival and, 175; legacy, 178, 183; as protégé of Liele, George, 91, 96–98, 100n2, 125, 145; as slave, 82, 97

Lewis, M. G., 148, 149, 150

Liberty's Exiles (Jasanoff), 14–15, 114, 118–19

licenses, for preachers, 99–100, 117–18, 123, 132–33, 136–40, 155

Liele (father), 2, 155

Liele, George. *See specific topics*

Liele, Hannah Hunt (wife), 47, 48, 140–41, 162–63

Liele, Lucy. *See* Price, Lucy Liele

Liele, Nancy (mother), 2, 155

Liele, Paul (son), 28–29, 95, 96

Index

Linton (Mr.), 171
literacy, 12–14, 18, 34, 51, 54, 128, 156
Long, Edward, 89
L'Ouverture, Toussaint, 115
Luke 17:3–4, 149
Lyon, George (Rev.), 77

Macedonia Call, 94, 131
magic, 83, 147. *See also* sorcery
Mann, James, 139
manumission, 8, 103, 135, 160, 162
Margaret (slave), 140
Marley, Bob, 59
Maroon population, Jamaica, 28, 34, 69, 115–16, 163, 165, 178
Maroon rebellion (1760), 163
Maroon Wars, 24, 35, 50
Marshall, Daniel, 40
Matthew: 18:15–18, 148; 25:45, 9
meat, 26
mediums, 146, 147
meeting spaces, 71–72, 91
Memorials (Clark), 82–83
Mercury (slave), 88
Methodist Church, 25, 29, 30, 50–51, 117
Methodists, 72, 73, 99, 115, 117, 150, 173
Middle Passage, 50
Middleton, Charles, 177
migrants, Jamaica with African American, 21, 31

missionaries: with Afro-Baptist faith, 119–30; with Afro-Baptist work, 130–34; Black, 55–57, 73, 78–79, 98, 102n52, 126, 133, 145, 175; British, 34, 76, 95–96, 100, 102n52, 106, 116, 125, 131, 138, 146, 175; buying and selling slaves, 134–41; children of, 77; class, 70–72, 93, 104, 130; Haitian Revolution, 115–19; *History of the Baptist Missionary Society*, 74–75, 82, 102n37, 176; Liele, George, and transnational faith, 111–14; slaveholding class and, 66, 68, 124, 175–76; as slave owners, 22–23, 60, 79, 107, 134–36, 140–41; slaves and, 66, 124; *Slaves and Missionaries*, 73–74, 98–99, 114–17, 145, 147
Missionary Society, England, 135–36
Moore, Matthew (Rev.), 2, 3, 16, 19, 40, 42, 118; at Big Buckhead Baptist Church, 43, 47, 107, 153–54; Liele, George, and, 155, 183; as Separatist Baptist, 86, 107
"Morant War," 179
Moravian Church, 33
Moravian missionaries, 20
Moravians, 57, 66, 91, 115, 150, 162
Morehouse College, 11–12, 48
"Mothers," 58, 73

Murray, Milledge Galphin, 5–6
"Myalism and the African Religious Tradition in Jamaica" (Schuler), 83
Myal religion, 21, 68, 70, 80, 96, 106, 156; Afro-Baptist faith and, 84–88, 90, 112; baptism and, 86, 89–90, 98, 147; dancing and, 67, 83–84, 89–90, 100, 174–75; dreams and, 69, 83, 111; Liele, George, and, 146, 147; revival of, 173–74; as secret practice, 69, 84–85; on slavery and sorcery, 105; spirits and, 83, 88, 89–90, 111–14, 119, 164, 174, 179

Nancy (slave), 140, 162–63
Napoleonic war (1802–15), 54
Native Baptist Church, 21–22, 34–35, 65, 73, 77–78, 169, 177–78; with freedom and slavery, 163–74; Liele, George, and, 111–12; membership, 173
native Baptist movement: class leader and ticket system, 71, 72–75, 76, 89, 151; enculturation of faith and, 78–85; with Ethiopianism and Afrocentricity, 181; indigenization, Afro-Baptist faith and, 70–72; Liele, George, as patriarch of, 75–78; with Liele, George, and assistants, 91–100;
preachers, 77–78; spirit and, 81, 85–90, 110
Native Indians, hanging of, 5, 24
Negro Baptist churches, 6–8. *See also* Silver Bluff Church
The Negro Church (Du Bois), 79, 81
Neptune (slave), 140
New Lights, 16, 40
New Providence, Bahamas, 9, 13, 14, 33
New Testament, 154, 158, 160, 179–80
nonviolence, 181
Nova Scotia, Canada, 1, 2, 9, 14, 31, 33, 104

Obeah (Obe, Obi) Worship, 17, 68–70, 80–81, 83, 92, 96, 113; Black, 147, 150, 151; Christianity and, 114; Liele, George, and, 146, 147, 148; as secret practice, 173; spirit and, 89, 111, 112, 164; white, 148, 149, 151
Ocho Rios Baptist Church, 131
Old Testament, 179–80
"One Love," 59
Onesimus (slave), 160–61
organizational structure, Native Baptist Church, 21–22
Original Baptists, 76
Osiek, Carolyn, 160–61

Paine, Thomas, 118

Index

Palmer, Wait (Rev.), 4–5, 7, 11, 156
Particular (Regular) Baptists, 16, 39–40, 51, 60, 65, 75, 152–53
Paul (saint), 158–63
Paul, John, 51
Payne, Ernest, 17, 24, 126, 143n26
Pearce, Samuel, 4
Peggy (slave), 140
Peter: 1 Peter 2:9, 39; 1 Peter 2:13–16, 128; 1 Peter 2:18–22, 128
Peter, Jesse. *See* Galphin, Jesse
Philadelphia Baptist Association, 39
Philemon (slave owner), 159–61
Phillippo, James Mursell, 20, 77–79, 91, 109, 136, 138–39
plantations: ethics, 41–44; preaching outlawed on, 126–27; slavery, 46, 62, 70, 83, 88, 163; sugar-and-slave, 56, 83, 86, 88, 90, 92, 97
planters: Christianity and, 59–60; class, 17, 33, 60, 74, 100, 123–24, 128
Pocomania, 179–80
police, 93, 177–78
preachers: with authorization from ecclesial leadership, 110; "Daddys," 57, 58, 71, 73, 75; licenses for, 99–100, 117–18, 123, 132–33, 136–40, 155; native Baptist, 77–78; non-Church-of-England, 84

preaching: Jamaica Assembly with restricted access to, 84; laws against, 29; outlawed on plantations, 126–27
Presbyterians, 48, 57, 115
Price, Charles, 178
Price, Lucy Liele, 162–63
Priscilla (slave), 88–89
prison: Baker in, 98, 116; death row, 28, 61; Liele, George, in, 12, 18, 23–25, 28–29, 47, 61–62, 68, 76, 96, 98, 103, 116, 122, 129, 154
protests, farmers, 177–78
Psalm 68:31, 48, 108, 181
Pugh, Alfred, 12–13

Quakers, 92, 93, 94, 106

Raboteau, Albert, 7, 179–80
Race Course, Jamaica, 14, 16–18, 62, 81, 91
racism, 46, 52, 59, 61
Rastafari, 181–83
Ras Tafari. *See* Haile Selassie
Rastafari (Edmonds), 180–81
Rastafarians, 59
rebellions: farmers, 177–78; slaves, 17, 34–35, 50–52, 54, 87, 106, 122, 129–30, 163–72, 181
Redd Pass, 13
Regular (Particular) Baptists, 16, 39–40, 51, 60, 65, 75, 152–53
Reid (Lieutenant), 178

Religion and Race (Lawson), 123–24
Religion and Society in Post-Emancipation Jamaica (Stewart, R. J.), 30, 70–71, 91
Revelation 5:1–5; 19:16, 182
revivalistic movements, 39–42, 48
Revivalists, 179–80, 183
revivals, 129, 168; Bedward with, 177–81, 183; Great Revival, 174–77
Revolutionary War, 7–10, 13, 15, 46–47, 52, 60
Rhode Island, 6
Rippon, John D., 4, 29, 42, 96; with British Baptist Missionary Society, 58; at Carter's Lane Baptist Church, 33, 37n51; on conversions, 35n8, 36n15; Liele, George, with letters to, 2, 11, 13, 17, 20, 25, 32, 34, 44, 76, 126, 133, 157
Robinson's Chapel, 134
Romans: 10:1, 23, 61, 76, 108, 129, 154; 10:10, 61
Rowe, John, 34, 94; Crooked Spring Church and, 130, 131; death of, 109, 125, 130; in Jamaica, 76, 78, 100, 123–27, 138
Rowe, John (Mrs.), 127
Russell, Horace, 23, 32, 94–95, 113, 130–31, 133–34, 161–62
Ryland, John, 125

Sabbath School. *See* Sunday School
Salters Hill Baptist Church, 55
Sandy Creek Association, 153
sanitation, 176
schoolhouses, 34, 54, 87
schools: churches and, 11–12, 28–29, 34, 54, 56, 87, 94–95, 127, 132, 139, 156–58; East Queen Street School, 31, 136; in Jim Crow era, 11; Liele, George, with, 12, 34, 156–58; for slaves, 62, 75, 130, 132; Sunday School, 57, 130, 132
Schuler, Monica, 83–86
Second African Baptist Church, Savannah, 10
sedition accusations: Baker with, 93, 116, 123, 126; Liele, George, with, 23–24, 28, 61, 116, 123, 129, 154
Separatist Baptists, 16–17, 19, 40, 65, 86, 90, 107, 152–54
Shannon, David, 154–55, 157–59
Sharp, Henry: Liele, George, enslaved by, 2, 3, 8, 40, 42, 43, 59, 104–5, 153, 155, 157; Liele, George, freed by, 103, 118; in Revolutionary War, 8
Sharpe, Sam "Daddy": with Baptist War, 34–35, 87, 106, 122, 129–30, 163–72, 181; Crooked Spring Church and, 176; execution of, 171; legacy, 178, 183; with nonviolence,

181; with resistance and religion, 180–81
Sherlock, Philip, 54–57
Sierra Leone, 2, 9, 33; Christianity in, 104; Freetown, 1, 4, 14, 31, 48
Silver Bluff, South Carolina, 2, 14–16, 33, 52, 67, 105, 118, 156
Silver Bluff Church, South Carolina, 4–8, 10–12, 14, 35n8, 48, 118, 156
Silver Bluff Church (First African Baptist Church of Augusta), Georgia, 11–12, 48. *See also* Springfield Baptist Church, Georgia
Simpson, George Eaton, 149–50
singing, 25, 43, 54, 58, 93, 101n14, 156, 174
sins: confession of, 16, 75, 182; as sorcery, 86–87, 93, 105, 146, 175, 179
slaveholding class: with Christianity and slavery, 109, 120, 123; compensation for, 172; Liele, George, as member of, 22–23, 60, 107, 140–41, 161–63; Liele, Hannah Hunt, as member of, 162–63; as minority, 14, 88, 106; missionaries and, 66, 68, 124, 175–76; missionaries as members of, 22–23, 60, 79, 107, 134–36, 140–41; Philemon, 159–61; with power over slaves, 128–29, 148–49, 159–61, 168–71; with violence against slaves, 10, 14–15, 88–89, 159, 171, 181
Slave Laws (1802), 94
slave religion, 69, 181
slavery: abolition, 116, 118, 121, 128, 164; Afro-Baptist faith and, 106; Anti-slavery Society, 164; apprenticeship system of, 172–73; Christianity and, 106–7, 109, 120, 123–24, 128–29, 141; as European sorcery, 105, 146; freedom and, 163–74; in Jamaica, 14–15, 18–22, 24–28, 33–35, 50, 54–56, 61–62, 66, 70, 76, 81, 87, 118; Jesus with, 22; Middle Passage, 50; plantation, 46, 62, 70, 83, 88, 163; plantation ethics, 41–44; religion used to dismantle, 151–52; sugar-and-slave plantation, 56, 83, 86, 88, 90, 92, 97; violence of, 54
slaves (enslaved people): with Africa and traditional practices, 145; Afro-Baptist faith and, 68, 74, 82, 85; baptisms and, 119, 150; the Bible and, 3–4, 9, 34, 50–51, 54–58, 110, 159; Bryan as, 9, 10, 47; buying and selling, 134–41; children, 61, 62, 130, 140–41, 148, 162–63, 172; as children of God, 9, 18, 19, 51, 53, 57, 129, 146, 159; Christianity and, 19–22, 25–27,

30–31, 41, 59–60, 91, 128–29; as class leader, 71; Consolidated Slave Law, 131; culture, 14, 24, 29, 44, 47, 74, 87, 126; in Egypt, 57; executions of, 171; freedom for, 7, 8, 13, 15, 32, 35, 49–54, 75, 87, 103, 108, 135, 148, 160, 162, 165–66; George as, 4, 5, 7, 11, 105, 160; with independent Black churches, 40–49; Lewis, George, as, 82, 97; Liele, George, as, 2, 3, 8, 22, 40–44, 49–50, 58–59, 68, 76, 103, 104–7, 148, 153–54, 155, 157; Liele, George, as owner of, 22–23, 60, 107, 140–41, 161–63; Liele, Hannah Hunt, as owner of, 162–63; ministering to, 3–4, 6, 7, 9, 18–19, 42–43; missionaries and, 66, 124; missionaries as owners of, 22–23, 60, 79, 107, 134–36, 140–41; obedience of, 128–29, 160–61; Onesimus, 160–61; rebellions, 17, 34–35, 50–52, 54, 87, 106, 122, 129–30, 163–72, 181; with Redd Pass, 13; Revolutionary War and, 7–8, 10, 13, 46–47; runaway, 4–5, 7–8, 24, 34, 50, 88–89, 165; schools for, 62, 75, 130, 132; slaveholding class with power over, 128–29, 148–49, 159–61, 168–71; survival strategies, 54–61; violence against, 10, 14–15, 88–89, 159, 171, 181; wills and bequeathing of, 162–63. *See also* emancipation; Haitian Revolution; indentured servant; Maroon population, Jamaica

Slaves and Missionaries (Turner), 73–74, 98–99, 114–17, 145, 147

sorcery: baptism as charm against, 150; European, 84, 86–90, 105–6, 175; magic and, 83, 147; sin as, 86–87, 93, 105, 146, 175, 179

South Carolina, 1, 24–25, 29, 46, 50, 104; Charleston, 8–9, 49, 51–52, 153; Silver Bluff, 2, 4–8, 10–12, 14–16, 33, 35n8, 48, 52, 67, 105, 118, 156

Spain, 24, 69

Spanish Town, Jamaica, 94, 98, 116, 123, 131–34, 136, 138–39

speaking in tongues, 67, 70, 147, 175

spirits: cotton trees and, 70; evil, 74, 86; Holy Spirit, 16, 85–86, 110, 112, 127, 153, 179–80; Jesus Christ as, 81–82; Myal religion and, 83, 88, 89–90, 111–14, 119, 164, 174, 179; native Baptist movement and, 81, 85–90, 110; Obeah Worship and, 89, 111, 112, 164; revengeful, 147

spirit (possession) seizure, 21–22, 55, 57, 66–67, 110, 113, 174–75

spiritual guides, class leaders as, 21, 73
Springfield Baptist Church, Georgia, 11–13, 48
Spurgeon, Charles Hadden, 133
Stanley (Lord), 172
Stearns, Shubal, 40
Stewart, Dianne, 68–70, 96
Stewart, Robert J., 30, 70–71, 91
The Story of the Jamaican People (Sherlock and Bennett), 54–57
sugar-and-slave plantation, 56, 83, 86, 88, 90, 92, 97
Sunday (Sabbath) School, 57, 130, 132
superfluity, 26
swearing, 26
"Sweet Beulah Land," 101n14
Swigle, Nicholas, 85, 94, 111, 123, 125, 131–32, 153; Gully Chapel and, 95–96, 122; in Jamaica, 91, 95; as leader, 95; Liele, George, and, 73; with split from Liele, George, 28–29, 73; as teacher, 156; Windward Road Church and, 34, 73, 75, 127

Tacky (Ashanti warrior), 163, 165
Taylor, Simon (Sir), 99
teaching, laws against, 29
Theology in America (Holifield), 51–52
1 Thessalonians 3:13, 128
Thistlewood, Thomas, 14–15

ticket system, class leader and, 71, 72–75, 76, 89, 151
Timothy, 26, 128, 161
Tinson, Joshua, 32, 136–37
Titus, 27, 128, 161
Tosh, Peter, 59
transnational faith, 111–14
Tripp, Henry, 131, 176
Trueman, George (Rev.), 77
Turner, Mary, 73–74, 98–99, 114–18, 121–23, 145, 147, 165–66
Two Jamaicas (Curtin), 108–9
Tybee Island, Georgia, 8–9, 52, 60

Van Broekhoven, Deborah Bingham, 104, 106
Vaughn, Samuel, 34, 92, 94, 117–18, 125–27, 131, 176
Vesey (Captain), 49, 50
Vesey, Denmark, 49–50
violence: executions, 5, 24, 25, 171, 178; nonviolence, 181; at protests, 178; of slavery, 54; against slaves, 10, 14–15, 88–89, 159, 171, 181
visions, Myal religion and, 69, 83
Von Ketelholdt, Maximilian August (Baron), 178
voodoo (Vodum, Voodoism) worship, 17, 151

Walker, Charles O., 16–17, 152–54
washing, of feet, 26, 152–54, 167

Washington, James Melvin, 39, 44–47, 59, 60–62, 107
Watts Hymnal, 160
Watty, William, 119–21
Wesley, John, 60, 72
Wesleyan-Methodist Missionary Society, 30
White, William J. (Rev.), 12
White gaze, 68–69, 84–85, 97, 123
white Obeah, 148, 149, 151
Whitfield, George, 16, 19, 39, 41, 44–45, 50, 60, 65; Christian cosmology and, 107; with Christianizing slaves, 128–29; Liele, George, and, 152, 183
Wilberforce, William, 118
Williams, Amos, 1, 9, 12–14, 33, 48
Williams, Caesar (son), 13
Williams, Elsey (daughter), 13
Williams, Judy (wife), 13
Williams, Lisey (daughter), 13
Williams, Prince (son), 13
Williams, Rachall (daughter), 13
Williams, Selina Bedon (wife), 13
wills, last: of Liele, George, 140–41, 162; of Liele, Hannah Hunt, 162–63
Windward Road Chapel, Jamaica, 76, 88, 92, 95, 97–98, 122, 125, 129, 133, 143n26, 175; Gibb and, 131; as hospital, 87, 99, 117, 138; Liele, George, with, 23, 75, 80, 91, 116; literacy at, 34; membership numbers, 78; repairs needed for, 32, 137; Swigle and, 34, 73, 75, 127
Winn, Lascelles, 92–94, 126
witchcraft, 20, 80, 83, 92, 108, 113
Woodson, Carter G., 7, 39, 41, 60

Yoruba people, 145
youth, early years and, 2–9

About the Author

Noel Leo Erskine, Emeritus Professor of Theology and Ethics, Candler School of Theology and the Graduate Division of Religion, Emory University, has been a visiting professor in ten schools in six countries. His books include *King among the Theologians*, *Black Theology and Pedagogy* and *Plantation Church: How African American Religion Was Born in Caribbean Slavery*.

Professor Erskine was baptized and ordained in a church in Jamaica, West Indies, which owes its foundation and theological existence to the ministry of George Liele, who lived in Jamaica for forty-two years. Following in the footsteps of Liele, Erskine, a Jamaican native who resides in Georgia, brings together both strands of Liele's life and ministry—in Georgia and Jamaica—through his writing in *Black Missionary in an Age of Enslavement: The Life and Times of George Liele*.

www.ingramcontent.com/pod-product-compliance
Lightning Source LLC
Chambersburg PA
CBHW021856230426
43671CB00006B/415